"**The point of so many of his plays,** which laudably never turn characters into mere mouthpieces for their author, is that what we all need, first and foremost, is to be heard— WHETHER OUR WORDS HIT LIKE A FLOWER OR A STICK."

– **Kerry Reid**, Chicago Reader

"**One of the most** MESMERIZING PERFORMANCES of the year came from Beau O'Reilly as Davies.... Colm O'Reilly and Jeff Bivens were uncompromisingly disturbed as Ashton and Mick, but Beau O'Reilly's disjointed transient Davies had an undercurrent of UNREALIZED THREAT that made you keep him in your eye, even if he was only fumbling around in the background. This was a great production, a study in how to convey absurdity to an audience in a way the audience can wrap its brain around."

– **Chicago Stage Review**

"**BEAU O'REILLY is living proof** that if you work at your art long enough, following your vision, different drummer or bliss, YOUR WORK WILL BECOME SUBLIME..."

– **Jack Helbig**, Daily Herald

published as part of the

curious theatre branch • contemporary
theater collection

beau o'reilly plays...

curious theatre branch • contemporary theater collection

Jenny Magnus & Beau O'Reilly **STUDIO PORTRAIT**
/ Curious Theatre Branch, Chicago, 1988

beau o'reilly
plays...

volumes 1+2

14 curious plays: 1991 to 2025

Beau O'Reilly

For more information on this book or to order, visit
www.jacklegpress.org

Published by
JackLeg Press
Washington, DC

Book Design by
Jason Greenberg / Art Works Design
Chicago, IL

First Publication Printing © 2025 Beau O'Reilly
ISBN: 978-1-956907-26-1

Library of Congress Control Number: 2025937916

Photo/Art Credits:
Over these 3.5 decades, many photographer/artists have
created documentation and shot publicity stills, actor
portraits and made promotional art for the productions
included in this book; I'm thankful to these Chicago artists:

Jeffrey Bivens, Joe Mazza, Kristin Basta, Paul Brennan,
Sue Cargill, Julie Williams, Phil Cantor, Jason Greenberg
& Iwona Biedermann

Front Cover image by Paul Brennan
Back Cover images by Joe Mazza
Frontispiece & Artist Profile images by Jeffrey Bivens

beau o'reilly plays

98 puppets in a revolving door...

volume 1
6 curious plays: 1991 to 2000

Beau O'Reilly

ACKNOWLEDGEMENTS

This book is dedicated to my partner in all things artistic Jenny Magnus... John-O!

With a shoutout to JW Williams
and Ginger & Pepper…

In Memoriam: Winifred O'Reilly, Beth Ann O'Reilly-Amandes, Matt Rieger, Ryan Wright, Michael Martin

My writing self exists because of you all, Yes!
That's true.

General Notes on the Text...

All introductions, synopses, settings, casts of characters and stage-directions are indicated in oblique (slanted) typeface.

Song lyrics in-text are indicated with quotation marks, bold titles and *(Sung)*.

Unless otherwise indicated, roles can be played by performers of any gender or age. Have at it actors, claim your characters!

More info about my work can be found on my websites, **beauoreilly.com** and **curioustheatrebranch.com**.

98 puppets in a revolving door...:

The end is in the beginning and yet we go on...   **– Samuel Beckett**

TABLE OF CONTENTS

volume 1

Sections / Plays

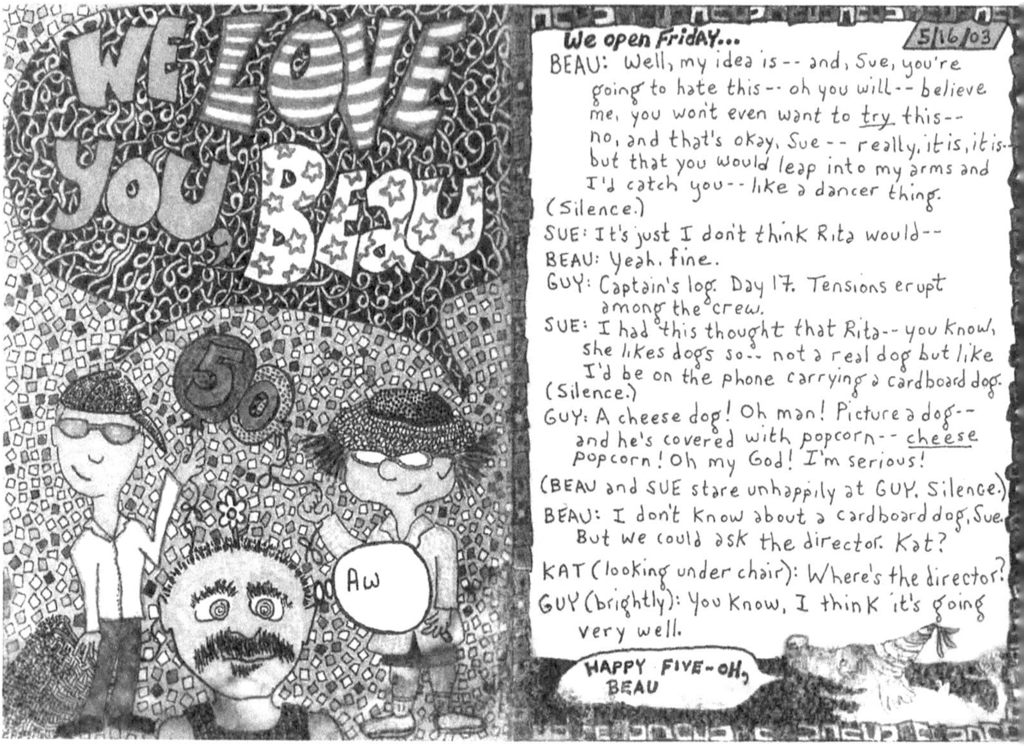

WE LOVE YOU, BEAU

AW

HAPPY FIVE-OH, BEAU

BEAU: Well, my idea is -- and, Sue, you're going to hate this -- oh you will -- believe me, you won't even want to <u>try</u> this -- no, and that's okay, Sue -- really, it is, it is -- but that you would leap into my arms and I'd catch you -- like a dancer thing.

(Silence.)

SUE: It's just I don't think Rita would --

BEAU: Yeah. fine.

GUY: Captain's log. Day 17. Tensions erupt among the crew.

SUE: I had this thought that Rita -- you know, she likes dogs so -- not a real dog but like I'd be on the phone carrying a cardboard dog.

(Silence.)

GUY: A cheese dog! Oh man! Picture a dog -- and he's covered with popcorn -- <u>cheese</u> popcorn! Oh my God! I'm serious!

(BEAU and SUE stare unhappily at GUY. Silence.)

BEAU: I don't know about a cardboard dog, Sue. But we could ask the director. Kat?

KAT (looking under chair): Where's the director?

GUY (brightly): You know, I think it's going very well.

AN

INTRODUCTION

Beau O'Reilly: Foreword, Forward!

by David Isaacson

January, 2025

Beau O'Reilly is a VOICE. A voice that booms when fronting a band, a voice that whispers when he's in story-teller mode. A voice alternately bemused or bombastic. And as you will see in these career-spanning volumes, that voice is equally protean on the page, as Beau the playwright conjures up ecstatic vernaculars for his panoply of dreamers and murderers. "I need language to land in adventure or rebellion. I need language to poke or sparkle," says the visiting lecturer in the semi-autobiographical *Dickie Giebel Gets His Exercise By Leaping To Conclusions* (2024). And when Beau the *actor* inhabits one of the parts created by Beau the *playwright*, the synthesis—melding the gravitas of a Burl Ives with the abandon of a Mick Jagger—has shivered the timbers of the small Chicago theaters he's been inhabiting these last four decades.

Some of Beau-the-writer's prodigious output is collected here in two volumes, and what invaluable volumes they are! The American theatrical avant-garde is very much alive, but the literary artifacts of that theater are hard to come by. Publishers are not predisposed to publish dramatic works. There's no money in it. Try to find the "theater section" in your local bookstore! And the anthologized work of a single playwright is an even rarer treasure. Who knows how many working playwrights are out there, whose contributions to our culture will never be fully known, appreciated, contextualized?

Performances are rehearsed for months, exist for a few weeks or for a few days, and then... are never heard of again. It's the nature of the non-commercial (or anti-commercial) arts, created in impoverished conditions, without much institutional support. But it is often a product of the artists' own inclinations. Writers like Beau are driven to create, always on to the next thing. If a show is a hit perhaps it will be revived the next season, at a slightly larger venue; but in general the artist is more concerned with charging into the future than doubling-back to the past. Even when the 2015 edition of Chicago's Rhinoceros Theater Festival paid tribute to Beau (a great opportunity for a retrospective), he came up with almost all new work instead of revisiting the glory of past hits. And when Beau's 2004 *Hit Me Like a Flower** got a second life last year, it was no conventional remount.

> **"I didn't have a copy of that play,"** Beau wrote in his program note. "In those days I never put anything on my computer, but with mine and Jayita [Bhattacharya]'s memories mostly intact, using pieces of old work scripts we cobbled it together… The play was fun to reinvent."

Archiving, for struggling artists constantly on the move to the next cheap neighborhood, becomes a luxury. Beau, with his less-than-pristine handwriting, limited typing skills, and scripts that morph throughout the rehearsal process, is a particularly difficult *archivee*. A finished working script is usually a tattered affair with pages framed by scrawls in the margins. As mentioned in his author's notes, one of Beau's most celebrated works, *Whiskey in Blue* (2000), had to be completely recreated for this volume from his notebooks and recollections.

And so it is a triumph of no small measure that these volumes now rest in your hands. Old filing cabinets were opened. Hard drives were searched. Memories were plumbed. And these plays now await you—fourteen of them, created over thirty-three years. That's a lot. I don't think any of the theater anthologies on my bookshelf—save Shakespeare—contain so many works. And yet it amounts to just a fraction of Beau's remarkable oeuvre. The total comes, I am told, to over eighty plays. But Beau is not some solitary practitioner: He is devoted to collaboration. He is co-artistic director of the Curious Theatre Branch, the company he founded thirty-seven years ago. He has been the primary curator of the aforementioned Rhinoceros Theater Festival for almost as long. He's part of a scene, a milieu, a movement. He has been referred to, by various theater critics, as the "godfather," the "elder statesman," or the "white-ponytailed president" of the Chicago fringe. So you now grasp in your paws the chronicle not only of a single writer, but a record of an entire era in American theater.

My bona fides, in assessing this oeuvre, are as follows: I've been a theatrical fellow-traveler with Beau for the entire period covered here. I've acted in a couple of his plays—**Crowtown** (1997)* and **Sex and Minutia** (2015). I wrote the screenplay for a short film that appeared before **Talking About Godard** (1999). My name shows up in **Tattered and Wincing** (2017). But even though I have attended most of these plays, it is quite the task to hold such a mass of work in one's consciousness and make coherent and succinct sense of it. And so I have enlisted as co-conspirators the critics of the city's leading independent weekly: the *Chicago Reader* (through the miracle of that publication's online archive and its well-designed search engine). Their writers have been there from the get-go, usually applauding and occasionally antagonizing Beau. Those characterizations I cited above ("godfather" etcetera)? All from the *Reader*.[1] I'll be sprinkling in more quotes from them as we go along.

> **"Beau O'Reilly's scripts** tend to feature type A personalities running circles around a character who's slightly out of step with the world: a henpecked introvert, a coolly rational observer, an easily agitated misanthrope."
>
> – Nick Green reviewing *Things That Go Missing*,
> a collection of three plays (2004)

* * *

Let's begin with clitorises and nutsacks. You will be hard-pressed to find another playwright who writes as consistently and brazenly about the body, about sex, about the squishy details of erotic desire. The eruption and the fading of that desire often drives the action, with unrequited love the overwhelming propulsive force of most of these works. And we are seldom kept in the dark about any lustful craving: Beau's characters wear their hearts on their sleeves, and leers on their lips. "There's a war going on," says Norman in **Hit Me Like A Flower**, "between the loved and the wanting love, a war of never getting what you need, and everybody's losing."[2]

There are plots, for sure, but the plots are never *de rigueur*, nor are any neat resolutions for the anguished characters. We are treated instead to what the *Reader*'s Tony Adler admiringly referred to as "multiple low-life characters sluicing around a cluttered set, propelled by great gusts of poetry." They are trying to live their lives in a world that is repeatedly described as harsh and wild;

they are trying to make their art, hustle their hustles, bed their lovers; and one gets a sense that, after the curtain rings down, the characters will simply continue those pursuits. "Things end, after 65 minutes," wrote Max Maller in his 2021 *Reader* review of **A Packet of Holiness and Joy Will Come to You? (A Fable)**, "much as they started: randomly and strangely." The randomness and strangeness are, of course, the point, because tidy endings are not Beau's thing. *Tidiness* is not his thing. He is focused on character as revealed through language, through an *excess* of language, language that critic Justin Hayford called "florid wordplay" and critic Mary Shen Barnidge called "broken-glass lyricism." When language is non-naturalistic, heightened, extravagant, *poetic* (as it invariably is in a Beau play), it provides a speedy route to the core of the characters, the *full* characters with their dream lives and life-histories and inner rap-sheets gloriously manifest to us. The excessiveness of language, on stage, can achieve the same kind of Aristotelian catharsis that theatrical naturalism can. Beau's works are a type of *introspectacle*, as defined by Jenny Magnus, who has co-helmed the Curious Theatre Branch with Beau from its inception:

> **"We have a word we've coined over the years;** the introspectacle. We are not so interested in the spectacle, because we could never really quite pump ourselves up to that level. It's always about, can we go deeper in to the work, can we just make more and more deep and beautiful and questing works?"[3]

* * *

Beau's plays, for me, fall into three categories: a) indelible, in-depth character studies, such as the evangelizing nudist Edward Hickock Collins in **Eddie: A Man in His Skin** (1997) or Leonard "Truck" Bloom in **Truck in Pieces** (2002);[4] b) plays with mid-sized casts, usually having some central action (a planned kidnapping, a road trip, a murder, an upcoming date with some French gangsters) to organize itself around; and c) sprawling works in which the collective id of entire communities are revealed through the sparks of their individual clashes with each other.[5] Of these latter plays, *Reader* critic Kerry Reid wrote, in her 2024 review:

> "I've been seeing Beau O'Reilly's plays for over 30 years. But somehow it never occurred to me until taking in the current revival of O'Reilly's 2003 play, **Hit Me Like a Flower**, how

much this bard of the Chicago alternative theater community has in common with American writers like Sherwood Anderson and Thornton Wilder. Like Anderson's **Winesburg, Ohio** and Wilder's **Our Town**, O'Reilly's plays excel at creating portraits of communities through characters who are stumbling through their little worlds, finding profundity, tragedy—and occasional flashes of grace—amid the most mundane and sometimes ridiculous of situations."

This rubric was there from the start. In the *Reader's* very first review of a Beau play (this one co-written with Jenny Magnus), critic Peter Handler wrote in 1988:

"[**Careening is a Skill***] is less narrative theater than a Brechtian showcase, as the Nothing Is Everything Man careens from one encounter to another. While the sum of the parts does not produce a clear story, it does make for provocative theater."

* * *

Can we pin Beau down, through his regional or literary allegiances? There's no question that there's a lot of Chicago in Beau. His are plays of three-flat walkups and The Biograph and the Paul Butterfield Blues Band and bus drivers to yell at and cops to yell at you. But they also retain the traces (and scars) of all the other communities he's lived in, in Crystal Lake, DeKalb, Champaign, and Madison. And at least a couple of these plays were written while Beau was a guest artist at the *Iowa Writers' Workshop*. So let us call him a decidedly **Midwestern** playwright.

And where to place Beau in the grand schema of authors? His characters help plot his allegiances through their literary spats: "I hate Hemingway." "I love Hemingway." Each writer referenced becomes a point along the X/Y axes of Beau's universe: Nabokov, Whitman, James Joyce, Joyce Carol Oates, Russell Banks, Henry Miller, Toni Morrison, Charles Bukowski, Beckett, Ruth Rendell. He loves Dylan Thomas and Loraine Hansberry and Bryn Magnus. He's got Pynchon's penchant for joke-y names and, as Jack Helbig pointed out in his *Reader* review of **Evil Triggers Down Amateur Street** (1991):

"In lieu of realism, O'Reilly is after a rich, multilayered work having more in common with Thomas Pynchon than David Mamet."

* * *

What's it all boil down to? "Compassion counts for much here. It's the basis of the structure of our judgment," says J.O. in **The Third Degrees of J.O. Breeze** (1995), and he urges that "your compassion and imagination could balloon and expand enough to include" the odious Captain. In **Whiskey in Blue** (2000), the appropriately-named part-time lawman Mercy pleas for understanding for the murderous TommyO. Truck Bloom's ex-wife Rita advocates on behalf of her ne'er-do-well, puppy-killing son: "Donnie deserves love. Everybody does. Donnie is part of everybody." The characters in these plays behave in thoughtless and even barbarous ways, bringing great pain to each other. And yet—we are reminded—we must have compassion even for those we hold in contempt, even the assholes, even the losers. Especially the losers.

> "Perhaps even more important than O'Reilly's comic talent is **his great capacity for empathy.** His characters are endearing even at their most unattractive—like when the hapless John is discovered trying to cheat Dude out of his share of the tips. It's this loving celebration of human foibles that gives the play its big heart."
>
> – Justin Hayford in his 1993 review of **Let the Dolly Do the Work**.*

* * *

All the works you'll read here bear the stretch-marks of their creation. When Beau's characters get annoyed in a café by a loud patron at the next table, it is an echo of Beau's writing process, created with pen and paper predominantly in public places, with the muck of the world swirling around him. And then, after Beau extracts narratives from those notebooks, these plays find their public incarnation, all of them (with the exception of the latest, **Dickie Giebel**) produced by the Curious Theatre Branch. And that is perhaps the defining feature of these works. Beau is not one to include a lot of stage directions, or to frontload his scripts with copious explanatory notes about the characters. He has left space for the creative force of his fellow artists. These plays came to full fruition in collaboration with an astounding, shifting group of actors dedicated to a mode of art both truthful and inventive. And now the plays sit here, in your grasp, ready to be explored again; to blossom in new incarnations. Theater-makers, go shiver some timbers.

:: *David Isaacson is Chicago playwright and founding member of Theater Oobleck*

--- --- ---

Illustrations by Sue Cargill for *Truck In Pieces*, 2001

FOOTNOTES:

* Note from Beau: These plays are not included in volume 1 or 2. In the final days of compiling the manuscript it became clear that, even with two volumes, there were just too many pages, too many plays. So I cut two of the longer plays, **Evanston: Which Is Over There** and **Hit Me Like a Flower**. A major part of my work—long plays with lots of story and lots of characters—now feels under-represented. Oh, those troubling page counts! So you can write to me and I will send you those two plays: available for the asking at beauoreilly2@gmail.com

¹ Those quotes are from the *Reader's* Kerry Reid, Justin Hayford, and Max Maller, respectively. But I might add that Tony Adler once covered all the bases in writing "Beau O'Reilly is at once RhinoFest's eminence grise and the master of its revels, its satyr and elder statesman."

² A quote astutely noted by Kerry Reid in her *Chicago Reader* review of the play.

³ From Mark Larson's invaluable *"Ensemble: An Oral History of Chicago Theater,"* Agate Publishing 2019.

⁴ Beau's in-depth character studies are under-represented in this book, and could fill another volume on their own: the pugilist Truck returned in **Truck on a Roll** (2007); Leon in **Wolfie 'n' Me at the Foul Line** (1994); the raving drunk in **The Spew Police... Suffergush Returns**; Flagg in **Not Only Sleeping** (2000).

⁵ The most expansive of these—the eight-and-a-half-hour **Madeline Trilogy** (2007)—is not included in this volume.

THE

PLAYS

Evil Triggers Down Amateur Street: A Play in Black and White

Premiered 1991
Curious Theater Branch–North Ave.
Chicago, IL

performed by

Mark Comiskey
Ian Lipski
Jenny Magnus
Beau O'Reilly
Colm O'Reilly
Anita Stenger

THE
PLAYS

INTRO

I was working at the Chicago Symphony, selling subscriptions on the phone… I was happy to get the work, my body relieved by not having to move furniture for a living any more and I was making enough money to pay for stuff for Colm and our household with Jenny Magnus.

*Me and Jenny had written three plays together by then and that day at work **ARSON FIX** was my first call and **JACK SUGAR** my fifth, by the time I got on the train I was writing it, it was a love and betrayal play, there were guns and a tree house, the kidnapping plan of the Stones came cause I needed a plot hinge, twenty years later somebody stole that device and made an HBO movie… if that was you, you can send me a check… I was listening to the Stones a lot, they were so very cool then, Mick sneering and risking all that heartbreak and Keith wrapped in scarfs and losing all his teeth and I already know that Charlie Watts was the secret weapon, which he remained til his death.*

*At thanksgiving day that year I was at the Magnus' house and we were watching **Double Indemnity**, a film noir in black and white, Bryn, Jenny's playwriting brother, sighed on the commercial and muttered 'Evil triggers down amateur street,' it really was a mutter but I heard it… I grabbed the title right then, Bryn was always a muse for me in those days.*

We did the play at the first **Curious Theatre Branch** on North Ave.; John Coyne built a beautiful treehouse set out of black and white paper, Miki Greenberg printed up massive cyberchrome flowers for the garden... The cast: Jenny M. as Arson Fix, Anita Stenger as Amanda, Colm O'Reilly as the gardener, Ernest, Mark Comiskey as the hapless Max were excellent, and my collaborators of choice for some time. I imagine we group directed, Ian Lipski stepped in as Pan, I played Jack and no one remembers who played Ruth and Ray, if it was you, give me a call. Bob Jacobson as Keith Richards & Lisa Black as Mick Jagger performed for the handheld video.

When it came time to put it in the book it was somewhat snakebit; scripts existed but more than one in different scene orders, so I went back to the handwritten notebook to decide what to do...

– *Thanks to Stefan Brün & AT Gruber for typing the script back to life.*

SYNOPSIS

*Two petty thieves, **JACK SUGAR** and **ARSON FIX** meet to plan a kidnapping of Mick Jagger and Keith Richards at the end of the 1980's. They recruit a kid, **MAX**, to drive and head to the treehouse where Jack Sugar lives with **AMANDA**... love swings wildly between Amanda and everybody, jealousy ensues, the earnest gardener—**ERNEST**—keeps the garden a blooming and magical place before guns are drawn and loyalties are tested... A NOIR play in black and white.*

SETTING

In front of the Tree House, on the street, in the Garden... everything is black and white as are the costumes initially, when Jack enters the Garden it blossoms with color... we did it with huge prints of flowers cast against the walls and ceilings in bright greens, purples, reds, & yellows.

CAST OF CHARACTERS:

AMANDA	*MAX*
ARSON FIX	*PAN*
ERNEST, the gardener	*RAY*
JACK SUGAR	*RUTH*

MUSIC

All Stones, all the time: 'Paint It Black,' 'Jumpin Jack Flash,' 'Midnight Rambler,' 'Sway,' 'Gimme Shelter...' The songs will cover the transitions at full sound and then continue in the scene, but at lower volume, under the action. The exception is the party scenes, where 'Sway' should remain loud throughout.

SCENE: FIX ALONE, STANDING IN A SPOTLIGHT
'MIDNIGHT RAMBLER' in the background

Fix: We started out real slow…Prairie fires down Tulsa
         way at four, five hundred a crack. Cattle farmer
         smoke games. Shit-on-my-fence-I'll-burn-out-your-
         family stuff. I showed Jack, a little kindling, just a
         pint and a half of gasoline, minimize that evidence.
         Jack had the knack and he picked up quick. Jack
         was a lifter, he taught me some moves. How to
         sweet talk your way into a guy's table, grab his
         wallet, and smiling always, pay the bill with his
         money! That was smooth with the two of us coming
         at it from different ends, we were living "The Life"
         and doing just fine. Still amateurs, but up and at
         'em. But it was Jack who suggested the grab and
         my ears were open… We were fowl shooting,
         hoping to bag us a fourteen-pound gander for our
         Sunday platter…

         *(JACK handing FIX a rifle, they shoot throughout
         the scene, geese dropping from above)*

Jack: I'd go with Keith, that's exact—every time. I reckon
         he is rock 'n' roll, that fuck-you rhythm grinding
         deaths head look.

Fix: Naw. Mick's got the looks. An' the clothes.
         He's the grab… He's the essential.

Jack: Without Keith they wouldn't—they couldn't even rock without him. Fix, Fix, Keith is what make 'em the best thing. It's Keith, it's gotta be.

Fix: What are you sayin? Naw. I thought you liked singers, lyrics... Mick is smooth, ten times the singer...

Jack: Happy! Best-song-on-the-best-album-ever." I need a love to keep me HAAAHppy HAAAHppy, baby woncha"—Keith sings.

Fix: You playing with me, Jack. You don't even think that! Happy?! "Gimme Shelter," "Shattered," "Paint It Black."

Jack: Well, Mick is exceptional, I don't mean... to say... ...umm "Paint It Black."

Fix: Mick is coherent, he's valuable. Grab Keith and who cares? Just replace him.

Jack: What? No! Fix! There are only two guitar players: Robert Johnson; Keith. Nobody else... Who would they get?

Fix: Jeff Beck, Jimmy Page, Eric Clapton...

Jack: Fix. Don't even joke.

Fix: When Mick-and-Keith pushed Brian in the pool it didn't even take 'em long to get Mick Taylor.

Jack: What? What? That never...fuck.

Fix: Easy Jack Sugar, easy, Easy. Just Charlie horsin'
        your leg. Fix loves the boys, you know I do…

Jack: Waal, that's exact. Y'all gotta—they're the best.
        (Pause) Keith wrote "Wild Horses" and
        "Satisfaction," those cool words.
        He wrote "Satisfaction" in his sleep.

Fix: Jack, he's a junkie. You can always replace a junkie.

Jack: Straight! Straight! He sweated it out on Mick's
        couch, for Chrissake, he lay there like a baby,
        Mick said, and all those blood transfusions.

Fix: Naw, Jack, c'mon—he drinks half a gallon of Rebel
        Yell a day, straight? He doesn't have any teeth…
        Mick's intact, he's the money guy…
        And his clothes…

Jack: Waal, I reckon we could take 'em both…
        "The Glimmer Twins" man, that's a big score…

Fix: In the end, we agreed that either would do…
        Fix could use the old contacts in the coke trade to
        get a glimpse at Keith and Mick's private domain,
        Jack Sugar would find us a wheel man…

        Jack could do the muscle work, and Fix would do
        the smart planning, but we needed somebody
        young and not too greedy with a heavy foot for
        those speedy getaways. Wouldn't take him long to
        find somebody who wanted to go to work for Jack.

        Everybody liked Jack, he came on very soft and
        sure… hair three weeks without a wash and sticking

every which way on his head, Jack with his southern 'yes maam' thing, smile almost a sneer, sharp in his seersucker suit, first time I saw him I wanted to touch his cheek, his body soft like a big baby's. There was a taste between us, you know like after lightning in the summer air, awake to the possibilities, but I never liked cock much, when it comes to the old push and shove, I like to do the entering.

SCENE: THE STREET

JACK SUGAR and MAX nonchalantly picking pockets. 'COUNTRY HONK' for the transition.

Jack: First crimes in the city are like flash-floods in the lowlands…you feel 'em comin' from far away… I'd felt mine coming for years, I was younger then y'all, skinny. I'd worked my way up from the deep south, that summer was one big hot moment that burned me dry…red…crisp. I was somebody's bad news…

Max: You were ready for it, The Life.

Jack: Yeah, yeah. She was maybe 40, swayin' like champagne, red eyes leaning against the lamppost. One of these old fashioned jobs, just swayin', a blurred look all over her.

Max: Nicely dressed? Money obvious–

Jack: Oh, she was nice. Face like ivory, jewel lips.

Max: Wow. Furs leather.

Jack: Dreamy. Very dreamy…
        The thing was, I was hungry no prospects.

Max: You were scraping, struggling just to get through
        the day.

Jack: Now that's exact… Yeah, yeah… I was scrapin' and
        her purse was open, everything presenting itself.
        The wallet was easy. I could have picked out every
        piece of kleenex, every lipstick, every hairpin; she
        never would have noticed.

Max: How much? How much did she have? "C" notes?

Jack: Once I had it, man, it was so very heavy, I had
        to keep my pace even, though, I was staggering
        under that wallet. I didn't want to startle her.
        I had to walk cool…

Max: What'd you buy? Get…

Jack: Chicken 'n' ribs, man, It was the best.
        Creamy slaw and corn on the cob.

Max: Meat fallin' off the bone?

Jack: That's exact. That grease was smooth.

Max: What else?

Jack: Headed right over to the haberdasheries:
        white linen, three pieces, creases like
        a razor blade. I was sharp.

Max: Yeah, very classy.

Jack: Broke by the next day but lookin' good.
         I moved uptown.

Max: Yeah… yeah…

Jack: Listen; what's the weekend hold for y'all?

Max: *(Coy)* Oh, people to see—downtown appointments.
         You know.

Jack: Coy, Max, coy. You could come up to the house,
         we could take the train, Jack'll show you how to
         work the club car… Would that please y'all?

Max: O, yeah, I'd be pleased. I could make some calls,
         shift some stuff around…

Jack: Commuter special leaves in a half-hour.
         Sweet pickin's that train.

Max: Yeah…

         (FIX in spotlight.'
         MOONLIGHT MILE' playing the transition.)

Fix: When Fix met Amanda Dupuy, I was all set to sulk and
         brood, to fight her for Jack's attention. But she looked
         at me and… I was shivered. Amanda Dupuy had this
         way of looking at me, her body thrust forward, face
         lifted, a flicker, a motion, lightning striking bush on a hot
         as flame summer night, one look and Fix was, hooked,
         burned and I'mean, I'm a flame queer and there was
         chili-pepper taste between us from the get-go.

Me'n Amanda met up, hiding it well from Jack, Amanda claiming a "mother visit," me taking a Stone reconnaissance, we met up in backwoods Maine, Big House Corners—once home for Arson Fix. Thought I'd catch a glimpse of Papa's ghost, but now it's just slow woodlands.

Amanda: Moon came up full that first night, champagne by the bottle, shots o' Old Fizz, exhalation in a cold Rebel Yell. How-ah-howl…

Fix: You wanta howl, I'll moon stuff your mouth, ma'am, much as I can and I can, Howlin' Wolf on the box when we headed into that juice joint.

Amanda: You and me, sloppy drunk…

Fix: Rollin' red lips 'round each other, hips grinding, all wet and flushing, burnin' face pressing nipples, we were quite a pair, your red-hot skirt hoisted up, the round cheeks bursting out black panties, my hands gripping hips, workin' my crotch to your crotch, our mouths in suck…

Amanda: That dance floor cleared and got deadly. Lumberjacks don't want to see no girls fucking in a public place. I sensed it pulling your head up.

Fix: The room all red eyes on rednecks.

Amanda: Sweety, I think we oughta cover up here, water in the desert, don't want any of those tough guys drowning on us.

Fix: As I tweaked a tit.

Amanda: The boys closed ranks, tightened up around us.
I was shaking.

Fix: Easy, baby, easy… We got a full hand.

Amanda: She had one of those sawed-off jobs, double
barreled, and when she cocked, the room iced.

Fix: I figured to explode the heads of the two tallest
ones, heads like sloppy melons me, I couldn't miss.
I pulled both triggers bodies dropped air went
out of that bag, I burned that place after, a little
kerosene, a flick of the bic and that whiskey burned
so blue and smokey, lumberjacks running out
the door, fire every which way we headed out,
sopped off to recanter the Stones and we went
back to Jack's to celebrate.

SCENE: THE TREE HOUSE
FIX and AMANDA making love on the couch,
clothing being slowly dropped on the floor.
'STRAY CAT BLUES' for the transition.

Amanda: Sweet Fix, hold my lips.

Fix: Your lips Amanda, on my hips, that's what I want.

Amanda: Like this, or this? *(Kissing)*

Fix: Soft sweetheart take it slow… uh… the buttons
stuck sweetheart, just let me…

Amanda: The flesh flows, Fix knows what there is to know, you
are marvelous… stroke my legs, very very slowly.

Fix: Give you the shivers.

Amanda: I like the Shivers... *(Sound on the road)*

Fix: Whats that now?

Amanda: Get up get up baby and go.

Fix: Go? That is not what I was thinking to do.

Amanda: He's due, Jack, he is due, he is here.

Fix: Ok, ok... I'm up, I'm up.

Amanda: Go out the back.

          (JACK and MAX enter staring at the the
          tree house, all black & white, shining like
          an old picture book paper castle)

Jack: This is my home.

Max: It's a tree. A fort?

Jack: A home. My home.

Max: You live in a tree?

Jack: Um Hum... the wind blows, the branches sway,
          the trunk bending: solemn and graceful, cradling...
          That's the best it gets... I love this tree.

Max: You love a tree? You're a thief, a...

Jack: Bad Guy! And I'm good at it, but being a Bad Guy extracts a cost; it drains the inner fire.

Max: Yeah?

Jack: Uh-hum. Amanda! Amanda Dupuy!
(*AMANDA comes out and they hug/kiss—very tender, touching faces with fingers*)

Jack: Amanda, sweet Amanda. I'm back.

Amanda Yes, Jack. I see that. And your trip? Lucrative, I hope—pockets full to the bursting now, Jack? We need no longer worry about the wolf at the door? Right?

Jack: That's exact.

Amanda: So we can... party! (*Stones begins to play 'HONKY TONK WOMEN'... they begin to dance.*)
Did you bring smoke, Jack?

Jack: Red Bud. And sensemilla.

Amanda: Red Bud! Yes. We had better smoke it.

Jack: And your mama? The split...

Amanda: Temporarily billowing with good will, all patched up and seaworthy Mamma...
(*To MAX:*) You, I haven't met.

Jack: Amanda... This is Max... Max the Magnificent.

Amanda: I am so charmed. Any Max of Jack's is a Max of mine. Can you roll Max? We're sure to smoke two. Are you tough, magnificent?

Max: Sure.

Amanda: Roll big, Max.

Jack: Tell us about your mother.

Amanda: My mother whom I have just returned from! She has four personalities, Max, all of whom visit with punctuality: in spring she is seasonally fecund, hair flying, lips smeared. She drinks Southern Comfort, smashes Toyotas, she emerges gashed but gay. By winter she is dried up, rolling and whining in front of the fireplace, cursing the empties as she smashes them into the fireplaces, ripping up all of Mamma's lace underclothes as she sits, then supergluing each piece to her thighs, the sensitive skin on her upper arms, under her chin, once she is so festively decked out, she waits for the postman, the plumber or her own darling daughter to appear at the front door, there to calmly rip away each piece without flinching… in summer she is the grand dame, the lilacs burst forth to greet her, the bluebirds swallow themselves with joy at her garden appearance, she wears only lettuce leaves and fingers herself but only when someone's looking… And then coyly as if itching… Are you a young man? You seem to be, the fall is worst of all, you may not be man enough… to hear about fall, Max, do you have a mother, Max?

Max: No.

Jack & Amanda: No Mother.

Max: No. Well yes, but not like that.

Amanda: What does mom do, Max?

Max: Perfume. The perfume counter.

Jack: Scenting up the housewives?

Amanda: Making their day a little easier!

Jack: Readying them up for the romance of the evening.

Amanda: Tipping the scale on that job interview!

Jack: Blowing away the C.T.A.

Amanda: Good work for mom, Max? You. Ever stink other dimes?

Max: Stink? No.

Amanda: Sniff. Stop by mom's counter for a good snort?

Max: No, I never see her.

Amanda: That's a shame. She probably misses you.
          My mom misses me when I'm away and she's in pieces.
          Are you here to work, Max?

Jack: Learn. He's here to learn, 'Manda.

Max: It's nice to meet you, Amanda. Jack told me-

Jack: Nice. Yes, it's nice. And it can stay nice. Manda is my sweetheart, my flower, my friend.

Amanda: Oh, and you are mine, too. Jack Sugar, you can sweeten my cup anytime! *(Kiss)*
Smoke now. *(They do)*

Jack: One hit to the body.

Max: Wow. Some pot.

Amanda: Smacking that pineal gland.

Jack: Dosing that third eye point...serious now.

Max: Yeah. Wow.

Jack: "Wow." Twice he said, "wow."

Amanda: What a youngster you've brought us, sweet Jack!

Jack: Chicka – chicka on display. Max, y'all are welcome in my house. Relax, enjoy.

Max: Yeah.

Jack: Walk in the garden.

Max: All right.

Jack: But don't smoke there and leave the butts. No, don't do that. And don't piss in the flowerbeds or tear up the grass, don't pick anything, Max, every weed has its purpose. Treat the garden like a temple, Max, pray in it, if you can. Or just sit.

Max: Sure, Jack. It's very pretty.

Jack: Pretty; Yes, it's pretty. And it can stay that way
         it has to. Here, you be a slob, it's a living room.
         Smoke away.

Max: Yeah, nice.

Jack: Nice. Again with the nice. Max, this is a great room
         for men. Go on and get reckless. Pick your nose
         and flick it on the mantle. Relax. Lounge around,
         but don't, do not scratch my Stones records.
         Especially Aftermath, it's in mint condition. Hell,
         don't even play that one. Y'all prefer the 70's
         anyway… "Some Girls" fan?

Max: I don't like the Stones, much.

Jack: What?

Max: The Stones. I don't like the Stones much
         pass the joint man.

Jack: (Dangerous pause) What?

Max: The Stones. You were talking about the Rolling
         Stones?

Jack: I know what I was talking about, Max,
         Mick - Keith - Bill Wyman - Charlie.
         "Beggar's Banquet," "Sticky Fingers."
         What did you say?

Max: I said, "I don't like the Stones much"…

Jack: Thrice. You said it thrice. Manda, he said…

Max: I guess, The Beatles.

Jack: Don't whine, Max. I can't abide whining…

Max: Abbey Road.

Jack: That Ringo drum solo? Wuss music, are you a wuss, Max?

Max: No. What?

Jack: Maybe stupid, Max. A stupid wuss.

Max: No… I…

Amanda: Jack Sugar. Cool. Cool. Get Cool.
          He just hasn't heard.

Max: Well, "Miss You"…

Amanda: Hasn't been exposed, Jack, in an ear-opening way.
          Jack. Come on. Play nice.

Jack: Nice. Again nice.
          (Pause) Yes. It can stay nice.

Amanda: Pot head on the boil? Come on, Jack…

Max: Listen. It's only rock 'n' roll–

Amanda: Jack likes the Stones. He really likes them.

Keith the most. A lot. *(Warning)* A big pile of like he has for the Stones. Especially Keith. Jack are you all right?

Jack: "I have to turn my head until my darkness goes…"

Amanda: Breathe and ease, Jack. *(She does.)* Oh, yeah.

Jack: Thats exact, Amanda. All right, I'm smokin.'
I'm holdin' it in… I'm letting it out… I'm all
right, Max… but i don't know about you, Max.
Magnificent Max. Who are you?
Why'd ya come here?

Max: What? What do you mean?
I'm Max, you brought me here, invited.

Jack: Literal Max… So straight, so simple…
lean over, Max.

Max: NO! Why?

Jack: I want to see your eyes, Max.

Max: No. *(Alarm)*

Jack: *(Enraging)* Lean the fuck over, Max, you twist,
or I'll snap you in half like a bread stick.

     (Grabbing and pulling MAX to him.)
I wanta see your eyes, you fuck-hole, you sick
crapper! *(Looks in)*
Are you treachery, Max, are you? Show me.

Max: Okay, okay. You're looking. You tell me.

Jack: Baby blues...baby fucking robin's egg blues.
            (Relaxing)
            Calm and look, Max. No panic, Max. *(Smiles)*
            Cool and snappy as a snow pea in July.

Amanda: Oh, y'all are all right, aren't you, Max.

Max: That's exact.

Jack: *(Very high and laughing)* So why am I worrying here?

Amanda: It's just The Stones thing, Jack.
            That's all, he can learn the Stones thing.

Jack: "Music appreciation?"

Max: *(Laughing)* Yeah!

Jack: *(Deciding)* We'll play the good stuff.
            ('SWAY' from Sticky Fingers: They all dance.)
            Oh yeah, that's exact. Charlie, the secret weapon.

Max: Who?

Jack: Watts, man, Watts. The drummer.

Max: Yeah. He's good, I guess, but I like loud drummers
            better. That Aerosmith guy, or, ah, Bonham?
            Zeppelin's.

Jack: Amanda...I'm being tested.
            I'm trying not to-Max, you're pushing it, MAN.

Amanda: Jack, he doesn't know we'll teach him, Jack.
        Go out and walk in the garden before Fix gets here.

Jack: She called?

Amanda: A little late, but moving.
        Go out. Breathe and ease, see Ernest.

Jack: The irises should be open...so blue.

Amanda: Go.
        (JACK exits.)

Max: Is he always like that? So–

Amanda: Fiercely attractive? Worse, he gets worse. As the
        moon moves across the sky, his spirit waxes, it wanes,
        he ingests large amounts of heroin, sleepless for
        weeks on end, veins bulging, nose distended, horrible.

Max: Junkie? I saw his arms; no tracks.

Amanda: He eats it. Usually mixed with venison stew
        or sprinkled paprika like over buffalo slabs.

Max: He hunts?

Amanda: Preys. Creeping on the critters, grabs 'em while
        they're all cud—choking 'em down fresh and raw
        for their spirit, their essence. He brings 'em home in
        warm messy chunks to me, the wandering wife. We
        have us a fine meal of fresh flesh and horrible heroin.

Max: You're teasing me. You've both been
        teasing me all along, since I got here.

Amanda: Not completely. At least half-truths.

Max: Which half?

Amanda: Ah, ha. There's a game.

Max: What about the job? The grab. Is there a job?

Amanda: Always. Idle hands…

Max: Cut it out.

Amanda: Oh, tuff. Do you have tattoos? Brass knuckles?

Max: I wanna know.

Amanda: As do we all. "A universal desire."

Max: This is starting to piss me off.

Amanda: Are you going to hit me, Max? Did you learn
         that from-Mom-at-the-perfume-counter?

Max: Forget that.

Amanda: Would Mom approve, Max? Of hitting Girls?

Max: No.

Amanda: I should say not. And I want you to think of me
         as "Mom" here, Max. I'll care for you, nurse your
         fever, cook your gruel, cuddle your uncertainty.

Max: I don't get you.

Amanda: No. I'm afraid you don't. My love hole is already overcrowded. I suppose I could slip you a nipple for the occasional suck, the oral soothe. Smoking always worked for me as a sensual placebo.

Max: What?

Amanda: Bong hits, we'll do bong hits. You'll worry no more!

SCENE: FIX IN SPOTLIGHT
'PAINT IT BLACK' plays for the transition.

Fix: Jack Sugar and Arson Fix, *(Holds up fingers)* like this. A glove and a fist. Me, I could just see it going on and on. But Jack was starting to slow down, often I'd catch him just staring off... Empty and mournful-like. He brought himself a little piece of land in the country, began to take the train to work, commuting to crime, reading Wilhelm Reich and Krishna Murti. He was still in "The Game," but more and more unsettled, squirming with "mystical regret," fast losing his edge. I'm thinking we need that big score, to get him right.

SCENE: THE GARDEN
No music as into the garden with JACK, ERNEST is gardening as all the colors of the flowers burst against the walls.

Ernest: Mulch and mud, oooh yes! Breathing the green, my nose is overloaded. *(laughs)* I get down to it, oooh, dirt and dung, mud me, mud my toes. I'm happy, here comes my garden patrone.

Jack: Ernest…there are people in the house, it's got
           me so fucking red hot in the chest, like a garlic
           afterburn. Ernest, man.

Ernest: Distress?

Jack: That's exact. Burnin' up.
           Expanding to damage, I'm all out of…

Ernest: We'll try "The Swan." A minute, a minute and a
           half, oooh yes. Wings spread and a flap *(They do
           THE SWAN)* Amen.

Jack: That settles me. Thanks be! Can we do more?
           I want to strengthen…

Ernest: The dew held tight this morning, Jack.

Jack: The irises?

Ernest: Glistened, gleamed. Single drops, the blue shone
           through. Like cats' eyes… The cabbage sparkled,
           brainy and witty this morning, oohh they were.
           Sunflowers shook, yellow drops everywhere.
           Oooh, it was so.

Jack: What, Ernest? It was so…what?

Ernest: *(Laughs)* Startling. Superb. So sublime a morning,
           even the potatoes muttered. The celery got down
           right perky.

Jack: Y'all could hear that? With your ears?

Ernest: Bells at midnight. Loud as a fist in the eardrum.

Jack: I want to hear that.

Ernest: Weeding.

Jack: Weeding?

Ernest: Weed while breathing…oooh, yes.

Jack: Grabbing the little chokers by the neck
            and twisting them off?

Ernest: Three steps. Grasp. Pull. Breathe. Grasp. Pull.
            Breathe. While bending…

Jack: Grasp. Pull. Breathe. While bending at the waist.

Ernest: The worker position. Oooh yes.

Jack: I think she'll leave me, Ernest. What'll happen
            then? How will I…live? Ever?

Ernest: Flowers close the night's push, but give them the
            morning, the sunlight…

Jack: Without her, I'll kill everything.

SCENE: A MINUTE LATER
FIX steps into the TREE HOUSE.
JACK is already there.

Fix: Hey, hey, Jack Sugar, how do you figure?

Jack: You found them.

Fix: Bermuda. Swordfish trawling and Buddhist
meditation, roadies. But no muscle. Mick and Keith
on tape. (Hands him video)

Jack: Fix. (Laughs. They hug, mafioso kiss?)
Y'all done me a good one.

Fix: A little high class schmooze and coke in the right…
places… We've gotta move fast, though…
he's expected. London, on the fifth.
You got the wheel man?

Jack: Kid with an outlaw tendency… no time but more
moves than I'd like… I'm not… sure…

Fix: We'll button him down. The two of us, huh?
And Amanda. D.

Jack: Soft 'n' sweet. She'll be pleased to see you…

Fix: Umhmmm. She will.

SCENE: THE TREE HOUSE
A few minutes later FIX and AMANDA trying
on clothes for the party. 'NO EXPECTATIONS'
transition music plays.

Fix: When Fix was four or five, my old man took me to
the show —almost every day—he'd pick me up,
throw me over his shoulders and rush me down to
The Palace… Do you like this shirt, the checks?

Amanda: Umm. Square cut?

Fix: Yeah, and the shoulders.

Amanda: Huge.

Fix: You're right. How about this?

Amanda: T-shirt hot! Breast emphasized.

Fix: Yeah. But the pants. It was film noir stuff: Philip
          Marlowe, Bogart, cigarettes dangling, cool hats,
          long shots. What about this shirt? Too short. Or…

Amanda: Ummm. No, it is lovely.

Fix: The shirt should be white, though.

Amanda: Here, try this one. On me it's tight, but…

Fix: Papa loved that tough guy stuff, trigger men
          and dames with doomed lips… So, how is it?

Amanda: The best looking.

Fix: But the belt should be–

Amanda: Thinner—with a big buckle, and of course black.

Fix: Right. The trigger guys had all this thin hair
          combed straight back…Richard Widmark,
          John Garfield, Humphrey Bogart, sneers, jowls,
          white skin in dark suits, not an ounce of tan
          between them.

Amanda: Looked like they'd cough to pieces after punching you out. Stone tough and over forty. Lungs full of glue and broken razor blades.

Fix: Everybody, take notice, heh. Arson Fix is well fixed!

Amanda: Yes she is! Should I wear the white dress, or the flowered print… or the silver lame, heh…

Fix: Let's see…let's see that silver lame… Yeah. The women, the dames: Lana Turner, Lauren Bacall, Bette Davis, perfect Lucifer red lips and smoking, God I'd've died to be the butt end of one of those languidly sucked sticks, the burn just so, slow smokey power those dames had.

Amanda: Well?

Fix: It's terrific, sweetheart, a million dollars. But–

Amanda: What, what? Too much hip?

Fix: How about the red?

Amanda: You think so, Fix? The red?

Fix: Tonight's a big night.

Amanda: What happened to Dad?
Why'd he stop with the movies and all?

Fix: When I was fourteen, fifteen…our house burned down… Fire moves very fast through a house, a home, minutes and it eats the world. Paper, pictures, clothes—they go first, plants choking in their pots. I'd come home early, Papa didn't know I was, he wouldn't have done it if he knew, I mean we lived in Maine... I was smokin' pot with Papa's corn cob pipe and very stoned. Papa was the Big House Corners librarian, he should have been at work, safe among the encyclopedias.

Amanda: Fix. Sweetheart, you don't have to tell I...

Fix: I could hear him sobbing upstairs. I huddled in the big chair. I didn't want him to know, I'd never heard him cry before, this was Big House Corners, Maine and my Papa wanted to be a tough-guy.

Amanda: Fix. Let me, oh, sweetheart.

Fix: He didn't see me when he came down the stairs, the gas can sloggin as he emptied it everywhere, I wanted to cough from the gas fumes, wanted to puke, him sobbing sobbing, as he bent to light the wood in the fireplace, splashing gas, I didn't say anything and the flames went everywhere.

Amanda: Fix. It's all right. You're all right now.

Fix: They found my Papa fright-faced, smoke dead lying in bed, wearing my mother's robe and panties, I wasn't there, I was moving.

Amanda: Fix, what about this red dress, sweetheart? Don't I smoke in this red shimmer?

Fix: The world owes you a living, sweetheart.

SCENE: TREE HOUSE

Hours later: everybody's eaten, drank and smoked... MAX especially—very blurry.
'PAINT IT BLACK' plays again.

Jack: And now my dears, it is exactly time to watch the video.

VIDEO: ***Camera zooms in,*** *obviously hand-held, searching the room for someone, finds KEITH bedraggled on the couch, arms and legs akimbo, bottles of Rebel Yell, full ashtrays, Bud big boys; on the wall: blues man Robert Johnson, ON THE STEREO: Howlin' Wolf's 'EVIL.' KEITH twitches and curses, the door opens and MICK comes in, dancing around the room, ups the blind, offs the record, picks up the guitar—Keith's—and starts to play, singing wordlessly, over the top and bopping in place.*

Keith: *(Waking)* Bloody wanker, I'm fuckin' sleeping. Here, you rotter, you twit.

Mick: Keith, I got a new song, all E--minor chords, E-minor seventh, very bloody moody. Howsabout?

Keith: Bloody AWFUL. Get rid of the first half, maybe somethin.' Try like a, just plain *(sings)* wah...

Mick: *(Trying)* I was liking it, the modal.

Keith: Modal. You aren't fuckin' Mozart, Mick, fuck the
            modal. And pick up the bloody back beat…

Mick: Well, away from the bump and grind, I was
            going… Try a little Latin, uh Celtic tinge.

Keith: Naw, just play the thang straight,
            like budda pa buh.

Mick: Budda pa–pa buh-da.

Keith: Naw, gimme that… You play like you're going
            Chinese laundry. You gotta harp?

Mick: I wanta play.

Keith: Blow, you blow good. I'll play.

Mick: Howzabout this.
            (MICK plays and KEITH plays) Buddha pa – pah,
            wah, … Beyoo—tee—full. Guess I know. Guess I
            knew, you…uh?

Keith: Huh—huh, babe. wah wah…

Mick: Huh — huh, babe. wah wah…

            – (End of Video Tape) –

Jack: That's exact and fine, Fix, what a gift.

Max: It was outta focus, uh—minicam handheld?

Jack: Out of focus? Max, that was Mick-'n'-Keith writing, a private glimpse... Don't y'all get that? It's like watching—

Amanda: Nureyev do knee-bends.

Jack: Carl Gustav Jung in a R.E.M. state.

Amanda: Isaac Newton meeting his McIntosh.

Jack: Beethoven rippling through his first "deaf scale."

Max: What?

Jack: Creative inspiration, Max, you numb... Manda, he's—

Amanda: He's young, Jack. He can learn. Roll joints, Max... play dance music Jack.

(JACK plays 'MISS YOU' singing along.
The conversations almost overlap, loud
over the music.)

Jack: "I've been walkin' Central Park, sleepin' after dark..." *(etc.)*

(JACK singing and swaying along, MAX rolling
joints. Very blurry, stoned, slow. AMANDA and
FIX in deep conversation... these conversations
almost overlap.)

Fix: My first was beautiful, Amateur Street empty, red flickers, street light, the only motion until I start to move...

Amanda: Big-city main street?

Fix: Nah, small town cricket quiet. Hush of innocence, the balls of my feet, hips swaying, just the motion rocking the gas from the can, little splashes barely hitting the ground, I strike the match…

Amanda: One urgent motion?

Fix: Nah, easy flip of the fingers.

Jack: Isn't she lovely, Max, the way she moves, the whole swing of her?

Max: Well, yeah, I guess…

Jack: You guess.

Max: Yeah. Sure she is.

Jack: Sure she is. That's exact. Her legs tapering, hmmm, doesn't that instep make you shiver?

Max: Her feet?

Jack: The toes. Little joys of flesh… finely shaped Tweekable.

Max: Tweekable. No, I don't care about her feet. Who gives a fuck about her feet?

Jack: A "fuck." A "fuck." You wanna fuck her feet? You're telling me that?

Max: No. No, I mean, I don't give a fuck. You know what
          I mean, I don't give a fuck. Hey, let's smoke the joint.

Jack: No, no. Let's follow this out… I don't know, now,
          do y'all fuck or don't you? Asexual?

Max: No, of course, I fuck.

Jack: Now. You want to fuck now. What?
          Y'all wanta fuck me?

Max: No, I fuck women.

Jack: Their feet.

Max: No.

Jack: Then what? You wanta fuck her feet or what?

Fix: Dance with me, Manda.

Amanda: But Jack.

Fix: Won't even notice. *(They dance)*
          Baby…Fix is remembering a big double bed
          pounding, your hands in motion, hot lava mama,
          throwing you all over room one-o-nine.

Amanda: My spine twisting and bird-burrowing to get
          the propeller thigh angle.

Jack: Or what?

Max: No. Her cunt. Her ass. Tits.

Jack: "Her cunt, her ass, her tits." Smug and sure, Max,
            announce your intention to fuck my girlfriend.

Max: No, I'm here to work. The grab.
            I'm here to help you.

Jack: I don't need your help in the love department, Max,
            I can do that work. Let's get exact now. I love her,
            not just her tits, her feet. And you think you can
            take her away from me?

Max: Jack. No.

Jack: That's exact. No. You think my fire is gone?
            Just an old dog with no teeth to rip you?
            (Music abruptly shifts to 'JUMPING JACK FLASH')
            (Sings) *"I was born in a crossfire hurricane…"*
            Max, you're a fuckin' snack, a fuckin' weenie and I'm
            the whole barbecue. Move on her once and I'll rip
            your cock off, I'll stuff it in your ear! *(Grabs his balls)*
            Don't think I can do it?
            I'm crushing your balls right now.

Fix: Jack, let him go.

Amanda: Jack, easy. Breathe and ease. Let go.

Max: Jesus, Jack.

Jack: *(Laughing)* Not to worry. He's still intact.

Fix: Sugar, you're fuckin' up here. We need this kid.

Jack: He can still drive, Fix, can't you, Max,
            even with your bruised balls.

Amanda: Jack. Get out of here…Go.

Jack: Okay, honey, I'm easy now, I'm easy.
        (Grabs bottle, stick, whatever and smashes
        MAX in the face repeatedly.)
        Let's just toughen up that pretty boy glam of
        yours, Max. You death fuck, you.

        (FIX and AMANDA pull him off)

        (Shouts:) Out Jack! (FIX drags him out)

Max: Jesus Christ, my eye, my face…

Amanda: Go ahead and cry, Max. Mom's here and she won't
        tell the other boys, no she won't come here.
        There's room in my lap…

Max: Get away, you bitch… you…

Amanda: (Light slap) Cut it out, Max, that's not nice,
        I didn't hurt, I can help. Come here.

Max: No.

Amanda: Come here.

Max: Ohhh… (He does and she holds him)

Amanda: Oh, that's better, isn't it? Just hug in, Mom will
        take away all the little pains, the humiliation…

Max: (Weeping) He really hurt me. That faggot.

Amanda: All right now, Max. I doubt that his sexual
preferences had anything to do with his ability
to crush your balls. Now what about "that beast"
or "that psycho?"

Max: I'm bleeding.

Amanda: Mom can clean it up with a little Mycitracin, there…
there. Turn your face.

Max: Nobody ever hit me that hard.

Amanda: Jack doesn't hold back when it comes to bad guy
stuff. What did you do that–?

Max: I don't, I didn't do anything.

Amanda: Now Max, there must have been something.
You didn't compare the Stones to Bon Jovi
or Metallica?

Max: No!

Amanda: Now, that face will be fine. A little rough around the
edges, is all… open your legs, I'll treat your balls.

Max: Well, Mycitracin…

Amanda: More like hands-on healing, open up.

SCENE: THE GARDEN
Moments later, 'PAINT IT BLACK' plays.

Jack: I don't want him…he's treacherous.

Fix: Jack, this is the Big One, the plum of the pudding, the hot enchilada, we need the help.

Jack: No, Fix. This is mine, my house, my big score, my sweetheart, I want it perfect, no outsider who's all cock and bicep. I want him out, he's out no fuckin' around, Fix. He's messing with the balance.

Fix: Jack, you're twisting things here,
         he hasn't touched her.

Jack: What, she told you? She talked about him?

Fix: Jack. Jack. You're brain's turnin' to grits on me.

Jack: He's out. Y'all know that.

Fix: Yeah, yeah.

Jack: No. No, Fix, not yeah, yeah. Know it Fix,
         really get it.

Fix: Jack. Don't. I'll hurt you,

Jack: *(Laughs)* That's exact?

Fix: You're walking the line with me…

Jack: I'll stay there. That's exactly where I want to be.
         No fuckin' around, Fix.

Fix: You talking' to me? No, that can't be.
Somebody else here, maybe?

Amanda: *(Entering)* Jack. Stop it. You're spreading piss and
nastiness, we don't fight with Fix, Fix is our dear,
our darling.

Jack: Witch. Flame queer.

Fix: Why you cracker barrel–

Amanda: Stop it now, everybody.
Max stays in, Jack, he knows about the grab.

Fix: What? He knows what?

Amanda: That is Mick–and–Keith in Bermuda.

Jack: You told him…

Amanda: No, I never did. He guessed, with you it's Stones–
Stones all the time. He figured it out. He can think.

Jack: Sweetheart. Did ya fuck him?

Amanda: That boy? That lump-of-smarts-Max? Oh sure,
Jack. First we did it on the table, then under the
table, dishes flying, fettuchini everywhere, me
moaning out Italian arias, then we moved to that
couch, the upholstery flying out, we skinned that
old couch clean, his sit bones have a big future in
the upholstery trade. Ended up in the medicine
cabinet, me crammed in and willing, aspirin
bottled, rubbing my nipples, toothpaste spreading
up and down my thighs as he power donged me.

He musta come all of five, six times in those three minutes, Jack, and me, I got close, very close, to ecstasy. Oh, I changed his life, Jack.

Jack: *(Laughing)* Launched his libido.

Amanda: Re-aligned his Eiffel Tower.

Jack: Polished his periscope.

Amanda: Jack Sugar, is that a woody I see pointing my way, Fix, lookie there, Jack Sugar's got his root in an uproar.

Jack: Just a little ol' hard-on, sweetheart.

Amanda: Fix, my dear, we must be thick. Jack doesn't have a mad on, it's a woodie thing! I'll be durned, thar, Jack Sugar, we can take care a that woody thing right now, I reckon.

Jack: I'd be pleased, ma'am.

Amanda: You just have ta ask, Jack.

(AMANDA leads JACK up the tree.
sounds of them fucking, lovemaking)

SCENE: THE TREEHOUSE
Next morning, 'PAINT IT BLACK' plays.

Max: Do I get a gun?

Jack: No, gun, exactly not, for you, we want this…

Fix: Smooth and professional, in and out, the Glimmer
          Twins untampered with, sharp…

Jack: Listen to Fix, here, Max, it's all about cool,
          we want to join our cool with theirs.

Amanda: They're our first rock stars, ya know that Max?

Jack: We'll be their first kidnappers. For Mick, minorly
          disturbing, that snakey charm; but for Keith–a new
          high, maybe danger cool…

Fix: Fix is doubtful of that, Jack. Remember somebody
          pushed Brian Jones in that pool.

Jack: Fuck, no fuckin. Keith n' Mick never did that…

Fix: Jack, Jack you bought all that "Alas, Alas,
          he is gone" bit? It was a con Jack Sugar,
          you should get that. You're a con man.

Max: How do we do it—uh—Knock 'em down?
          Baseball Bat?

Jack: No, the Psychic Charm Show.

Fix: No, The old snow job.

Amanda: Chanting and disguises, you mean? Superglue in
          the lock of the limo? Gee, Mick, I'd love to show
          you my Tarot Deck, it's just down here in—in—this

little ole dungeon. In my basement, here, slip into the comfy handcuffs? I don't think that will work, guys…

Max: We just go…somewhere and they come out and we box 'em, uh, bag 'em.

Jack: Grab!

Fix: Snatch!

Amanda: Kidnapping—Major criminal F.B.I. urgent. Have you guys ever…

Jack: Well, uh, Miss Fanny Tanny back home. She had this toy poodle, just a little thing, I just picked it up and stuck it in my pocket. Held it for ten days. It was smooth. It kept biting me though.

Fix: And they payed?

Jack: They would of. That little thing chased our mailman and got pancaked by the milk truck… come on, i was only fifteen… who have you'all grabbed?

Fix: Fix followed the Patty Hearst kidnapping very carefully, the lessons apply. Boldness. Clarity. Calm.

Amanda: Sex. We'll seduce them.

Jack: What?

Amanda: Poontang: The ribald joys, the erotic mystery.
Me 'n Fix, we'll fuck 'em into captivity.

Jack: No, fuck that.

Fix: No, that won't ever–

Max: Why don't we go where they are, get some guns,
you guys shoot 'em in the foot, I'll drive up, stuff
'em in the trunk, drive home?

Jack: Shoot 'em in the foot… stuff 'em-in-the-trunk?
What about the body guards? Press Corps?
Groupies? Management? Where are we gonna
stuff them, you dumb—

Fix: Fix know what we need, practice. A trial run.

Amanda: A kidnapping warm-up before the work-out.

Jack: Yeah, it's sharp. That's sharp. Practicing for the
grab. Yeah.

Amanda: No room for the sloppy flap when it comes to
Keith 'n' Mick.

Jack: That's exact.

         (Loud knocking, repeated,
         JACK & FIX draw big guns in a big manner.)

Max: Someone's at the door...

Jack: What?

Max: The Door.

Jack: What? There can't be anyone at the door.
          Max, You–

Fix: Fix hears someone knocking, cops?
          Jack, who knows?

Jack: No one knows anything… Manda?

Amanda: Visitors from another planet? Psycho-selling
        vacuum cleaners, maybe. Dr. Vicious seed
        catalogs? Could be… I'll go and see.
        (Knocking more frantic) I'll hide the pot first.

Max: I'll hide the pot for you, Amanda.

Jack: I'll hide the fuckin' pot, Amanda, the door.
          Play the wife.

Amanda: I don't have an apron…
        buttons & bows, maybe, or a shower cap
        and robe look, I'll go get some props.

          (More knocking)

Fix: Someone get the door…
          (Cocking gun and pointing it at the door)

Max: Maybe they'll go away.

Jack: No. They won't go away, Max, open the door.

Max: It's not my house.

Amanda: I'll go, I'll go. I'll take a dishrag or–

Fix: Do it now. *(Pointing gun)*

Jack: Get the door. *(Pointing gun)*

Max: I've got it. *(Opening)* Hello! Can I help you?

Ruth: Yeah. Live on the ground floor like normal people
         do. I almost broke my neck climbing up in the
         dark, fuckin' heard of handicap fuckin' access?
         This whole place is sue-able.

Max: It's a tree. It's not dark.

Ruth: To the blind it's always black soot at midnight, or
         did you think the white cane & dark glasses was a
         fuckin' fashion choice? Where the fuckin' chair?...
         to sit...You do sit? Listen, bud, I'm bleeding and
         crippled and need to sit down.

Max: Oh, right there. *(Pointing)*

Ruth: Are you "pointing," Is that a point I feel?
         I'm fuckin' blind, bud. I don't get the fuckin' point
         and don't you condescend to take my arm and
         lead me, you liberal shit... Use words, paint a
         visual road-map. The chair is right–left–center...
         It is one foot–two feet–three feet away. Come on,
         come on, make a sentence.

Max: The chair is two feet – fuckin' to your left.

Ruth: Brav–fuckin'—O.

Amanda: You're bleeding.

Ruth: Went through the fuckin' windshield. Ray, the
          walking penis, grabbed at my crotch just once too
          often, I punched him. He punched the brakes…

Amanda: How odd. I've got Mycitracin, soothes
          without scarring.

Ruth: Sure. Got any whiskey? The shock is wearing off.

Max: We've got pot.

Amanda: Roll big, Max. How's your arm, honey?

Jack: No pot. Hello Ruthie. What are you doing
          in my house?

Ruth: Well, I might be an unpleasant presence, Jack,
          a hopeless cripple with a bad attitude, stumbling
          on your woodland paradise by mistake…

Jack: You might be but you're not.

Ruth: Not today… you can put away that "Smith &
          Wesson," Arson Fix, I'm not the danger here,
          I'm a blind person. It's Ray you should worry
          about… He's a fuckin' fruit bowl and his gun
          is easily as big and nasty as yours…

Fix: Hello Ruthie, how's the girl?

Ruth: Hotter than you could handle, honey.

Jack: Your husband. Where is he?

Ruth: We fuck-but-we-do-not-marry.

Fix: Where's Ray, Ruthie?

Ruth: Out cold at the steering wheel, last I saw. You
          people took his money. That was bad. And then
          you burned his Porsche. Again, bad.
          Ray's an evil shit.

Fix: Jack, I thought no one knew where you lived?

Jack: Go get Ray, Max. Bring him in.

Max: Me... I?

Fix: Take my gun. *(Gives)*

Jack: How did you find the house, Ruthie?

Ruth: I didn't. I don't drive much, as I have a tendency
          to run over things. The blindness, Fix, or did you
          forget?

Jack: Who else knows, Ruthie?

Ruth: No one else. Ray works alone. He asks lots
          of questions. People remembered you.
          On the train, In the town. And the
          giant flowers are hard to miss.

Fix: We can use this. Nobody will know...

Jack: Grab practice—yes, but… it's easy, too easy
           maybe, Ruthie, do you have people?

Ruth: Oh, no—bad blood—all crippled on to death.
           Just Ray and me… Him I don't love he's petty
           and sadistic.

Amanda: You take care of him.

Ruth: I fuck him for money and do his books.

Amanda: How odd, why stay with him if you don't like—

Ruth: Are you a "babe?" You sound like "a babe."
           Patchouli girl and perfect floating "babe" breasts,
           huh, you wouldn't get it at all… Horribly maimed
           eye sockets does not exactly lead one to graceful
           romantic relationships.

Amanda: I'm sorry. My mom was maimed.
           Crazy harsh like you, but only in the fall.

Ruth: Crazy brains and ravaged eyeballs, that's bonding,
           we are bonding now.

Jack: Ruthie, we're kidnapping you and Ray.
           Consider yourself held.

Ruth: A mistake. But, we'll wait for Ray.

           *(MAX and RAY enter, RAY is holding MAX's gun…
           He is very pleasant throughout.)*

Ray: Ruthie, I am up. Up and ready to boogie-woogie.
           You shouldn't have left me in the ditch like that
           tho, Pal, put the gun down.

Ruth: I figured you'd survive, Pal.

Ray: You were right. I'm as vibrant and vigorous as ever.
           I took Max's gun away, Jack, and it was really easy.
           Give me yours or it's Max ventilation time.

Jack: I don't care about Max, Ray.

Amanda: Jack, give him the gun. He's serious. Jack.
           (JACK gives the gun)

Ray: You too Fix or I shoot the babe, once in the
           stomach, and then again in the head, just for fun.
           (FIX gives up gun)
           Jack, Pal. You took my money and you didn't say,
           "please..." And then Fix burns my Porsche.

Jack: Natural selection, boy, I'm a better bad guy than
           you. Your money just naturally came my way.

Ray: Jack, Pal. I treated you straight. You dicked me.

Jack: You were shooting people and leaving 'em on
           my tab. Cops were coming to me, looking for
           someone to incarcerate. That wasn't cool with me,
           Ray. I had to let you know so I took your money,
           all your money, I had to do it.

Fix: Fix, on the other, enjoyed burning your Porsche,
           Ray, it blew up so lovely, all flaming chrome.

Ray: You pals dicked my manhood. Now I am a petty
           and vengeful person. And I wonder, what have
           Jack Sugar and Arson Fix got that I want?
           (Staring at AMANDA)

A shockingly lovely girl, dangerous to look at, any reasons you shouldn't be my girlfriend, girlfriend?

Amanda: I'm spoken for, pal, I'm with them.

Ray: Sure you are but I've got the gun, come on, girlfriend, I just want to borrow a piece or two of you, I'll give 'em back. Tell that dyke to stop moving around, she makes me nervous.

Jack: Fix. Don't. I'll get him.
(Movin' slow)

Ruth: Ray, you shit. Leave the Patchouli girl alone. I'll fuck you.

Ray: Poontang is not the point, Ruthie, no.

Ruth: Don't let him touch you, patchouli girl, he's nasty.

Ray: Some girls like nasty. How about it, girlfriend? Pull out the old birth-control, it's in and out time.

Max: Hey, now...you stop.

Jack: Stay put, Max. I've got him.
(Continues to move on RAY, very slow)

Ray: You? You have nothing.

Jack: That's exact wrong, Ray, I'm as dangerous as I wanna be, boy, and right now...

Ray: Stop moving.

Jack: I know you, your soul is full of mud, it is a cesspool,
          I see in you, I know, I know, I'm a shit bog too,
          don't look away, there's nowhere else to look—
          I'm already in you.

Ray: Jack. Pal, I'll just–

Jack: No. No. You won't. Stare into my eyeballs, Ray,
          and you'll see your face staring back. Can you
          shoot that?

Ray: (Mesmerized) I will.

Jack: When? I'm on you now, my hands on your face…
          (FIX pulls a 2nd gun and shoots RAY's gun
          out of his hand) Awww, Fix.

Ray: My hand.

Jack: Fix. Goddamnit. I had him…

Fix: Exact and ventilated.

Jack: I was doing just fine, thank-you.

Amanda: You were the one who said no guns, Fix.
          How many guns do you have?

Fix: Guns for every occasion, sweetheart.

Amanda: And, Jack, you were great too. And Max.
          Everybody was great.

Ruth: Very impressive. Balls for everybody.

Jack: Let 'em go.

Fix: Jack, no.

Jack: They can't hurt us, Fix... just let 'em go.

Fix: No. Max, put 'em in the shed?

Jack: Not in the shed, Fix we don't, the karma,
           violence will color our actions. No, Fix.
           We need to stay clear here.

Fix: Karma? Clear? Jack, are you going soft on me!
           It's rabid Ray and ruthless Ruth.
           They were gonna hurt Amanda.

Jack: Good won out, Fix. The balance is restored.
           Ray, take off!

Fix: No, Ray, don't take off. Max, take 'em to the shed.

Jack: Max. Do like I say.

Max: No, Jack. I've got the gun.

Jack: What?

Fix: That's right, Max, and you can keep it.
           Take 'em to the shed.

Max: Guns work! Yeah. I'll use it on Keith and Mick.
           The grab.

Amanda: Oh, Max.

Ruth: Still on the Stones thing, huh, Jack?

Jack: Max. You numb-nut.

Max: What did I say?

Fix: The grab, Max. You told Ray about the
         Keith 'n' Mick grab.

Ray: Jack, Fix, I can help. I'm good, I'm lethal…

Jack: We'd be countin' bodies. No. The grab's off.

Fix: We need this, Jack.

Jack: Fix, it's off. Fuckin' Max.

Fix: No, Jack. Max, take them to the shed…

Ray: Wait. Pals. I was teasing. Just a hard tease.
         Ruth, tell 'em…

Ruth: Right, Ray. You shit-bag. It was very funny.

Fix: Move out, Max.

Jack: I'm not liking this, Fix.

Ray: Jack, I've got money. We can go get–

Jack: Help the lady, Max.

Ruth: I can walk. I can walk.

(Pause. JACK sits, rolls joint?)

Fix: We've gotta bury them, Jack, you know it.
The grab—

Jack: Off and over... I'm done with the blood thing, Fix.
I'm tryin' to control.

Fix: Jack. *(Gunshots)*

All: Max!

Max: *(Coming in)* I took 'em to the shed. No problem.

Fix: No problem? You shot them. You killed them.

Max: I thought—

Fix: You're the wheel-man, Max. You don't think.
I told you take 'em to the shed. We have a shed.

Jack: Cadaver Manufacturer *(Sadly)* Dumb Max has
got the ventilator blues.

Amanda: I liked that woman...Max.

Max: I just pulled the trigger and they fell down.

Fix: *(Taking it)* It's a tool, Max, not a cock.
You don't play with it.

Jack: I am doubting the whole escapade.

Fix: Fix is in agreement.
          Max was some great choice, Jack Sugar.

Jack: You're blaming me? You gave him the gun.

Fix: I didn't think he'd shoot it.

Max: Fellas, I didn't know.

Jack: No whining, Max, I can not abide the whining.

Max: I was just.

Amanda: Max, please shut up. Jack Sugar,
          we can use the cards. They'll help us.

Jack: Second sight. Yes. What about it, Fix?

Fix: Hocus Pocus, Jack and Amanda.

Amanda: Fix. Sweetheart.

Fix: *(Relenting)* All right. But Fix won't touch 'em.

Amanda: You pick the card, Jack.

Jack: *(Meditates)* I am pleased... *(Picks)*
          The Hanged Man.

Fix: Great. A hopeful sign. Dead on the end of a rope.

Jack: Card of change. Maybe out of indecision?

Fix: Bad odds, we'd better bury the bodies.

Jack: Tarot is mystery, often inversion–

Fix: You are really getting spooky weird, Jack.
          Max, where are the bodies?

Max: In the garden. Blood on the Irises.

Jack: You killed them... in my garden?,

Fix: Jack, come on—the bodies—we've gotta hide
          them: Max'll wait.

SCENE: THE TREEHOUSE
MAX is on AMANDA's lap, smoking a large joint.

Amanda: I was five when Momma smashed her first Toyota,
          not even drunk, just hyped hysterical twisting her
          head left and right, I hit the windshield but I was
          little and it didn't break, my shin-bone did.

Max: Mom, I just wanna do things like a rich man.

Amanda: Red, puffy, hurt at first. They gave me a big big
          cast and I slammed around in it all summer,
          climbing the trees, swimming the waters.

Max: Get the best spit polish in town.

Amanda: The doctor said it would never grow,
          that poor bone, they'd break the other leg,
          I'd have a short stride.

Max: Have my steak well done instead of the
          hamburger special…au gratin.

Amanda: A short stride, Max, my torso would grow,
          but Mamma said "No," she drove all over the
          south; revivals, tent shows, faith healers, voodoo
          dungeons; but nothing worked, I was active, each
          week I worked a little more cast off 'till it was just a
          glob of plaster round that shin…

Max: I had a nose bleed, once.

Amanda: You're a constant surprise, Max, I mean that. Jesus.

Max: Did you get…

Amanda: Better? Yes. Summer was almost over, the days
          were cooling, leaves curling, Mamma was getting
          desperate, her fall-persona would be coming,
          the irises of her eyes were like basketballs.

Max: Was she…?

Amanda: Beautiful. Her face a scarlet fist, hair wild, under a
          September Blue Moon. She carried me to a clear
          spot in the woods, she laid me down. Biting the
          glob of plaster off in one bite, she laid her hand
          on the poor bones and keening for all the world
          to hear, drowned that shin in tears… that's some
          mommying,

          *(JACK walks in unnoticed, points gun and pulls
          the trigger, AMANDA screams softly, she knows
          the gun is not loaded.)*

SCENE: THE GARDEN

ERNEST is standing on one leg.

Ernest: Mr. Sugar, red sky at morning.

Jack: Sailor take warning… but I am no sailor.

Ernest: A warning is a warning…
what do you need Mr. Sugar?

Jack: The Crane.

Ernest: Hmm, yes, but humming not whooping.
Would you join me in this pose of balance…

Jack: I am too jacked up, I need transformation,
shedding of the tense and anxious–

Ernest: We will do the caterpillar, a week or ten days
we will start on that cocoon right away.

Jack: No, no I need something now. Tear me up
only it'll take some evil thing coming out of me,
not a place to think like the garden.

Ernest: The worms crawl in the worms crawl out…
Garden wasn't always like this, came out of the
wilderness once just like the rest of us…
the primitive powers know all about the evil.
Do the Goat.

Jack: Udders? Hoofs? Naw, I need–

Ernest: Pan god of the old ways. Horn and tail, Mr. Sugar,
but I won't join you. Your own dark place is
what you want, not mine.

Jack: Pan? The pipes of pan, Brian Jones collected the
         pipes in the hash field of Joujaka Pan?
         You all can do that, call him up?

Ernest: Oh no—not me, but you can.

Jack: Show me I'm the burnin bush, I'm the burnin bush,
         I am the fuckin volcano. I need power Ernest.
         Now. Why not the snake, we should do the snake.

Ernest: Too soon, Mr. Sugar, you have to purify before
         you can rule, too soon for the snake.

Jack: I need it now. I'm gonna—

Ernest: Have you looked at the moon flowers, so bloomed
         under the orb, that shining. Power there, beauty.

Jack: Not what I need, I wanna kill him,
         what about the ogre?

Ernest: Too strong, too grotesque... why not climb the
         Willow. You want to hear it weeping?
         You could hear it, Mr. Sugar, I know you could.

Jack: No, no goddam you Ernest—you have got what I
         need, give it to me

Ernest: Here it comes–then squeeze everything in all of it
         now and then hurt yourself from the inside.

Jack: I wanna be harsh, I wanna be harsh, I wanna be
         harsh as I can be… I'm chanting now harsh, harsh,
         harsh… I'm asking for something primitive here,
         come on you fuck, you puck, you pan.

(*Enter PAN. 'SYMPATHY FOR THE DEVIL' plays.
Pan dances.*)

Pan: If a man be soft, ghostly shouldn' he stay that way
         mostly.

Jack: Lucifer Lucifer, you the devil.

Pan: No, no much older, not much bolder. Older than
         that dying oak, or the fat on that old christmas
         bloke. Or the stones that river choke.

Jack: Ok, ok, you're pretty old.

Pan: Ancient begat at the first crack at the dawn of
         time / before the first water lily tickled first water
         lily / before lack of first breakfast rumbled thru the
         first belly swelly / before the pox, before trouble,
         before the first ox, before bubble before–

Jack: Ok, Ok I get it but do you have the power I need?

Pan: Over horn toad's croak / over a lovesick mammy
         goat / …oo–la–la–power to tickle / power to poke
         / I can puss your pickle / nanny your bananny /
         provoke your joke.

Jack: Naw, I want action. (*Whispers*) I wanna do evil…

Pan: Call a weevil, a weasel, a wart, or a wastrel.
         Get some teeth, some grief, some longing,
         some smell.

Jack: I want to kill somebody.

Pan: To make an enemy ghostly / He needs patience, mostly.

Jack: I called you here to–

Pan: Ye called the wrong dervish / I'm not at his service / I'll pull his tail, goose his gonad / Flatulate you frequently...

Jack: I'm gonna do this.

Pan: Be soft, be sweet, hug the flowers with your feet.

Jack: No. Fuck. No... I'm gonna kill.

Pan: Don't confess to me. I'm not a forgiveness tree, you want evil, it's your upheaval.

Jack: What can I do...?

Pan: Hurt yourself inside / Don't stop 'till someone's died...

          (JACK loads his gun)

SCENE: FIX IN SPOTLIGHT
'SYMPATHY FOR THE DEVIL' plays.

Fix: That was the minute, the minute right after four a.m.; so thick we almost sat in it, the dark purple and heavy. Now, all five of us poised and stretched tight, that's when Fix coulda stepped in and blown the game wide open, grabbed Amanda and headed out, hand-in-hand, toward a happy ending. I knew it too. Sat in that moment, weighed it, calculating... Fix didn't move, I stared at the sky and the morning came, streaking like a hot coal...

SCENE: THE TREEHOUSE
FIX enters. 'SYMPATHY FOR THE DEVIL' plays.

Amanda: Hello, Fix, my touch, my darling.

Fix: Sweetheart...*(They kiss)* Stay here, Amanda, Fix doesn't trust this grab. Get sick. Faint or something. I've got a bad...

Amanda: No, sweetheart, we're not worrying, are we? Mick'll be easy! You know they will, we'll collect our wad and no more Amateur Street, queens for a day, eh Fix.

Fix: It's Jack. I don't trust...

Amanda: *(Laughs)* Jack's a pussy, Fix.
Putty in my hands, you know that.

(JACK enters)

Fix: Not this time, Manda, he's been in the garden, all night...

Amanda: Breathing and easing, Fix, meditations with Ernest. Fix, you got a chicklen inside ya? You're shaking...

Jack: Good morning, criminal elite. I've got guns for
           everybody! Where's old calm-and-cool Max...?

Amanda: Just getting up.

Jack: Let's go see him, all of us. Time for a side of
           Beggars Banquet before the train leaves.

Fix: Jack, I wanna talk.

Jack: On the train, Fix, let's rock first... Max, open them
           baby blues, come on boy, time waits for no one!
           Power! Max! A day of infamy.

Amanda: Big time, Max.

Max: Is there any pot left?

Jack: Of course, Max, but we need y'all clear for the
           grab, no pot 'till after.

Max: Fuck you, Jack.

Jack: Max, you sweet thing. Say it again.

Max: Fuck you, Jack. And your fuckin' ugly lezzie cunt
           girlfriends, your fuckin' bullshit games, You're a
           nothin', a blot, a hole, I'll shit all over you. You and
           your faggot Stones, butt-banging poseurs.

Jack: O my Max. Such rich language. Anything else,
           Y'all dying to say, Max?

Max: Where's the pot, old man?

Jack: Dead Max! *('MIDNIGHT RAMBLER' up and loud.*
           JACK shoots MAX repeatedly. it should take a
           while before MAX falls.)
           "And it hurts."

Amanda: *(Sadly)* Aww, Jack…

Max: *(Dying)* Mom? Mom…

Jack: Y'all fucked him, Manda.

Amanda: No, I never did do that…

Jack: I see him on you…Manda.

Amanda: Nothing, Jack…there's nothing there.

Jack: I won't have it, Manda.

Amanda: Like a doll, a stuffed doll, just a little thing, Max.

Fix: Move away from him, Manda, behind me.

Jack: Y'all not in this, Fix.

Fix: Wrong, Jack Sugar. You figured it all wrong. Fix is
           the promiscuous spark, the rooster in the wood
           pile. *(Kisses AMANDA, who stares blank)*

Amanda: Fix, Max is broken now, gears all bloody.

Fix: Just down to little ole you and little ole me,
           Jack Sugar. That's the game.

Amanda: Sweetheart, do you have any Band-aids? Or tape?

Jack: Fuckin Fix is the fuck!
         (*Laughing*) I'm gonna tear you.

Amanda: Jack. Cut it out, Jack.

Jack: Get over here girl.
         Your fuck buddy's got some bleeding to do.

Fix: Amanda get behind me now.

Amanda: I...no...Sweetheart, it's just Jack, let's just–

Fix: Amanda—move. He's an animal now thinking with
         his cock. He'll hurt us.

Amanda: No, it's just Jack.

Jack: "Just Jack," "Just Jack,"
         Amanda, I'm your man, your beau, c'mere.

Amanda: No. She's my.

Jack: Clit-tease, sweetheart, nipple rub. That's all. I can
         really–How could you do this? We are one person.

Amanda: Jack, she's the ace I love her.

Fix: Amanda get behind me, now, it's time to break
         this cracker barrel open... Jack Sugar, I'm a better
         fuck, and a better shot.

Jack: Amanda (*He grabs her*) you want tongue fucks all
         your life? No, this can't be—

Amanda: No, Jack *(Slaps him)*

Jack: Hey!

Amanda: You don't decide me, Jack, I decide me.

Jack: *(Weeping)* I can't…I won't be alone…
          Sweetheart… you're inside me… my heart… in…
          in.. You were inside there. I felt you there with
          me. Working on me. Skimming off the top layer
          of crap 'n' disappointment 'n' hurt. Discarding all
          that that piles up on peopled crushes their rubbish
          of broken hearts into a pile of ugliness and scar
          tissue, we made new skin, babe, rubbing, easing
          every hurt o it, forming a new muscle out of tender
          sweat and touch. You knew you were in here. I
          know you did how could this…? Amanda. You're
          hurtin' me. I won't be alone, no, I want you here…
          I'ts our garden our house… Fix is—

Amanda: C'mon Jack, What's a little sex between friends?
          We're friends. Fix, the bed's big enough.

Fix: Fix is no sideshow freak, Amanda.
          He doesn't need us to get off. Look at him.

Jack: She's smoking girl, she'll burn you out.

Fix: Jack, you weak thing, shut up.
          You're done deciding and Fix is gonna finish you.

Amanda: Fix, honey, he's my friend.

Fix: Decision time, 'Manda, this is it. The kill, the
          high point, don't you feel it? Gripping you

deep, that life and death danger thing?
Honey, Fix is burning with it. I'm gonna take
him out and then it's just we–

Amanda: No, Fix, honey, he's just a man, a "Hanged Man..."

Fix: Out of the way. Now!

Jack: Fix, you fuck. *(He jumps at her. FIX shoots twice.
          professional, accurate.)*

Jack: "And it hurts." *(Dropping dead, music fades)*

Amanda: Jack. C'mon, Jack, get up, Jack. Cut it out now.

Fix: Sweetheart. Come here. Let Fix give you a good
          one Baby.

Amanda: You're going to give me a good one? This is Jack
          Sugar… so full of holes, how could you do that?

Fix: Go out to the garden, Amanda. Fix has to hide
          the bodies. Fix will come there.

Amanda: Queen of flames, don't come there.
          Don't touch me.

SCENE: FIX IN SPOTLIGHT
'GIMME SHELTER' plays underneath.

Fix: Maybe Fix didn't have to shoot him then, coulda let
          it go, painful-misunderstanding-between-pals kinda
          thing, but with Jack playing poison and   my

rooster-ism up, there was nothin' for it. And maybe I wanted to get to this, the final shot, crackle and smoke, bannisters exploding. Arson Fix, the flame queer, working miracles with her darling on the heating garden... But I never got that. By the time I got there Amandine was gone.

SCENE: THE GARDEN
Leaves are dropping steadily and thick.

Amanda: Jack is gone. And Max. A stiff.

Ernest: Fall is beginning, too. The morning sky,
red crimson beauty.

Amanda: In fall, my Momma pounced on every strong gust, every cold blowing pitch of wind, she ran with them, up and down the narrow yard, the red oak leaves racing with her. Back and forth, her eyes ballooning, and sockets popping until, exhausted finally, my Momma would flop, giggling, in the garlic patch. Oh, she was a nut ball.

Ernest: Good instincts to ward off the evil.
Garlic does that, oh yes.

Amanda: Possession? You think so?

Ernest: Well, splits. *(Sadly)* If I could have known her,
we could have done The Birds, The Dove—
for grace, Jackdaw—for laughs, Ravens—
for wisdom. If I would have known her,
we could have flown together

Amanda: What? "Could–have–dones?" Ernest, she's alive.
Looney-binned. But present still. We could go.

Ernest: Help. We could help. Oooh, yes. Let's do that.
We'll need supplies, do you dig?
(Excitedly pointing)
We'll need supplies. Forget-me-nots for memory,
Peppermint for ease, Potatoes for substance.

Amanda: More. More. She's very hardcore.

Ernest: Aloe vera for healing, Deadly Nightshade
immunity, Sweet Basil and an apple a day.

Amanda: On! On! We'll dig the world.

— THE END —

A publicity still from the rehearsal process of

EVIL TRIGGERS DOWN AMATEUR STREET:

A Play in Black and White, 1991

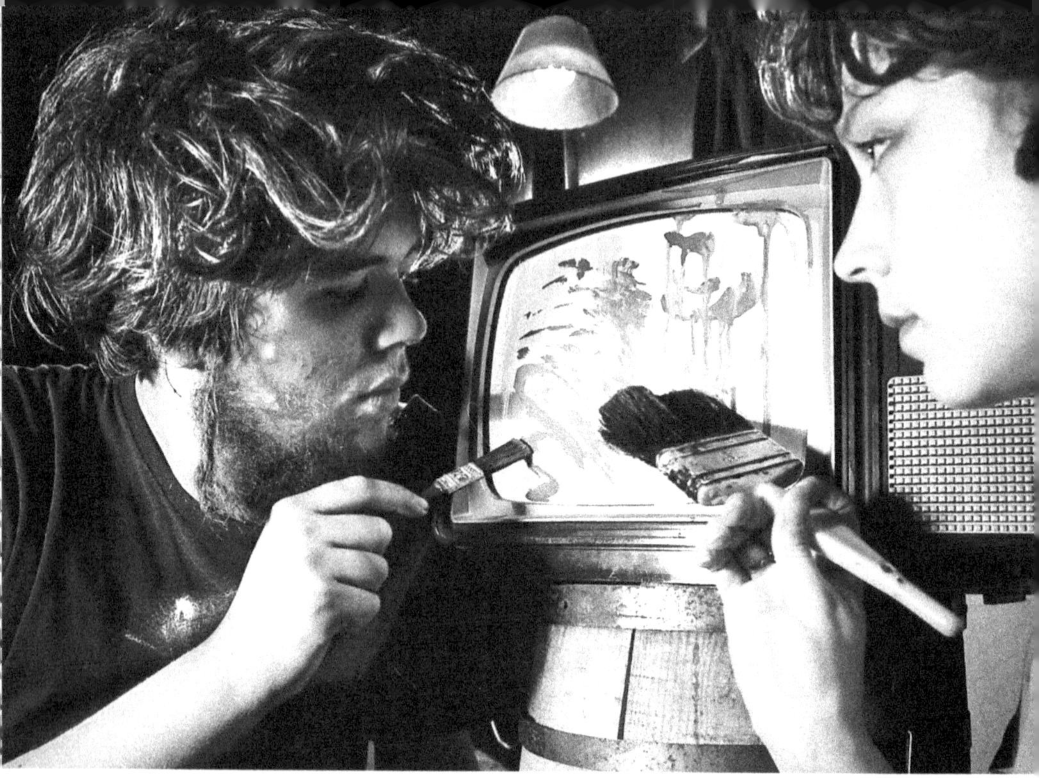

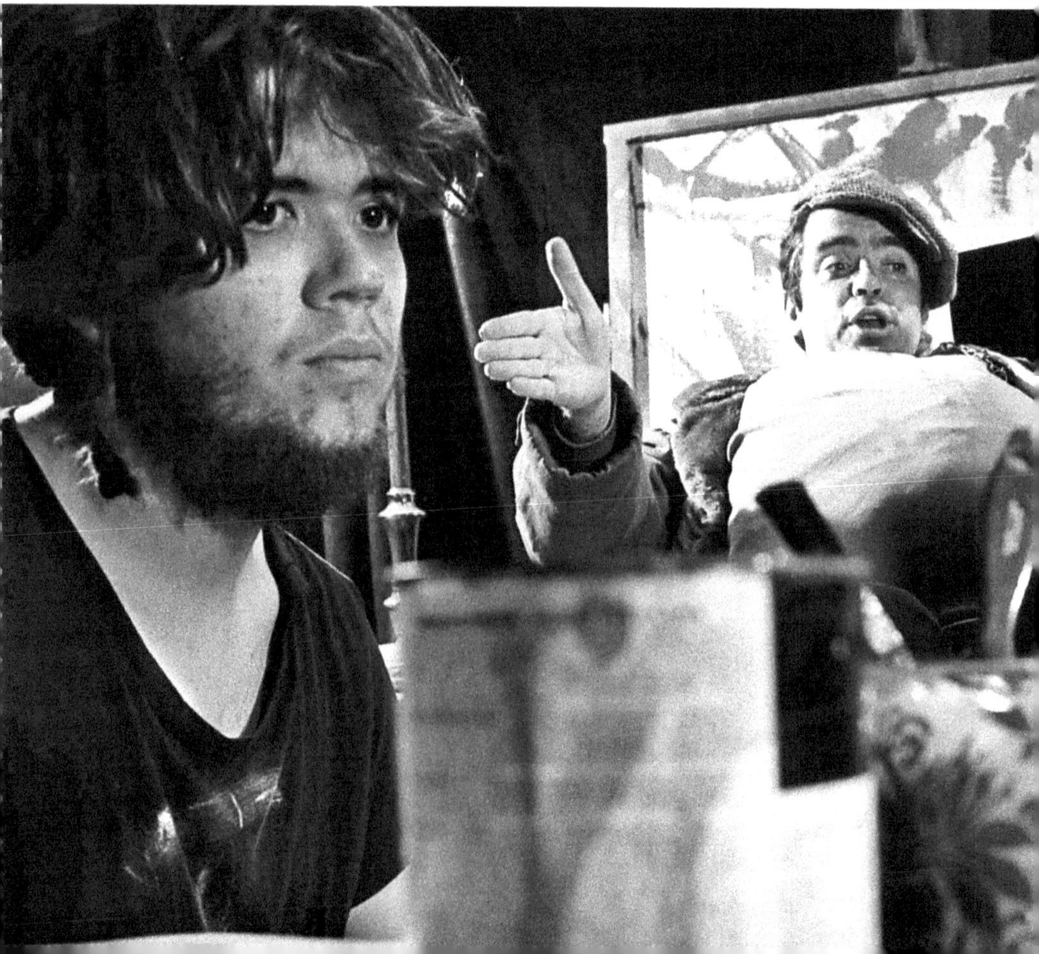

Dying is Private
the Satch and Mo play

Premiered 1992
Curious Theater Branch–North Ave.
Chicago, IL

performed by:
Beau O'Reilly
Colm O'Reilly
Anita Stenger
Spencer Sundel

INTRO

My third solo play, written the year my father died and my large family was very much on my mind… We were working with group direction at this point in the company, an effective and invigorating way to work that takes a lot of time.

Colm O'Reilly played SATCH, I believe his first lead role and Anita Stenger played MO. It was the two of them who brought the play to life; they were excellent, with me running along behind playing multiple roles, something I never did again….

Spencer Sundel did the sound from a room above the stage and played the MAN WHO COUGHS, John Coyne did the set. Not many people saw it, I think… It remains one of my best scripts and I think we should have done it again… we didn't.

Curious was like a house afire in those days, running from show to show. I left all the character and set description here, a practice I soon abandoned. Let the show show you the facts, writer… not the organizing principles.

SYNOPSIS

Two young painters living almost chastely together talk and paint while various members of Satch's large family drop in with news from outside. A biker pays Mo an unwelcome visit, the man who coughs lives upstairs.

CAST OF CHARACTERS:

SATCH: Young artist with a thing for color, a fascination with shapes, numbers, and their combinations. Prefers the dark and the security of indoors. Likes Mo but is clumsy and unsure of himself with her.

MO: Photographer, painter, older than Satch and much more worldly wise, has been freaked out and frightened by the world. She is pleased to have the comfort of a world with Satch, but longs, at the same time, to break that world open.

DEE-DEE: Satch's oldest sister, matriarch of the family, sharp, condescending. She is certain that Satch is highly intelligent and creative but not so sure about Mo. Terrible taste in clothes. Fortyish.

MORTECAI: Satch's oldest brother, big man, big presence, a storyteller with a flair for the theatrical. As warm as Dee-dee is cold. Fortyish.

BERTIE MCD.: Biker, mechanic, violent when bugged. He's always getting bugged. But he respects "love" "marriage."

R. BROTHER NED: *Satch's most repressed and worried sibling. He has a family duty and he will do it, no matter how uncomfortable he becomes. Thirtyish.*

THE MAN WHO COUGHS: *Artist, seer, one foot on the other side of the grave. Thin, greying, coughing, dying, calm. He has wisdom to pass on and he has chosen Satch and Mo to receive it.*

THE SET

Small, crowded room, Satch and Mo's studio... The walls and floors are covered with their painting, which they constantly paint, scratch out and paint again...

The room is lit by candles, cluttered, small, claustrophobic. The play is done in three quarter staging with the audience seated as close as possible. The feeling should be that we are all in Satch and Mo's studio.

Satch and Mo's bed is almost vertical, with only the slightest angle to it so that when Satch and Mo climb in they are actually leaning against the wall, their "lying down" is uncomfortable and self-conscious. This is to emphasize the uncomfortableness that Satch and Mo feel when in bed. The bed is lit with reading lamps.

There are windows in the studio, more and more of which are opened as the play proceeds, flooding the dark and candle lit room by plays end with more and more light...

SCENE: THE ROOM IS VERY CROWDED

Paintings, objects, blown up photos. Arty, not bric-a-brac. Special pieces of clothing strewn every where...an easel.

D.D: Do you drink tea?

Mo: I do. I love tea. Satch doesn't. He only drinks coffee. Strong coffee. And Barq's rootbeer, and Budweiser... Cherry cola.

D.D: Corporate food, you mean? Crap. Liquids should be healthy and small, and small-business oriented, I think. Do you agree with that? Mo?

Mo: I don't-

D.D: Have any political opinions? Convictions? I wouldn't be proud of that.

Mo: I'm not... I–

D.D: I have strong political convictions. All of our family does. Even Satch, despite his current Eeyore Existentialism. Is "Mo" short for something? Mo-rbid? Mo-rphine?

Mo: No. I don't do drugs.

D.D: But you have a death fascination.

Mo: No. It's... Maureen. My birth name is Maureen.

D.D: Well, My advice... Maureen... Is, lose the death fascination and do the drugs. Crap looks better in an altered state. That is, unless you need your memory?

Mo: Of course I do.

D.D: For your work. Not just Nostalgia. For your work. You do... What?

Mo: I paint.

D.D: Lovely. Beauty out of crap. Bravo. My personal thanks… always, always for the creative act.

Mo: You're welcome.

D.D: That is, if you're good. And to be a good painter. Well, one has to be a great painter. Is Maureen a great painter, Satch?

Satch: She's…

D.D: A hesitation, in our family, always a condemnation.

Mo: This is pissing me off.

D.D: Crap. He thinks your paintings "crap"

Satch: Her work has a strength in color and form. But lacks an emotional connection. She needs to live more before her work will really move me... But her work is strong, growing.

D.D: On the either/or scale of things, crap.
        You think it's "crap."

Satch: I don't think it's crap. I think it's developing.

D.D: That's not good enough.

Satch: That's what it is, Dee-dee.

D.D: *(Smiling)* I'm glad to see you, Satch.

Satch: I know, Dee-dee. It's good... to see you... It's good.

D.D: I didn't expect anything, you know.

Satch: I know.

D.D: I wasn't even sure you'd open the door.

Satch: I will always open the door for my sister.

D.D: Pleased to hear that. Yes, I am. Is it true?

Satch: I've taken an oath... A personal oath.

D.D: It's an ethical issue, then.

Satch: Yes. An ethical issue.

D.D: Do you like my hair? The blond.

Satch: It's very... bright.

D.D: I'd heard you had a lover.

Mo: Who from? The peeping postman?
          The voyeuristic crossing guard.

D.D: I can tell it isn't true.

Satch: We keep all the windows shut.

Mo: What did you say? *(To Dee-dee)*

D.D: Well, you're not a great painter. Crap. He thinks
          it's crap. Satch would only love a great painter.

Mo: I—

Satch: Dee-dee, I don't have a lot of friends, you know?
          Mo is the only one.

D.D: And she's touchy. *(Sigh)* Well, I'll go.

Satch: Good. you go.

D.D: I'm happy to have seen you.

Satch: I'm happy, too, Dee-dee.

D.D: Call me.

Mo: I'll call you.

          (Dee-dee leaves)

Mo: She's terrible. Is she always terrible?

Satch: No, she's not. She's my sister. It's not about
         "terrible"… Mo, maybe we should… live with
         other… people.

Mo: Where? There's no room. Where? …Why?

Satch: Two is a bad number.

Mo: Bad? Bad? What, misbehaving, rotten?

Satch: Bad. Bad.

Mo: Inappropriate, unethical, fashionable, gauche?

Satch: No. No. It's dangerous. I don't like it. I hate it.

Mo: I don't agree with you. Two is balance. One plus
         one. It's the basic composition. With two we can
         recreate the world.

Satch: That's the problem. Exactly the problem.

Mo: The problem. The problem. There's only one?
         Is it specific? Generic?

Satch: Shut up. Shut up now. I'm talking about a problem,
         something bad and dangerous, and you…

Mo: Okay, okay, I get it. You're talking about "two"
         and recreating the world, who would want to?
         Is that the question?

Satch: It's awful. It's terrible.

Mo: "It." "It." Which "it"?

Satch: Stop that. Stop it. I don't want to learn anything.
Stop it.

Mo: Don't get mad, Satch. It's just tools. Words. The
mouth. The brain. Don't get mad at tools, Satch...

Satch: I'm not mad about tools. I'm mad about you, Mo.
I'm disturbed, upset, and you're commenting..

Mo: Okay, Okay, I would like to recreate the world.

Satch: You would? Why? Why? How could you ethically
choose to continue...

Mo: Not "continue." Reconvene. Start afresh. In
everybody. Every interaction. There's some hope...

Satch: Hope of avoiding awful...

Mo: Hope. One of the big three. Lodged between
Faith and Charity. Try to picture...

Satch: Advice, advice. Make a rule.
Dialogue without learning directives.

Mo: Just helping, Satch...

Satch: That doesn't. Okay?

Mo: Okay. (Pause)

Satch: What are you doing now?

Mo: Pausing. I'm pausing...

Satch: Stop that, too.

Mo: We could lie down.

Satch: I don't want any of that reconvening.

Mo: Just lying down. Okay.

          (They do. MO begins to touch SATCH.)

Satch: You said... Is that reconvening?

Mo: Touch. It's touch. Isn't that okay?

Satch: I was thinking. About shapes. How they move.

Mo: In relation to each other?

Satch: Yes. That's how you know.

Mo: What?

Satch: That they moved. You look at the other one.

Mo: That's what you saw? Thought.

Satch: Mass always shifts, changing the angles. I have to
          hold my head funny just to keep track...

Mo: And you're just lying there thinking about seeing
        shapes move.

Satch: When it's two.

Mo: Two? What two?

Satch: Two bodies, two shapes. And a lot of angles to see.
        Numerous and many are the angles two objects
        can make. At least that's how I see it.

Mo: Do they move when no one's watching them,
        do you think?

Satch: No. I don't.

Mo: Why not? That doesn't make any sense, shifting
        is shifting. Eyes shouldn't make any difference.
        Something...

Satch: Happens. You see it, you trust your eyes. You
        believe. Something happens, you don't see it.
        What's to trust?

Mo: Accumulated knowledge. Memory of observation...
        You should work on your memory. Take herbs.
        ...or something.

Satch: Are there plants for that?

Mo: Yes. And yoga. Hypnosis.

Satch: I hate hypnosis. Human bodies. Always move.

Mo: I took shots. Gang boys. Today.

Satch: In pairs?

Mo: Well... They were...

Satch: They always are. Show.

Mo: *(She does)* Look. Two Sheiks. Two Vikings.

Satch: Vikings, red. Sheiks, black and orange.

Mo: Right! Satch. You remembered.

Satch: I like the jackets. Did they see you? That's dangerous, I think.

Mo: Telephoto lens. And they don't care about me. "Is he Viking, man?" "Naw, naw, Sheik." "He looks Viking, man." "Naw, naw, Sheik." This shot has got one of each. See how they stare one past each other, as if the sidewalks have tunnel vision.

Satch: Could I have that one?

Mo: You want one of my pictures, Satch? I thought you hated the art of photography.

Satch: It's not an art. It's a low level technology. Point and push...Mo. Tourist voyeurism. But I told you. I like the jackets.

Mo: I could make us jackets. Red and black, some purple maybe. that would be very sharp.

Satch: Vikings, the Sheiks, they would stomp us on sight.
           No, don't make us jackets...

           *(The sounds of manic, painful coughing come
           through the ceiling. Long and uncomfortable.)*

Mo: Satch.

Satch: Don't talk about it.

Mo: Satch.

Satch: Just go to sleep...

Mo: But he's...

Satch: In his own world. It's private.

Mo: I can't sleep.

Satch: Shhh.

Mo: Touch...

Satch: Sure.

SCENE: THE NEXT DAY

*SATCH is drawing and singing at the easel...
MO comes in and dances around the room
putting things down.*

Mo: Good morning Satch... Is there anything?

Satch: What?

Mo: Treats...

Satch: There's nothing. Carrots. Green Potatoes.

Mo: Make us lunch.

Satch: No onions. No greens. Grains. I can't do
         something from nothing.

Mo: Go to the grocery.

Satch: I hate the grocery. The lines, the lights.
         The "buy me" packaging.

Mo: We've got to go sometime.

Satch: Late at night. We'll wear sunglasses and
         shop efficientiy.

Mo: Let's go dancing. You want to dance, Satch?
         There's this polka place...

Satch: Parlor. A polka parlor.

Mo: You wanna go, babe?

Satch: I don't feel joyous and lighthearted, that's what
         you need for polka... And don't call me "babe."

Satch: "Sweet" "Dar'link" "Honey-crust" "Lover"

Satch: Ick.

Mo: Let's go dancing. There's this waltz place...

Satch: Palace. It's a waltz palace.

Mo: I've been waiting to try it. It's our exercise,
         our workout program.

Satch: Dancing is two.

Mo: Not always. Kick lines.

Satch: We're two.

Mo: What are you saying?

Satch: There are two of us... Two.

Mo: Call someone. You call someone. Call your
         brother, and his darling Danny Depthmeir.

Satch: They don't dance. I don't think my
         brother could, even.

Mo: He talks about it. "Dancing" all the time...

Satch: On stage. When he was young.

Mo: Well, he's hardly old. Call him.
         It can rock. Nothing fancy.

Satch: I like my brother.

Mo: But if they come, "it's" four.

Satch: What? What "it"?

Mo: You're "it." The dancers. You, me, Mortecai,
          Danny Depthmeir. Four. Two units of two each.

Satch: Stop that.

Mo: Well, Aren't I right, Satch?
          Two plus two equals four. Basic math.

Satch: Shut up.

Mo: Aren't I?

Satch: That's a private thing I told you. A fearful
          awareness. You're not supposed to...
          I don't care about "four."

Mo: So. You're accepting two now as good.
          "Two and two, oh good" Like that right?

Satch: No. No. I don't... You can take your meanness
          and shove it in the crappy old garbage, Mo...
          Who made you "Queen Louse"?

Mo: We'll call someone else, too. Your sister.
          That'll make five.

Satch: My sister and I will fight.

Mo: But you'll dance. She's a dancer. It will be
          rock'n'roll. Everybody comfortable. They're your
          family, you love them.

Satch: Okay. Okay. Okay. I'll call them.

Mo: So. Go do it.

Satch: Not now. The sun is out of control. Later. After dark.

Mo: It's just every old daytime, Satch.

Satch: After dark. I don't like it. But, Mo, listen.
            If they come, I want to get along. You and me,
            I mean. It's hard enough.

Mo: Okay, okay. I'm fine with that. Touch?

Satch: Sure. *(They do)*

            *(The door begins to knock, very loud, insistent.
            they are both startled, MO scared)*

Mrs. S: Hello, Mr. Mo... Are you in there Mr. Mo... It's Alice
            Schlindy, Mr. Mo. We need to talk... Open the door.

            *(SATCH runs to door, hammer in hand,
            and nails it shut)*

Mrs. S: Mr. Mo? Mr. Mo? What is that pounding?

Satch: I can't get the door open, Mrs. Schlindy.
            Do you have a handyman? It's stuck...

Mrs. S: Stuck. Pull, Mr. Mo, and I will push.

            (They do, the nail holds.)

Satch: It's no good Mrs. Schlindy.
         If you had a handyman he could-

Mrs. S: I'll come around to the back...

Satch: No, no, Mrs. Schlindy. There's flu at the back door.
         Influenza. You'll catch germs back there.

Mrs. S: Influenza?

Satch: A lethal dose. Let's talk through the door.

Mrs. S: It's about the rent, Mr. Mo.
         You haven't paid since August.

Satch: Oh no, Ma'am, I paid a hundred in September.
         I have the receipt.

Mrs. S: It's February, Mr. Mo... aren't you working?

Satch: Well, sometimes, Ma'am.

Mrs. S: What about the others? Aren't there others?
         People living with you?

Mo: Don't tell her.

Satch: No, Madam, just visitors.

Mrs. S: You owe me twelve hundred, Mr. Mo.
         Why don't you go out and look for work?
         The K-mart is hiring. There is all those yogurt
         places, you're young, Mr. Mo.

Satch: I'm sorry, Ma'am. I've been looking,
          I'm sure something-

Mrs. S: I can't support you. Do you expect me to
          support you? I can't support you.

Satch: I don't expect that, Ma'am.

Mrs. S: I have property taxes on all my houses,
          and my condo, and my Florida home.
          I've worked all my life, Mr. Mo.

Satch: I'm sure you have, Mrs. Schlindy.
          I'll pay it all, I promise.

Mrs. S: When? Now? When?

Satch: Soon. Really soon, Mrs. Schlindy.

Mrs. S: You have to give me something, Mr. Mo.

Mo: Here's fifty. *(Gives over)*

Satch: I'm sliding fifty under the door, Ma'am.

Mrs. S: That's fine, dear. Just keep it rolling, would you?

Satch: Can we get that handyman, Mrs. Schlindy?
          We've gotta fix that door.

Mrs. S: Oh. Well. You can take care of that, dear.
          Just send me the bill.

          (She goes away)

Mo: That's it? She actually went for that again?
        I am amazed by you.

Satch: What? We paid.

Mo: Barely. She must like you.

Satch: I pay. I'll always pay. She knows me.

        (Pause. Satch draws, Mo wanders.)

Mo: I'm gonna buy that chopper, the old red one
        we saw.

Satch: Chopper?

Mo: Bike. Motorcycle. Hog.

Satch: Hog? They call it that?

Mo: Yes, Satch, it's a hog. A grunt. Mmmm-squeal.
        A roaring male porker.

Satch: Ugh. But is it red?

Mo: Yes. It is. Red with yellow stripes. Very chic.

Satch: I'd like to see that.

Mo: You will. I'm buying it. I'll ride you.

Satch: Yes? Really? I don't know how.

Mo: I'll ride. You just hold on.

Satch: To that bar?

Mo: No. No. To me. That's the sissy bar.
           We'll get rid of that.

Satch: Money. We don't have any money.

Mo: My mom. My birthday. Her credit. There's a new
           gang. The Vicious Circle. They ride in pairs. Girls
           driving the choppers as much as guys. We'll drive
           by and you take the pictures. Can you do that?

Satch: Sure. Sure. Just point and push.
           Will they think we're from another gang?

Mo: I don't think so. They're arty types.
           We'll wear black and we should fit right in.

Satch: They're an art gang?

Mo: They are. I'm gonna go get that chopper.
           Call your brother.

Satch: I'll call. Mo.

Mo: What?

Satch: If you get a head injury and become a living
           vegetable who just jerks off all the time,
           do you want me to stay with you?

Mo: (Laughs) You mean, like, married together, Satch?

Satch: Uh-huh.

Mo: Sweet. You're sweet.

Satch: Well, should I?

Mo: No. No. You can leave me and find another.
        Be happy, Satch.

Satch: But who will take care of you?

Mo: Well, medical professionals. Vegetable caretakers.
        (Kisses) Don't worry. Call your brother.

Satch: Sure.

SCENE: LATER THAT DAY

*SATCH and his brother are playing bingo, each
with three cards. MORTECAI pulling the numbers.
MORTECAI is a huge man with a big picnic basket.*

Mort: B-22.

Satch: Bingo: one card, Bingo: two cards!

Mort: You are very lucky to win at that bingo, Buddy Boy.

Satch: Well, I never win.
        Except when I play with you, Mort.

Mort: You won four times in a row, two cards each time.
        That's so... even numbered.

Satch: Surprised, I'm not.

Mort: This time you win a huge and tasty chicken
           sandwich, and a can of a Pepsi, honey bun.

Satch: Do I win ice? I like ice.

Mort: I'm sure it's cold enough. I-18.

Satch: It's not, though. I think it's warm.
           And it will foam up.

Mort: Yes. That would be bad. Just sip it.

Satch: Well, what kind of Pepsi is that?

Mort: Pepsi. Just plain old, bunny. N-8.

Satch: A Pepsi. It does not look like a Pepsi.

Mo: Well. They changed the can. They put lips on it.

Satch: That's a woman's face. With lips on it.
           They changed Pepsi.

Mort: I guess they did.

Satch: I liked it better the other way. Didn't you, Mort?

Mort: I like lips, bunny-boy. Whenever.
           If you know what I mean.

Satch: I liked it better the other way.

Mort: Still, you're very lucky to win. They'd charge you
          a dollar for that sucker... G-12. You could win it
          again. I have cake, bunny.

Satch: Why wouldn't Dee-Dee come? Did you call her?

Mort: Well, she hates the family right now. She said you
          could call her, if you wanted to see her...

Satch: I don't have a phone. Or quarters.

Mort: Have you seen her blonde?

Satch: I saw her right when she dyed.

Mort: Did you see her with that black dress?
          Her head looked so yellow.

Satch: Well, pastel bright.

Mort: Not a soft color at all.

Satch: Dee-Dee doesn't care about soft.

Mort: With the dark hair, Dee-Dee could wear
          just about any color.

Satch: Red, orange, burnt sienna, cat's eye green, and
          cobalt blue...
          (Reading his crayons, bingo forgotten)

Mort: I suspect she would look great in anything, then.

Satch: Pale orchid.

Mort: Now, with the yellow? Ugh.

Satch: You think so?

Mort: I don't think that would work at all.
          She shouldn't even try.

Mo: *(Coming in, hepped up)* Mortecai!
          This is... No one ever comes here, hello!

Mort: *(Big and hearty)* Hello Miss Mo!

Mo: Are we going dancing?

Satch: No one else would come. Out and out refused.

Mort: They were busy, honey bun... Danny has work,
          and Dee-Dee is in a fashion crisis.

Satch: Refused out right.

Mo: Is she still a blonde?

Mort: Yes, and on her it's not a healthy decision.

Mo: An unfortunate fashion choice? From Dee-Dee?
          I'm stunned.

Mort: A great beauty gone trashy. It is sad.

Satch: She hates the whole family now.

Mo: The whole family? I thought you guys were it...

Mort: Oh, no. Is that all he told you? No. There's fourteen more of us... There is Scrag, and Scud, and E-Y, the twins: Adesti and Fidelis, Little Dickie, and Aunt Fig, Rough Annie, and Dynamite Darling Dynamite, Pony, and K-K-Katie, Henry, and Bambino, and R. Brother Ned.

Mo: All those? Satch, you never...

Satch: I only see Mort and Dee-Dee... I don't fit with everyone else... I'm odd...

Mo: They do sound like your average janes and joes. Geez, Satch.

Satch: Exactly.

Mo: Aren't we going dancing?
I got that chopper, and I met a biker, he–

Satch: Where?

Mo: Out there. Through the window.

Satch: *(Rushes to see)* That's it? That's it! Red with yellow. Mo, it's beautiful.

Mort: It is darling, Miss Mo. Dainty. A very dainty motorcycle. How sweet for you guys.

Mo: So, let's go. Would you say, Mortecai, polka bar or waltz palace. You choose.

Mort: I'd love to, dear, but... My knees got bad. All those years in the business. It's not that I'm heavy so much as the wear and tear. The nightly tango wears down the cartilage and I hurt when I walk. Of course, *(Pursing up big and preening)* I don't have to walk, I'm a star. Let them come to me.

Mo: *(Disappointed)* I wanted to dance.

Mort: We can dance here, Miss Mo.

Satch: Turn on the Glen Miller, and the Tito, and the Fela. We could dance all night...

Mort: And I brought treats.

Mo: Cake?

(Music up. They dance.)

(Later, champagne and sandwiches.)

Mort: It's the way of a showbiz family, of course, you know that, honey... You had to tour and you started young. I learned to tap before I learned to pedal a two wheeled bicycle. I toured Europe for two years, The Patches Henry Orchestra...

Mo: Why did they call him Patches?

Mort: In those days a tux was required. You had a working tux, with two working pairs of pants...

Satch: Patches was broad in the beam.

Mort: An ass as big as the great outdoors.

Satch: He'd wear the pants out. Both cheeks.

Mort: So he'd patch 'em up

Satch: By hand. He was a bad sewer. Plus, he didn't care.

Mort: He thought the tails would hide his butt.
         But it was so prominent, that butt...
         You looked at the bandstand-

Satch: And all you saw were patches wrapt round
         the moon...

Mo: Were you there, too?

Satch: I know the story.

Mort: Of course, I was large, I've always been large.
         My mother was large. At twenty one, I was very
         large, but light on my feet... But of course, I had
         the gift. We all had. My aunties were Ziegfield
         girls. Not one of them ever walked on stage
         weighing less then two hundred and twenty five
         pounds, They were big women, and bitchy.
         You had to be. But light on their feet, of course.

Satch: Aunt Florence, Aunt Nell, Aunt Mim.

Mort: They had the gift, and that counted for a lot
         back then. We all have it. Satch has got it.
         He just chooses to hide it under his painting thing.

Satch: *(Sings)* I'll be calling you-oo-oo,
         If you want me to-oo-oo…

Mort: Patches Henry liked my voice. I was hired to
         play bass, but when the tenor got the clap in a
         complicated bordello arrangement, Patches asked
         me to sing the ballads… Of course I had the voice
         for it, and I knew all the material, in those days you
         had to… It was expected…

Mo: Would you sing one for me, Mort?

Mort: You couldn't afford me, darling…
         Are you forgetting, I am a star?

Mo: Just warble a quick one…

Mort: My dear young woman, would you invite Picasso
         to dinner and ask him to doodle on a doily? On a
         doily, between the redsnapper with red sauce, and
         the crab rialto flambet? No. You would not.

Satch: You have to woo a star, Mo… Flirt.

Mort: My dear, there is nothing between your thighs
         that could possibly sustain my attention.

Satch: Flatter. Pander. Be overly attentive.

Mort: Listen to an old man's story. In those days, big
         band Singers were all suspected of being "fem,"
         and of course, we all were. It wasn't like it is now.
         We faggots were very closet cases, nobody loved
         us, unless it was another one of the boygirls, and
         even then I was never sure. My size, you see.
         I had a stage name Patches gave me.

Satch: Mitchie Blintz!

Mort: Mitchie Blintz the blazing tenor from Brooklyn, New York. A nice jewish boy.

Satch: We never lived in Brooklyn.

Mort: Brooklyn was romantic.

Satch: We had one jewish grandparent from Romania... We lived in Chicago.

Mort: It was show biz, bunny. Every night I had to win that crowd, fight the fleet for respect, and I got it, too. Standing ovations out of those suckers. Basses full of red blooded American boys screaming themselves hoarse. For me, the fat fag in the front...

Mo: Why did you ever stop?

Mort: Patches Henry was of the mail order persuasion, of course. He had a thing for trombone players, claimed they were especially well endowed. Musically we were always short on trumpets, but well stocked in the bone section... Now I've always preferred drummers, they move so well, don't they? I did have a tuba player once, with balls like avocados... That was a sweet suck, ummm... Anyway, Patches got caught flagrante with his trombone player of choice by a whole car of military brass, out on the end of a frenchified lover's lane... Patches spent the rest of the season in the brig, it was obvious what him and the bone boy were up to, but no one questioned the car full of military brass, what were they after on lover's lane? Well, we steamshipped it home, flat broke... That's the business...

Mo: I'm sure you were one of the greats, Mortecai. You are still so grand, a fine figure of a man... Mesmerizing...

Mort: I am liking her... I will sing for you Miss Mo.

          (Sings "Bye Bye Blackbird" and dances)

Mo: Oh! Bravo! *(Applause)*

Satch: Your high notes, Mort, *(Bows)* a shiver.

Mort: I am pleased to please you suckers. And now, a true star always senses his exit. My dears, adieu, adios! My darling Danny Depthmeir is waiting.

          (He sweeps out)

Mo: How old is your brother?

Satch: Oldest. He's the oldest.

Mo: Is he sixty? No one says "fem."

Satch: Well, forty-five, maybe.

Mo: Big band singing, Satch? For years?
          He's talking about the forties.

Satch: He was in Europe. Different things are
          popular over there.

Mo: You believe that story?

Satch.   He's my big brother.

Mo: Does he love his darling Danny Depthmeir?

Satch: Yes.

Mo: Does darling Danny Depthmeir love him?

Satch: We can hope so.

Mo: What about Dynamite Darling Dynamite?

Satch: What about her? I'm drawing now.

Mo: Is she your sister or what?

Satch: My sister.

Mo: Why didn't you tell me about her?

Satch: She explodes at things. People.

Mo: And the twins? Adesti and Fidelis.
          Did your parents name them that?

Satch: No.

Mo: Who did?

Satch: Mort and Dee-Dee. I'm drawing now.

Mo: What about E-Y? Who's he? Do you like him?

Satch: He's a professor of ancient Greece.

Mo: Do you like him?

Satch: Ancient Greece, Mo, ancient Greece.
          How would I know?

Mo: Where's your mom, your dad.

Satch: Heaven and hell, respectfully.

Mo: Wait. Which is where?

Satch: Stop it... I can't draw. You are keeping me from
          drawing, Mo.

Mo: I just want to know about them.

Satch: They are too many. It takes forever. I lose energy.

Mo: You don't want to tell me.

Satch: Hello! Hello! Am I alone here?

Mo: I want to know.

Satch: Here are two. Me, you. We are not the same digit.
          You could never know.

(Long pause. MO mopes)

Mo: I met a biker...

Satch: What like?

Mo: Raw. But sweet. Bow legs and patchouli oil.

Satch: *(Very sarcastic)* Did you reconvene?

Mo: I just could have, Satch.

(Pause)

Satch: *(Worried)* Are you dissipated?

Mo: Wrapt in gloom... We could go to bed...

Satch: Sure.

(They do)

Mo: Touch?

Satch: Well, okay.

Mo: A favor. You're doing me a sensual favor?

Satch: I said okay.

Mo: Begrudging skin on skin.
I hate that most about you...

Satch: (Getting mad) Make a rule! No. Analysis at
         bedtime… Nightmare producing Queen Louse.

Mo: Before I came here, I always had room on board
         the bed. What do you do? do you deflate and
         spread out all over or what is it?

Satch: I lie down. I just lie down.

Mo: Like an air balloon.

Satch: Before you came, I always knew where
         my stuff was. Where is my stuff?

Mo: What?

Satch: My… sunglasses. I need those. There's a constant
         glare. And my notebooks, I can't even think unless
         I know where they are. And my cufflinks.

Mo: Cufflinks. Cufflinks. You don't have any cufflinks.

Satch: Because, you're saving them under the cufflinks
         protection act. Right? Where?

Mo: I didn't touch them. I don't know where they are.
         You don't have any cuffs.

Satch: Of course I do. See there. Wrapt round my wrists.
         Everybody… knows.

Mo: Buttons. Buttons. Your cuffs have buttons. they
         don't need links.

Satch: Sometime they might. I'll have them.

Mo: Never. You'll never need them.
         This is anal. You're anal.

Satch: Fuss-budget.

Mo: Forget-hole. Loser habitual.

Satch: I just want a place for my stuff. It doesn't have
         to make your sense. It's what I want.

Mo: A place. Fine. But you want piles. You make piles
         all over the house. The house is a mess of your
         piles, and they drip. Into my stuff.

Satch: You have a place. A desk. A chest of stuff.
         A room of your own. I just want a place to
         pile my stuff so I can find it.

Mo: Make a rule. Make a rule. You order confuse.
         You space disability.

Satch: (Jumping up and pointing) This is my stuff. And
         this and this and this. All my stuff in 'three piles.'

Mo: That's two too many. It'll start creeping in.

Satch: I need three. Three.

Mo: Look, Satch? How about a bag. A bag can hold
         a lot of stuff. In the basement.

Satch: No! I'm furious now.

Mo: The garage.

Satch: I want to see it.

Mo: Under the sink.

Satch: No. No. No. No. No.

         (Upstairs the man starts coughing long and hard,
         harsh... It is worse than before. MO and SATCH
         come back to bed)

Mo: Satch...

Satch: Shhsh, now.

Mo: He sounds horrible. Worse. Is it emphysema?
         Lung cancer?

Satch: I don't know. You don't know.

Mo: Shouldn't we find out?

Satch: It's his home. Private.

Mo: He sounds like he's dying. Is he dying?

Satch: Dying is private.

Mo: What?

Satch: Dying may be the only thing that is.

Mo: Private?

Satch: Yes.

Mo: But don't we help?

Satch: Respect is help. Respect him.

Mo: But...

SCENE: MORNING
SATCH drawing, MO writing at desk.

Mo: Road trip, Satch. Road trip.

Satch: Why?

Mo: There's the Gang Pictoral Catalog to consider.
         You like that. Project.

Satch: Well, I like the pictures. I don't know about
         the gangs. The people.

Mo: I'll do the people. It can be a snapping tour.

Satch: Point and push.

Mo: Holland has these rival gangs. The Blue Smokes
         and Raj and the Razors. My mom will buy us plane
         tickets. The Blue Smokes! jackets are–

Satch: Blue with grey?

Mo: Yeah. How did you know that?

Satch: I have a nose for color.

Mo: Great! you'll be great on this coming trip.
        The Blue Smokes are all dutch boys, and
        they wear these tulip thorns in their ears...

Satch: That's great. What about the Razors? Raj...

Mo: They all wear Nehru jackets, and they're Pakistanis.

Satch: Dutch Pakistanis? Nehru jackets?

Mo: Like George Harrison in "A Hard Days Night."

Satch: Those bangs.

Mo: I guess so. Red jackets.

Satch: That would have to be.

Mo: California has got the Hells Belles. All tough girls
        gangs. They ride these old Harleys, and they
        won't fuck a fella unless he's older than their bikes!
        Colors? (thinks) Green and brown?

Satch: Green and brown?

Mo: Green and brown?

Satch: Earth tones, maybe. They're very tough.
        I'd like to see that.

Mo: And there's the One Ear Under Gang, they wear these floppy hats. Rasta hats that hide where they hacked off their left ears... they're terrorists.

Satch: Terrorists? Scare me... Where are they?

Mo: Everywhere.

Satch: That's scary stuff. It's too much.

Mo: Colors?

Satch: (*Thinks*) Mud and honey purple.

Mo: What? That's not a color.

Satch: That's what I saw... Mo?

Mo: Yes?

Satch: Are all these people... happy in crowds like that? Gangs.

Mo: I guess... Does that baffle you?

Satch: Yes...

        (*Pause*)

Mo: Satch... That guy. The biker. I invited him over.

Satch: Why?

Mo: To help me tune that chopper. For the road trip.

Satch: Does he have to come in?

Mo: I want him to.

Satch: Oh, reconvening?

Mo: He's just a person. A biker person. An interesting biker person who can help our chopper. Okay?

Satch: I'm drawing.

Mo: But is it okay?

Satch: I'm drawing.

        (Long pause broken by a funny knock)

Mo: Satch. This is going to be him.

Satch: How do you know? It could be anybody.

Mo: Who else could it be.

Satch: The handyman. To fix the door. Go around the back. The door is broken.

Mo: We don't have a handyman.

        (Door is kicked open, BERTIE MC D., full smooches MO... SATCH avoids seeing)

Bert: Hey hey, beautiful, how are ya?

Mo: Satch, it's him.

Satch: Who?

Mo: My friend. This is the guy. Bertie Mc D. The biker. Say hello.

Satch: Hello. Hello.

Bert: How are ya?

Mo: Bertie has a sixty-seven Harley.

Bert: Sure. It's a bear pig of a bike. You like Harleys, slim? I juiced this baby. Jacked up the vee-oh-locity, trimmed down the chassis, goosed up the va-room. Oh, she's flyer.

Satch: What color.

Bert: No comprendo, amigo.

Satch: The bike. What color.

Bert: Black. With red trim.

Satch: The leather is red?

Bert: As your momma's pickled beets.

Satch: I've gotta see this. *(Goes to the window)*

Mo: You can't see that bike from there.
          It's around the corner.

Bert: You wanna spin it, slim?
          Here, take the keys. Go for a run.

Satch: Can you draw it? Sketch it on this pad,
          and get all the details.

Bert: I know every inch of her, slim.

Satch: *(Excited)* I've got three colors of red. Scarlet.
          Crimson. And blood.

Bert: Lets see the blood red. *(Drawing the bike,
          painful and concentrated, tongue sticking out)*
          There's the girl...

Satch: Well. Amazing. It's all trim.

Bert: That red just jumps out at ya.

Satch: Can I have this? I want to hang it up. Can I have it?

Bert: Baby, I've just been art-collected.
          You want a snake? I do a snake, like,
          a tattoo serpent, if you want...

Satch: Okay. Do you want another color?

Bert: Blood red!

Satch: Yes!

Mo: Satch...

Satch: Wow! That's great! It looks like a tennis ball...
          A gob of spit...

Bert: Nooo... It's a python. And this here is the rattles.

Satch: A python with rattles! Wowee, you're a living
          rorshact test, Bertie Mc D, Can you draw a cat?
          Whiskers?

Bert: Rorshact? What's rorshact?

Mo: The ink blot test. Bertie, lets work on the chopper.

Bert: I'm drawing, pretty.

Satch: Oh, yes, He's drawing, pretty. A little teeny red
          kitty cat for our wild avant-garde collection.

Bert: *(Dawning)* Are you boning me? You're fuckin
          boning me. Slim!

Satch: No, no, no. This is naive art... It's raw, it's vital...
          Your use of color... I have nose for color...
          An astounding use of blood red.

Bert: Oh, I'm raw and vital, alright. You fucking weird art
          pansy fuck, Maybe I oughta make you eat that cat,
          huh?

Mo: Bertie... He doesn't mean anything.
          He's an eccentric is all.

Satch: A fly-around-the-room-pansy-weirdo type is all,
          Bertie. *(He runs around the room)* I'm no threat
          to your manly forearms and sweaty brow.
          Not now. Not ever.

Mo: Satch. Stop it.

Bert: What the fuck! What the fuck?
          (Tracking Satch around the room)
          You fuckin' fuck, I'm gonna stuff you...

Satch: Oh, never that. I'll fly out of here first, I'll flee,
          filled with fear. *(Runs out the door)*

Bert: What the fuck was that about?
          I was liking that kid. what the fuck.

Mo: He gets... nutty.

Bert: Well, it's time to up the thorazine,
          he's gonna get himself mashed.

Mo: He's hurt. Jealous. No one ever comes here,
          and I brought you.

Bert: Jealous. What? I thought... Roommates, right?
          Bohemian and asexual arty, right?
          Isn't that what you said?

Mo: I didn't say...

Bert: You implied...
          You indicated you were unattached.
          Didn't you?

Mo: I did. It's just-

Bert: What? He slipped you the joy package?
        You bunning his sausage?

Mo: No. We're best friends. We sleep together, but...

Bert: In the same bed? Without the fuck?
        Is he sick, or what?

Mo: No. Just sensually... quiet.

Bert: Jesus. Listen beautiful... I don't want to fuck up
        a marriage. It's a marriage, right?

Mo: I guess... It could be.

Bert: I would find fuckin' out... If it were me... It's a
        marriage. I don't want to fuck it up. My parents
        were married, for fuck's sake, and my gramma,
        I don't want to touch that kind of a situation.

Satch: (Rushing in swinging a broom wildly) Aaaargh!
        (Slam)

Mo: You don't have to...

Bert: Now. Slim, I'm half way outta here. Drop the club.

Satch: Aaargh! (Slam)

Bert: Goddamn it you little shitter! (Grabs SATCH,
        they wrestle, falling down)

Mo: Bert. Get off him. Get off, you thug-brain.
          *(MO jumps on BERT, all fight and wrestle, BERT
          emerges, lights lighter and holds it to SATCH.)*

Bert: Don't, slim. I'll put it upside your head. I swear.
          Everybody stops. I'll burn him, goddamn it.
          Everybody. *(Pause)* Alright, slim, I'm leaving.
          I'm going. I only kissed her the once. But I gotta
          know... Did you hurt my bike? Did you beat it?
          Don't say yes.

Satch: I wanted to.

Bert: Did you hurt her?

Satch: It shone, flame-red, on the sidewalk. Color.
          I... couldn't do it...

Bert: Good instincts, slim... You two met the big bad
          wolf today, you know that. I coulda chewed both
          of you up. But I respect love, I do... Take love
          seriously, play burrow the banana, mouthin' the
          spot... Let out that ojazz. You two have got it so
          corked up, something will blow... I know, I'm an
          animal, too. *(Leaving)* You gotta exercise that shit.
          (Gone)

Mo: Are you alright. Satch.

Satch: Sure,

Mo: What are you... What do you think?

Satch: That was three.

Mo: Three.

Satch: Bodies. Human shapes. In this room. Three.

Mo: You're right.

Satch: Dangerous.

Mo: Could have been lethal. I'm sorry.

Satch: It wasn't two. Or divisible by two. Not four,
        not eight… Not even at all.

Mo: What?

Satch: I thought. Two bodies in space. Facing off.
        That was the primary scene. The animal equation.

Mo: No. One is primary, It has always been primary.
        And one plus two equals...

Satch: Please, Mo. Don't start with me.

Mo: Three. Doesn't it? Two is still there.

Satch: No, I'm serious about this.

Mo: So am I.

Satch: You're not.

Mo: I'm just saying… The trinity. Father. Son. Holy…
        Mom. dad. Baby. New. Middle. Old. Faith. Hope.
        Charity. Three is basic a lot… Admit that…

Satch: I'm considering.

Mo: North-South-East. Morning-Noon-Night.

Satch: Wait. Wait, North-South-East? Fast?
          That's mocking. You're mocking.

Mo: I'm just saying, approach these numbers
          with an open mind.

Satch: I'm considering that.

Mo: Two is just male and female. Me and you.
          That's what confusing you.

Satch: Look at this picture. Two disappears in three.
          That's frightening. Isn't that frightening?

Mo: Two is still there.

Satch: You look at this picture.
          How many people do you see?

Mo: Well...

Satch: Three. You see three. Not two and one. Right?

Mo: Well, I could see two and one.

Satch: But you don't. You never would.

Mo: Approach mass in space with an imagination.
          Satch. You're an artist for christ sake. I would.
          I could see two and one.

Satch: This is terrible.

(Pause)

Mo: Seven. Seven.

Satch: What?

Mo: Think about seven. There's a numerical possibility.

Satch: Lord Jesus, have mercy on my simple soul.

(Both begin to laugh, MO first, SATCH joining in.
Gales of laughter)

Satch: You wanna lie down and play "burrow the banana"
(Still laughing)

Mo: "Mouthin' the spot?"

Satch: Where did you get that guy?

Mo: At the bike shop. He's a biker.

Satch: He drew rattles on his python! (laughing)

(Coughing begins, loud and raspy, awful.
SATCH and MO move towards each other.
Four eyes up at the ceiling. They climb into bed)

Mo: Satch.

Satch: Shh, now.

Mo: He's choking...

Satch: Tomorrow we'll start the road trip.
         You'll drive and I'll shoot...

Mo: He's strangling...

Satch: I can do the cover if you want.

Mo: His lungs will wear out...

Satch: It can be a woodblock, maybe, or meltéd crayons
         pressed into wax.

Mo: What?

Satch: The cover. For the Gang Pictoral Catalog...

Mo: The man is drowning with himself.

Satch: I know... *(Moving towards her)* Pray. He's got an
         angel. Or a soul with wings, inside of him, waiting
         for the chains to fall free.

Mo: That's really very Christian, Satch...

Satch: My momma raised us up right. Come over...

Mo: Are we reconvening?

Satch: Come over...

SCENE: MORNING

SATCH wakes up first, gets out of bed, something is different. He watches her until she wakes up, then he moves quickly away from her to his easel, begins to paint, avoiding her. She comes over, he rebuffs, she is hurt. Angrily she sets up a slide projector. She begins to show slides.)

Satch: Who's that?

Mo: Me. Thats me.

Satch: What are you doing there?

Mo: The Scotch collide

Satch: Scotland? Youre in Scotland?

Mo: Scotch whiskey, Satch, whiskey on a daily basis.

Satch: I loot, mon begora...You look like Scotland.

Mo: The pounds were sobbing off me.
             (Changes slide) My body going from this...
             to this, the drying liquid look.

Satch: The liquid dry look.

Mo: All the water and blood squeezed out of me.
             Burned dry by hundred proof liquid fire.

Satch: Whats that blue?

Mo: Blue? What blue?

Satch: There. On your hands. Your cheeks.

Mo: *(Looking fascinated)* Veins.
           My veins shining through skin.

Satch: Great. That is such a great color.

Mo: Yeah? The more I drank, Satch, the more those
           blue veins got molten.

Satch: "Molten." Got "molten."

Mo: Hot blue turning to hot purple. You like colors,
           Satch, here. *(Changes picture)* A gouge of color.
           Me puking sick rainbows of the wild young parts of
           myself...I puked at the camera, an action shot.

Satch: I'm sorry Mo.

Mo: There are a lot of colors in there Satch...splatting
           out. *(Changing picture)* There, see? Hot purple.

Satch: Molten purple. I never imagined that.

Mo: I was burning with a drunken enthusiasm
           (Switches) and this, this is my black on white
           phase. Black lipstick, stockings nails. White white
           skin, and hair. Death rocker. You like?

Satch: Black on white, its ok, I liked the molten purple.

Mo: *(Changing slides)* You want to see my lovers,
           Satch? Romantic snaps?

Satch: (Turining away) I've got work.. I'm working.

Mo: They're not scary, Satch. Just lovers. Or love
          speculations maybe, the "ers" implies longevity...
          don't you think?

Satch: I don't know.

Mo: Let's just look, and see. We'll start with Johnny.
          Johnny had everything. A noble brow, a sweet
          and salty mouth and this downy soft touch, and
          a bouquet of the sweetest, cooling words.

Satch: Popsicle. Ice box.

Mo: (Returning) What?

Satch: Lemonade, tree shade...cooling words, Mo.

Mo: Cool, right.

Satch: Hand held fan from the Tang Dynasty.

Mo: But it wasn't enough. (switches) Here is Ray.
          Let's look at Ray. Dead eyes and a cock like a
          tuber, a root vegetable, leaping a string vines
          inside me. He had dead eyes and a poison
          baritone.

Satch: That executioner's brow.

Mo: He wasn't enough

Satch: He would not be.

Mo: I loved this girl. Sally Moment, coal black hair, never right bangs, flaming red lips and violet iris eyeballs. Sally Moment, who moved like a dancer, all tiny waist and muscled thighs.

Satch: You danced the cha cha cha, the fandango, the swim.

Mo: She was quite a dancer.

Satch: She'd have to be. With those iris eyeballs. (*Picture flips*) You're smoking.

Mo: Cigarettes were all in the way one held them, that was what Sally said. And I held them all. My heart stretched...and...

Satch: And what? What?

Mo: What?

Satch: And what?

Mo: I scotch flipped. Each of my lovers a shining whistle stop that highwayed past, their faces, their stances, a flash bulb picture at night, me moving away... I flipped and landed in New York. The room was so yellow. Yellow walls, yellow sun, yellow... room. And I was upping the yellow, bringing in mirror after mirror, yellow flowers, sun fiowers, roses and daisies. I was bathing in light, a golden glow washing me and surrounding, until I took on golden feathers, and golden fins, and I was sheathed in bright, living color...

Satch: Beautiful, you were beautiful.

Mo: Terrible. There were so many terrible things out there– It was New York, and New York was a terrible, open wound, the streets, the parks, the subways were brewing and growling towards a huge psychic civil war. The crowds all scam and snatch, the piss and shit smells rising in a nauseous gaseous cloud, The city choking with dying, their rag, their baskets, their misery in bundles, faces blank or twisting in rage, filling my windows with visages that were huge, and showed everything, every pore overblown and blotching, terrible faces showing everything. I covered the windows with yellow paint that would let the light, only the light through.

Satch: Mo don't tell me. You don't have to tell me.

Mo: But a moan can't be colored away. At night the weeping and crashing of inner bones filled me up, and I couldn't block it out. But I was being pulled and dragged toward it, standing on the sagging New York stoop in the gray light of early morning, and I wanted to take them in my arms, the whole suffering crowd, and hold them, and nurture them, suck all disease away from them and take it in myself, me becoming a marvelous atrocity flypaper, holding in every cancer and misery... The light shifted and the crowd moved towards me, their hands outstretched, and a light kindling in their eyes, and I knew I couldn't do it, and die doing it, and I flipped, and I ran, and ran to Chicago, this slushy city, painting, and photography, whatever.

Satch: Beauty out of crap, Mo. Kiss?

(They kiss long. Broken apart when SATCH walks out. MO surprised, but not upset, begins to paint. Long pause.)

(Door opens soft, and in comes R. BROTHER NED)

Mo: Oh, I... Can I help you?

Ned: Brother Ned.

Mo: I'm sorry?

Ned: I'm R. Brother Ned. I'm brothered with Satch. Is he... home?

Mo: Oh. Ned! Hello, I've heard so much...

Ned: You have? Satch must like you...

Mo: Yes, well... We're friends. He's not here.

Ned: He's out? Dee-dee, that's my sister, she says Satch never goes out... Is he... alright?

Mo: I hope so. Dee-dee. I know Dee-dee.

Ned: She's our sister. She's a blond. Right now, anyway... You live here?

Mo: Yes. We're... roommates?

Ned: Really? Where do you sleep?

Mo: Well...

Ned: Don't worry. I'm not Catholic about that...
        This is nice... So much light here.

Mo: Well, the window's open.

Ned: Yes, it is...

        (Long pause)

Mo: So. What are you doing?

Ned: Waiting for my brother. *(worried)*
        He'll come back won't he?

Mo: I hope so.

Ned: You didn't fight... Or did you?

Mo: Oh, no! ...We... no... We're going on a trip...
        A bike trip...

Ned: You better check the tires, then. I have a tire
        gauge, if you wanted to borrow it. Is it a Schwinn?
        Your bike...

Mo: Oh, no. A chopper.

Ned: Motor bike.

Mo: Yes.

Ned: You have helmets, I'm sure?

Mo: Oh, I'm sure.

          (Pause)

Mo: Listen. Why are you here?

Ned: Well, my brother lives here.

Mo: What I meant is... Is something wrong, Ned?

Ned: Yes... Yes. Something is wrong.

Mo: What is it?

Ned: My brother... is...

Satch: *(Entering)* Mo, I gassed up the bike, I changed
          the oil, and I drove it. Mo, It's go cool, runs like
          a bird... I– *(Seeing Ned)*

Mo: Satch. Your brother is here.

Satch: R. Brother? What...? You're here?

Ned: The tires are important, Satch, did you check
          them? I can lend you my tire gauge...
          You shouldn't be on the highway without that.

Satch: R. Brother. Forget the tires. Who?

Ned: Don't go without checking those tires, Satch.
          Miss, help me out here and agree. It's not safe...

Satch: Damn it, R. Brother, Who is it?

Ned: Mortecai, Satch.

Mo: Oh, no.

Ned: His heart. It was all that weight, you know. It just
          strained him. He must have been coming from
          here, we think. They called Dee-dee's. He had
          fallen in the street, carrying his picnic basket.
          You know, he loved a good picnic, The local gang
          boys found him, carried him to the hospital...
          Didn't even take his wallet, apparently...

Satch: Vikings or Sheiks? Which gang?

Ned: I don't know. How would you know?

Mo: The colors.

Satch: Vikings, red. Sheiks, black and orange.

Ned: Sheiks, then. We tipped them at the hospital.

Satch: I knew it would be the sheiks...

Ned: Dee-dee asked me to come. You don't have a
          phone... Dee-dee asked me to come...

Satch   Sure. Dee-dee would.

Ned: There's a funeral. Tomorrow, I guess. Everyone's
          coming home...

Satch: Who will sing, without Mortecai?

Ned: Dynamite Darling Dynamite would like to. It will give her something to do.

Mo: So she won't get mad, explode?

Ned: Yes, she's a tenor...

Satch: "Lili Marlene." Marlene Dietrich.

Ned: "Falling in love again." She loves those songs.

Mo: That will be... great.

Ned: Yes. *(Long pause)*

Ned: Satch.

Satch: *(Who is crying)* Yes?

Ned: I love you, sir.

Satch: Okay.

Ned: I'll come in the morning.

Satch: Okay.

(Ned goes. The coughing continues)

Satch: Mortecai was the first one in each swimming summer. He always said that water was the most natural of states for him, the most natural of men. We trooped to the beach, the big and middle kids bounding ahead, and our momma calling them back to catch the small kids, all caught up in a small kid wander: from gravel to pop bottle to leaf… Road tar hot, so hot that bare feet had to hop- oh, oh, oh- just to keep from blistering… The giant brother scooping first one and then the next… Hot and sweaty but hugging tight, rolling against your roundness. The first flash of water against summer skin was the best wet slap… the coolest ever… Under the water, all the voices of my brothers, my sisters got distant, wrapped in gauze and thickened by water into sudden old men's voices, they talked in slow motion. Looking through water green I could see them all floating up above me, blotchy white of new summer bellies and thighs crashed away by blue cut-offs and flashing red hair, by paisley swimsuits of yellow and lavender no painter would ever choose to paint with… I could have stayed under all day… Watching my brothers and sisters filling the lake world. But at a distance. All our lives, I kept looking for a distance. You were all too much my family, I loved it, it was an excruciation.

SCENE: SUNLIGHT AGAIN, *more if we can get it.*
Another window open. SATCH is up, suit and tie, pacing. MO is painting.

Mo: Satch.

Satch: What. Yes? What?

Mo: The coughing. It stopped.

Satch: What? When?

Mo: I just noticed it. I think we should go up there.

Satch: Now? When?

Mo: Of course. Now. Maybe he's... dead.

Satch: I have to go to the funeral.

Mo: I know, babe, but... It's up to us.

Satch: What? Up to us. What is up to us?
          And don't call me babe.

Mo: No one else knows anything.

Satch: We don't know anything.

Mo: I know, but... I think we should go see, Satch.

Satch: 'Well. Okay. *(Starts to go)*

Mo: 'Wait. What's that? Listen to that...

          *(Sounds of a trunk being dragged across the floor
          and then bumped down the stairs)*

          He's coming down the stairs. Here.

Satch: Lord jesus christ of the sacred heart...

Mo: What did you say?

Satch: Catholic. It's a catholic thing. I'm praying.

           (Both are backing towards the bed)

Mo: Don't. You're scaring me.

Satch: I'm scaring you? I'm not scaring you. It's him...

           *(Both huddling in the bed as he comes through
           the door, very white hair, white face, dragging a
           huge trunk behind him. once through the door, he
           coughs hard, as if he's been holding back, blood.)*

Man: *(Barely above a whisper)* A favor. A boon... this
           is my work, my writings... could you... watch over
           them? I'm... a dead thing and you two are young
           and you have an esthetic. *(Laughs)* I smelled the
           paint... *(Coughs)* It kept me awake.

Satch: I'm sorry.

Man: Oh, no. No. I wanted to stay awake. I had work to
           do, stories to finish. *(Throws open truck)* You see.
           Fat notebooks full of me, my... inner voices... I'm a
           dead thing, now. Will you take them. They have no
           armor... on... their own... they're small...

Satch: Okay.

Mo: It would be an honor, sir. Can I ask,
           are there angels, where you are?

Satch: Wings on your soul, sir?

Man: No. No... It's a fight to feel the light... this is a lovely room. where you live. I feel the light here. you're artists. I love that...

Mo: It's kind of a mess right now. We've been–

Satch: Busy. My brother... died.

Man: Yes. I saw him go...

Satch: Was he... alright.

Man: Well, he was dead... but singing. "Pack up all my cares and woes, here I am singing low, bye, bye blackbird, where somebody waits for me, sugar sweet and so is she, bye, bye blackbird, blackbird, bye, bye."

Mo: Would you like to sit down sir?

Satch: Take a load off, sir?

Man: Nice of you, but I'd never get back up again, would I?

(Long pause)

Mo: Sir?

Satch: Sir?

Man: It is really terrible that it isn't even raining. Terrible. I love that sound, rain on rusty gutters, and Beethoven... and the way the world turns. That was three good sounds…Goddamnit, my mother made the best biscuits out of bacon fat and white flour… And my grandmother died begging for fresh banana creme pie. I could never top that… the light is going. Turn up the light.

Satch: It's a cloud, sir…

Mo: A thick cumulus cloud, sir.

Satch: Rain is coming… It's blocking the sun…

Man: And I am goddamn gonna miss it…
          (Falls over, dead, thunder)

Satch: He should have waited.

Mo: Too tired, I guess. Satch. He had a list of three good sounds, Three was his number.

Satch: No. Two. The food was to two.
          The biscuits and pie.

Mo: He regretted the food. Losing it.

Satch: He regretted it all, I thought.

Mo: I want to go with you to the funeral.

Satch: Okay.

Mo: I want to see Dee-dee, and E-Y, Bambino, and Henry, and Pone, and Scragg, and Scud, and Rough Annie, and Aunt Fig, and Little Dicki, and

R. Brother Ned, and the twins, Adesti and Fidelis.
Who did I forget?

Satch: Dynamite Darling Dynamite.

Mo: That was a mistake

Satch: Yes, It was.

SCENE: **SATCH AND MO ARE READING THE
READINGS OF THE TRUNK**

Mo: How many (*Reading*) "Resistances to
Excruciation?"

Satch: Seventy-nine.

Mo: Why so many?

Satch: It's what's needed, I guess...
There must be excruciations everywhere...
"The Excruciated Masses."

Mo: Or maybe... only seventy-nine people
have excruciation.

Satch: What?

Mo: One a piece.

Satch: That can't be true.

Mo: He's appealing to the individual excruciated need.

Satch: We'll find out, we'll find out. Go.

Mo: "Charms and Herbs to Soothe the
Poisoned Heart?"

Satch: Thirty-seven. "The most powerful being
The Chaplin Smile Mantra and peppermint."

Mo: Does it divide evenly?

Satch: The Chaplin Smile?

Mo: No. The category. Half herbs and half charms.

Satch: Of course not. Thirty-seven is an odd number.
They're remedies. Mixtures.

Mo: One part herb, two part charm.

Satch: It varies. They vary.

Mo: But there two different elements, right?
An even number.

Satch: Mo, please.

Mo: I just want to be clear. Two, right?

Satch: Two, yes. Next.

Mo: "Reasons for the Metaphysical to Enter
the Daily Practice"

Satch: Twenty two. And please don't say it.

Mo: It's even. Two-two the ultimate "even" number. The whole rest of the trunk is odd.

Satch: It's metaphysics. Odd enough as it is. Maybe "Reasons for" needs a solid base.

Mo: But it's twenty-two. Doesn't that freak you out?

Satch: Somewhat.

Mo: Somewhat?

Satch: People died. Mo, I can't keep getting freaked out by numbers.

Mo: You're changing.

Satch: I'm trying... What's next?

Mo: "Mantras for Charging the Erotic in Comfortable Couple."

Satch: Eleven. The category begins with odd places and ends with funny fruits.

Mo: And the other nine?

Satch: I know 'em all, Mo.

Mo: What are they? tell.

Satch: I don't want to.

Mo: Shy. You're shy.

Satch: I'll show you. When we're convening.

Mo: Wow. You really will?

Satch: I really will. Next.

Mo: "Hard and Fast Rules for Creative Endeavor."

Satch: Eleven.

Mo: Again with the eleven.

Satch: Right.

Mo: But that's two categories of eleven. Eleven twice.
         Twenty-two. Two-two. The ultimate even.

Satch: I'm ignoring you.

Mo: That's an impressive trunk full of stuff. Bravo.

Satch: Nothing, next to nothing. Now, we've gotta
         apply the knowledge...

Mo: We?

Satch: You're in it. He died in our living room.

Mo: Apply it? He didn't say apply it.

Satch: It's knowledge. There's a mission here...
       He loved this stuff...

Mo: But we don't have to "love this stuff."
       We've got our stuff to do.

Satch: We can keep reconvening, honey.
       Don't worry about that.

Mo: What?

Satch: Reconvening, well just...

Mo: No, no. You called me "honey."

Satch: Sweetheart, sugar lump, good'n'plenty…

Mo: You hate that.

Satch: That was before we opened the trunk. It's all in
       there, Mo,.. All we've got to do is spread it.

Mo: Zealot. You're talking like a zealot.

Satch: A "trunk zealot" yeah that's good.

Mo: No, that's bad, it's terrible, We're just on
       a bike trip. The Gang Pictoral...

Satch: When a person knows something, well, you can
       just swallow it... Swallowing when you should be
       spewing, That'd give you a sour vinegar mouth.

Mo: I'll risk it... Satch we're out... We've never gone
           out... We could be a couple on a road romance...
           It's about us, this trip...

Satch: I've got to see the brothers and sisters...
           I've got to... I think they're suffering...

Mo: Suffering what?

Satch: Grief. Loss. Angst. You know.
           Mortecai made me promise.

Mo: Promise.

Satch: To see them all... if he died. Mortecai was a
           big star. He left me his big star phonebook.
           R. Brother brought it.

Mo: All right, Satch. Sid Caeser, Yehudi Menuhin,
           Tony Bennet, What page are they on?

Satch: Two. *(Pause)* Two!

Mo: Satch this is not like you...

Satch: It's just a page, one after another...

Mo: Where do they live?

Satch: Trenton, Oswego, Venice Beach...

Mo: All over? How many are there?

Satch: We can still do the gang pictoral...

Mo: How many did you say?

Satch: Fourteen. Where are the Hells Belles
        parking these days?

Mo: Well. In San Francisco.

Satch: Venice Beach, it's on the way.

Mo: I did want to meet Dynamite Darling Dynamite...

Satch: Mystic Mountain, Montana. Just a slight detour.

Mo: Well the One Ear Under Gang is around there...
        Hiding in the desert...

Satch: Committing small terrorist acts.
        (Laughs happy)
        And Raj the Razors...

Mo: That's Holland. They're in Holland...

Satch: Well, my brother Scud is in Holland, delivering
        the mail... We'll go to Holland.

Mo: They have mailmen in Holland?

Satch: Of course they do, Do you think they just leave it
        lying around in the street? (Etc. as they leave)

— THE END —

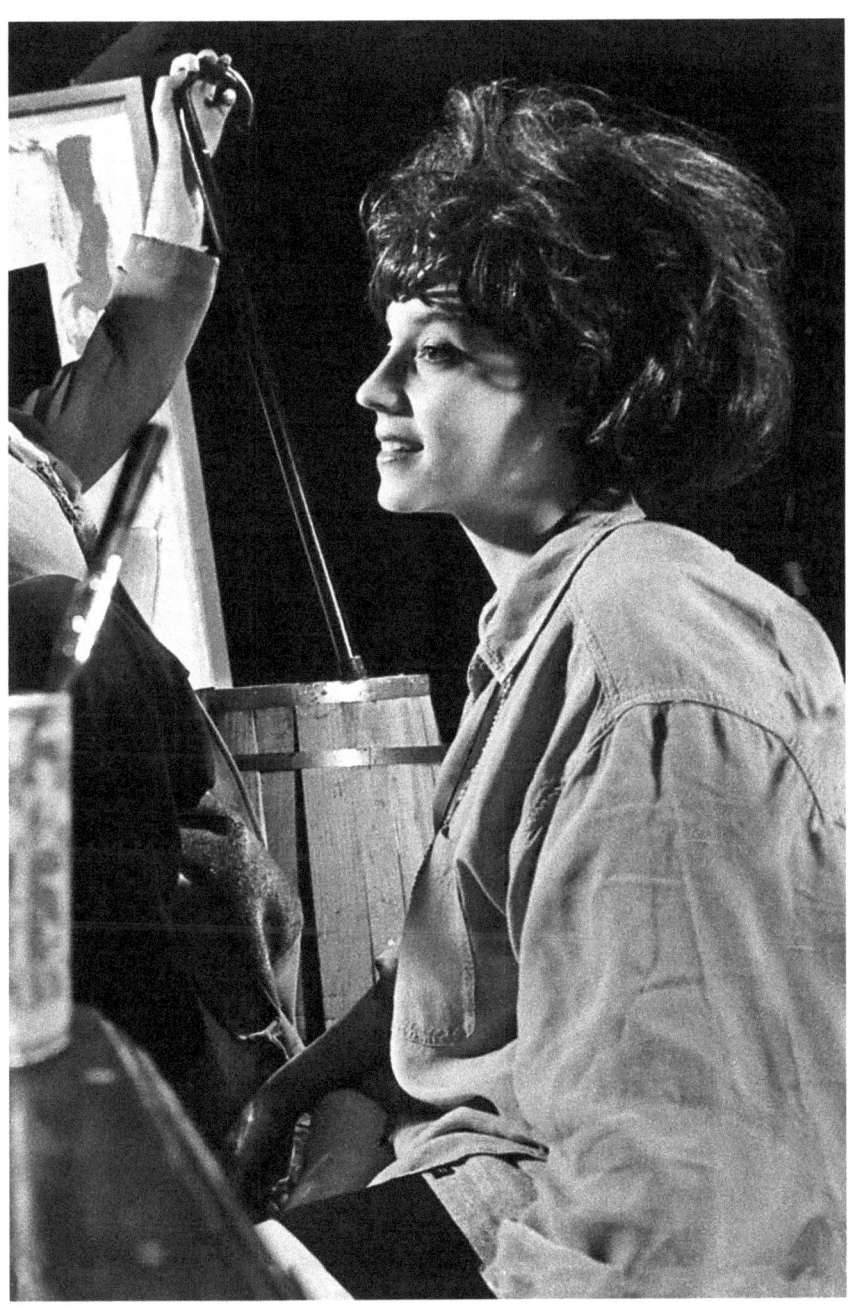

Anita Stenger in **DYING IS PRIVATE: The Satch and Mo Play,** *1992*

The Third Degrees of J.O. Breeze

Premiered September 1995
The Rhinoceros Theater Festival, Chicago, IL
&
August 1998
NY Fringe Theater Festival, New York City

performed by:

Marianne Fieber
Bryn Magnus
Beau O'Reilly
Colm O'Reilly
Ben Raynor
Paul Tamney
Danny Thompson
Dana Wise

INTRO

I wrote this in two weeks straight; every couple of days I sat down to continue it. I wrote a final scene where the two characters, Horace and Doris, who have yet to meet, are in the space ship headed toward a new beginning hinted at in the play. Space travel seemed very faraway then, not so much now… I cut that scene after the first reading, the scene seemed too explainy and I like my plays to hold on to some mystery; what's really going on here?

The play came out of conversations between me and two friends. The three of us were very close, that friendship was overwhelming with good questions and sexual tension… in retrospect we should have stuck to the good questions! They were both smart, not young anymore and thoughts on character, good character, how do you define it, know when you are working from it or are off the mark, were a big part of our dinner talk. Everything exploded between us over a few bewildering months and this writer really wanted to know why. The production ran, off and on, more than most of my plays… played at the old Mary Archie, Lunar Cabaret, the New York Fringe Fest… Paul Tamney always played JO, I played The Captain, even though most of my heart went to Doris, Danny Thompson replaced me for the New York turn, Ben Raynor, Colm O'Reilly, Bryn Magnus all played Horace, Marianne Feiber and Dana Wise played DORIS, a play of mine has never been served better… group directed, I think. A rolling chair; two tables, macadamia nuts… The press liked it. Somebody actually said it was the play they had been waiting for from me, so I promptly wrote '7 Pounds of Mud,' which me and Jenny and my mother liked just fine!

SYNOPSIS

J.O. is an ethical investigator assigned to interview applicants for an off this planet new life. Assisted by THE CAPTAIN, HORACE TREELANDER and DORIS DOHENY are put through their paces answering questions designed to reveal their ethics and 'Oh so personal' lives.

SETTING

A long table with two chairs. To the left a card table with a typewriter on it. J.O. BREEZE—a dwarfish man properly dressed in a suit and tie, and THE CAPTAIN—a large man dressed in military gear conduct interviews in this room.

CAST OF CHARACTERS:

J.O. BREEZE

DORIS

HORACE

THE CAPTAIN

SCENE: ACT I

Lights up on J.O. BREEZE, seated at the long table. THE CAPTAIN is seated in front of the typewriter. Enter HORACE, already packed for the trip.

Long pause

Horace: Good evening. *(No response)* Am I in the right place? I hope I'm in the right place.

J.O.: Macadamia nut? Fresh Macadamia nut?

Horace: No, thanks *(Pause)* I don't eat Macadamia nuts, usually.

J.O.: "Usually"?

Horace: I'm sorry?

J.O.: You said "usually." Didn't he, Captain, say usually?

Captain: *(Reading)* U S U A—

J.O.: There. You see. You said it. Usually.

Horace: Yes, I know I said usually. I just didn't understand, why you pointed it out, the word. U-s-u

J.O. I know the word, Mr. Uh *(Looking at clipboard)* T-reeelll-ander. I don't need you to point it out.

Horace: That's Treelander.

J.O. What is it?

Horace: My name. How you say . . .

J.O. Wait, now. Am I misspelled? T-R-E-E-L Ander.

Horace: No. That's how you spell it.

Captain: THEN WHAT IS THE PROBLEM, PUNK.

J.O.: Oh, Good. I thought I was misspelled.

Horace: No, it's not the spelling. It's the pronunciation.
It's Treelander. Usually.

J.O.: Usually.

Horace: That's right. That's how it's pronounced.

J.O.: But I didn't pronounce it "Treelander."
I pronounced it "Treell - ander."
I simply read the letters. In other words.

Horace: You were wrong.

J.O.: "Were wrong."

Horace: You pronounced it wrong. A person's name,
that's important. How you pronounce it.

J.O.: Do you think so, really.

Horace: I do. Yes. It's a dignity issue.
A personal dignity issue.

J.O.: Usually.

Horace: What?

J.O.: Is it a personal dignity issue "usually"?

Horace: I don't understand.

J.O.: "Usually" or... *(Pause)* In other words...

Horace: No. No. A name is important always... I think.

J.O.: Good. On this point, you do not waffle. You are
not a waffler on the issue of names and dignity. I
was beginning to dismiss you... as a waffler.
A word of advice?

Horace: Sure. If you're offering advice, I'll take it.

J.O.: Drop the "usually" in the future. It makes you
appear wishy-washy. An equivocator no one likes
wishy-washy. Equivocating.

Horace: I guess it comes from being careful around people.
I'm often misread. People think I'm simple and
straight ahead. I'm not simple or straight ahead.
I'm convoluted about... a lot of things. Painfully
convoluted... *(Pause)* ...usually.

J.O.: When do you eat Macadamia nuts, Treel-ander.

Horace: Never. I never do. Actually eat them. I mean.

J.O.:   A ha. Now we're back on it. Why?

Horace: They're difficult to open.

J.O.:   Difficult to open? You come here on very
          important business and you tell us in the first five
          minutes that you find opening a nut too difficult
          a task. In other words, you present yourself as a
          marshmallow who would rather starve than work?
          Where's the dignity in that?

Horace: No. No. It's just... I don't like nuts, that much. I
          didn't think it was important...

J.O.:   And you're certainly not a hundred percent on
          the name thing either, Treel-ander.

Horace: Wait. I thought I was clear.
          You said no wishy-washy.

J.O.:   Yes, yes that was good. Bravo.
          Big Bravo for you on that one Treel-ander.
          But you offended earlier on.

Horace: How? I couldn't have. I was being so careful...
          I'm very careful with people I don't know.
          I never offended, consciously or subconsciously.
          I'm like a priest. A very careful priest.

J.O.:   Think back. Now. You were offensive. How?

Horace: On the Name thing? I stood up for myself,
          that was good. Perhaps...
          That was a problem for you?

J.O.:   Read it to him, Captain.

Captain: "NAME IS IMPORTANT" BLAH BLAH –
           "PERSONAL DIGNITY" BLAH BLAH –
           "A NAME IS IMPORTANT ALWAYS."

Horace: Is that it.

J.O.:   I'd say so.

Horace: But that's what I think. I was speaking up,
           expressing my needs. You were pronouncing
           it wrong.

J.O.:   "I" "I." "My" "My." This is sad. Treel-ander.
           Do you stare at yourself in the mirror all day,
           delight in your own reflection in every
           passing car window? Is that you?

Horace: No. Definitely not. I don't have the ego for that.

J.O.:   Then why are you doing it here?
           And I note the "definitely" Treel-ander
           and I give it a small nod of approval.

Horace: Thank you.

Captain: *(Screaming)* YOU NARCISSISTIC LITTLE WORM
           PRICK

Horace: I don't understand.

J.O.:   It's true. *(Pause)* Are you squirming.
           You're squirming.

Horace: I'm uncomfortable. This man is yelling and you're... I don't know what you are.

J.O.: You feel, what?

Horace: Helpless? Annoyed!

J.O.: One gives you points, the other takes them away.

Horace: I don't know which is which. But that doesn't freak me out. I expected difficult. That these questions would be difficult. My mother used to say you can't give birth without burying the placenta. Ha-Ha
(Pause – no one else laughs)
I guess that wasn't funny. She's kind of a ghoul. My mother. I expected this.

J.O.: Expectations. What are your expectations. Treel-Ander. From me? That I help you out here. Or that I continue on, hardnosed and with harshness. Which do you expect?

Horace: I don't know. Honestly, I don't.

J.O.: Help, then. You're a drowning man. What is my Name?

Horace: I don't know.

J.O.: The Captain's then?

Horace: I don't know.

J.O.: Why don't you know?

Horace: You didn't tell me.

J.O.:   Ah Ha! Because you didn't ask. After all this fol-
derol on the dignity of names you didn't think
to ask the names of the two perfectly legitimate
beings involved in a discourse of a very serious
nature with you...

Captain: *(Screaming)* YOU SNOT NOSED CRETIN

J.O.:   It is very damaging Treel-Ander.

Horace: It was your interview. Up to you to identify...
yourselves. I thought.

J.O.:   I began, I believe, our conversation with a long
pause designed to test your mettle. It is easily
checked, Captain.

Captain: *(Reading)* PAUSE, LONG PAUSE.

J.O.:   To which you replied, Captain?

Captain: GOOD EVENING.

J.O.:   Not "I am So and So Treel-Ander and you are?
Pleased to meetcha'" I was forced to look your
name up.

Horace: I was nervous. The interview is important to me.
I thought you were... I don't know.

J.O.:   We were Buddhist. Simply able to wait without
aggression.

Horace: *(Laughs)* I didn't think of it like that.

J.O.:   That would be understandable and If that was
          the real reason, an acceptable excuse...
          But you didn't think that was it.

Horace: I just didn't expect Buddhists, in your line of work.

J.O.:   What else could it be?

Horace: I can't think of anything else. I know that's
          pathetic of me. There must be something,
          but what else could it be?

J.O.:   What else could it be? Well, many things.
          My partner is a psychotic sadist with a tendency
          towards drool and I myself am one of nature's
          near abortions, a grotesque with a spine like a
          slinky and a camel's hump that crowds my brain
          and makes me look cross-eyed. My height is no
          taller than the average footstool, perhaps you've
          noticed. In other words, I am a troll-like creature.
          Perhaps you thought us sub-human, the Captain
          and I.

Horace: God, no, I never... That never crossed my mind,
          I didn't notice. Your physical... things.

J.O.:   Then are we to believe you are narcissistic,
          hypocritical, wishy-washin' and a blind, dumb
          person as well?

Horace: No. No. I. No. I'm just not... a noticer, my mother
          says "Head in the clouds, heart in heaven!"
          That's pleasant for my mother. I'm sure you're
          both fine... people.

J.O.:   *(Finger waggling)* Here, politeness may not be your friend. Treel-Ander. *(Long pause)*

Horace: I am sorry, truly sorry. For not acknowledging, the two of you, your humanity sooner by asking your names. Perhaps we could start again.

J.O.:   A pretty apology and worth some points. Gentleness, humility, and a little groveling. Perhaps you've balanced the scale. Treel-Ander. And we can go on. Captain?

Captain: FUCK HIM UP THE ASS WITH A RED HOT FIREPLACE POKER AND THROW HIM OUT IN THE STREET WHERE THE TRAFFIC CAN DO WHEELIES UP AND DOWN HIS PRETTY BOY HEAD.

J. O.:   Long winded for the Captain, but... overruled. A pretty apology and I'll accept it as such. In other words, we begin again.

Horace: Good evening, gentlemen. I'm Horace Treelander and I have the pleasure of speaking to whom?

J.O.:   Bravo! Bravo. Pretty. J.O. Breeze, Investigation peephole observations, psychiatric pronouncements, and relationships counseling– my specialties.

Horace: You're a doctor then?

J.O.:   Well, a friend of the mind and a relentless pursuer of the body.

Horace: Some of my best friends are in therapy and I myself, have recently taken a turn on the couch. It's quite a mind blow. Therapy. Like sticking a vacuum cleaner up your brain and turning it on full roar, it just pulls everything off the shelves, out of the closets of your mind. Everything that you thought was cleaned up and safely put away in there is now just a pile of crappy old garbage. Cracked and sodden, leaking across... everything you know to be true.

J.O.: What is that, Treelander?

Horace: What?

J.O.: What is that you just said?

Horace: I was just describing my thought process.

J.O.: Really? That spew was a process?

Horace: Yes. Yes. It was what's in here, about therapy.

J.O.: Captain?

Captain: PSEUDO PSYCHO FREUDO BABBLE CRAP!

J.O.: I'm forced to agree with the Captain, Treelander.

Captain: STEAMIN' SHIT ON A PLATE!

J.O.: Yes. And badly served up, Treelander. Sloppy and badly constructed. Pointless. Make note, Captain.

Captain: BOOGER ON TOAST!

J.O.: Enough now, Captain.

Captain: THREE WEEK OLD PANTY STINK

J.O.: Captain, hold something back. We'll need your forcefulness later and who knows, even you might run out of tasteless things to say.

Captain: NAH!

J.O.: Nonetheless, Captain, restrain yourself. I must insist that you do... Treelander wants the hook we mustn't let him worm away. You were saying, Treelander?

Horace: Yes, well...was I?

J.O.: Chaos in your brain... things falling off shelves, something, does it warrant repeating?

Horace: No. I guess not. I just thought you'd... It's difficult to describe... I used to be very orderly, mentally *(Smiling)* I could tell the difference between a hawk and a handsaw when the wind was right. But now, I'm confused and all the therapy confusing me more. It's like when you're cooking soup and the spicing isn't right. You panic, adding more and more things to get it to taste right. But it never does taste right, it's just wrong, with more things in it.

J.O.: Yes. I'm sure you have a deep understanding of the suffering of all mankind. Treelander.

Horace: *(Modestly)* Only as to how it relates to me.

J.O.:   "To me." "To me." Yes, how it relates to "you."
           We'll get back "to you," Treelander.
           But we werent' talking about you.

Horace: *(Surprised)* I thought we were.

J.O.:   No. We weren't. We were talking about me.
           J.O. Breeze. At your insistence.

Horace: No. I did not insist.

J.O.:   It's easily checked. Captain?

Captain: "YOU'RE A DOCTOR THEN?" BLAH BLAH. "HE
           INSISTED" BLAH BLAH.

Horace: But I didn't say that. He just wrote that in.

Captain: THE INSISTENCE WAS IMPLIED

J.O.:   There you have it. "Implied insistence."

Horace: But that isn't fair.

J.O.:   This is not Quantum Physics, Treelander. Career
           Counseling is an interpretive art. It's not one of the
           hard sciences. It may be the real genius quality of
           our work here. Interpretation.

Horace: It seems warped somehow. He's got a lot of
           responsibility and he's kind of a sick fuck.

J.O.:   You have a sloppy mind, Treelander, undisciplined.
           There is a lot you could learn from our sick fuck,
           the Captain. My advice. Follow him closely...

Horace: That would surprise me.

J.O.: Yes, I'm sure it would, Treelander. But let's take a break from you. Just a pause to let you settle over the scene. Like hoarfrost on the pumpkin after the first touch of winter... or don't you want to listen to my story? You think you could survive that?

Horace: Sure. I'm quiet interested in you.

J.O.: Bravo. You get points for that, Treelander, and pretty points they are, too.

Horace: God, that's good. It's been awhile since I got some points.

J.O.: Yes. You have been starving here.

Horace: Is it my attitude? Mostly?

J.O.: Your attitude. Your execution. I note here that we are back on your favoriet topic—you. Did I breathe between now and the last time we were on your favorite topic—you. I don't think I even had a chance.

Horace: God, I'm sorry. Please go ahead.

J.O.: My father, as you can see, was a freak of nature. When his eyes stared off into space, they went north and south... simultaneously. His head was as twisted as my back, two noses, a mouth like an underground garage, a brain that pulsed like a souffle rising with every hideous indrawn breath. ... My mother was an acrobat with a perfect little body. All skin and muscle, 2 breasts, 2 thighs, hair on the back of her neck that rose at the sight of my dad and his little grotesque Winky the Two Nosed Boy booth at the circus... My mother's love of father was the first experience of what I came, in later life to refer to as an impossible alchemical coupling, how they ever achieved coitus... Well, they never told me. Mother loved father even though she couldn't look at him without shaking in horror and perhaps my father couldn't look at her either, as his eyes were always looking North and South simultaneously, gazing off to either horizon... It's possible father never saw mother shudder, but I did. Those eyeballs wide with horror were my bedtime stories. Macadamia Nut?

Horace: Uh. Sure.

J.O.: *(Big smile)* My mother appeared to love me, too, despite or perhaps because of my grotesqueries. She taught me an impossible tumble and acrobat act she knew... You've been *(checks clipboard)* married. Fianced, what?

Horace: "Deeply and Irrevocably in love."

J.O.: Good. Then. How many times would you say.

Horace: "Deeply and Irrevocably"?

J.O.: Yes, that.

Horace: Six or seven times.

J.O.: Which is it. 6 or 7 times.

Horace: 8. 8 times.

J.O.:   Eight times. Would you describe all eight of
          these times, these "deep and irrevocable times,"
          as marriages?

Horace: Yes, I suppose. I would.

J.O.:   You "suppose?"

Horace: I would. I definitely would.

J.O.:   Good. Good. You progress Mr. Treelander...
          your mother's name...

Horace: Martha. Martha Louise. My Father's name is Erwin.

J.O.:   I didn't inquire after your fathers name,
          nor your mothers, for that matter.

Horace: I was showing some initiative.
          I thought, you might be giving points.

J.O.:   Bravo. Bravo for some. But for you I may
          have to take points back. I think I will.
          (Wagging finger) I'll have to.

Horace: Sure.

J.O.:   What do you prefer to eat,
          prefer instead of Macadamia nuts?

Horace: Oh, the normal stuff.

J.O.:   Cabbages and kings? Pickles and Ice Cream?

Horace: *(Laughing)* None of that.

J.O.:   *(Hardening)* Pork on a stick…

Horace: Nothing like that.

J.O.:   But "normal stuff."

Horace: Sure, I'm a pretty normal guy.

J.O.:   What do "normal guys" eat?

Horace: Thai Food, Enchiladas.

J.O.:   What else.

Horace: Vegetables. I try to limit my cheese.

J.O.:   "Limit your cheese." In other words.

Horace: I'm health conscious. I used to have problems,
          constitutionally. A heart murmur, skin boils, a
          hacking cough. I've cleaned up, healthwise.

J.O.:   A health conscious. Normal guy. Macadamia nut?

Horace: All right.

J.O..:   A health-conscious normal guy
          with eight failed marriages.

Horace: I'm not proud of that...

J.O.:   No. You wouldn't be..

Horace: I fully gave my heart. Each time.

J.O.:   And took it back, each time.

Horace: I didn't think of it like that.

J.O.:   But how else could it be? You'd given it, you
         needed it again. So you could give it away again.
         You took it back.

Horace: The heart isn't one thing.

J.O.:   You gave your heart, you took it back, gave your
         heart, took it back. Gave your heart, took it back,
         gave your heart, took it back, Gave your heart,
         took it back. Gave your heart, took it back. It must
         have been exhausting for you.

Horace: It's an allegory. You don't really hand over your
         heart. Reach into your chest and rip the fucker
         out each time.

J.O.:   That's some image!
         "Reach into your chest and rip the Fucker out."
         Bravo on the image, Treeland. Captain?

Captain: HYSTERICAL SOPHOMORIC CRAP.

J.O.:   I will probably eventually agree with you, Captain.
         But for now I'm dazzled, Treelander. You've
         dazzled me. Did you take it down Captain?
         In other words, did you do your job?

Captain: *(Reading)* "REACH-IN CHEST AND RIP FUCKER
          OUT EACH TIME."

J.O.:   Could you highlight it for me? Perhaps little stars?

Captain: *(Sarcastic)* "LITTLE STARS."

J.O.:   *(Equally sarcastic)* For me?

Captain: THAT'S NOT THE JOB. FUCKING LITTLE STARS
          IS NOT THE FUCKIN JOB.

J.O.:   I am prepared to show you one of Mother's
          vaudeville routines, now, if you're interested.

Horace: To me?

J.O.:   In other words...

Horace: I'd like to see one of Mother's vaudeville routines,
          sure.

J.O.:   Good. That's points, Treelander,
          real points for you.

          *(J.O. BREEZE does the vaudeville that is wonderful
          and at a certain point he works HORACE into it.)*

Horace: That was great. Really great. Thank you,
          J.O. Breeze. I love tumbling with the guys.
          This was better than that. This was great.
          Thank you, J.O. Breeze.

J.O.: And you, Mr. Treelander.

Horace: You can call me Horace.

J.O.: I don't think so. But you can call me sir.

Horace: Sir?

J.O.: I like that better.

Horace: What was that about, the routine. I thought, it was friends, we were... friends. Connecting, bonding. Friends don't insist on Sir. We were friends.

J.O.: Oh, God, no... This is an important interview and you have yet to pass. Treelander. No. I was just demonstrating my physical prowess, just in case. Haven't you forgotten something?

Horace: What now?

J.O.: The Captain.

Horace: Oh, oh. I say, sir. I don't think we've been properly introduced.

Captain: BLOW IT OUT YOUR PISSHOLE, ASS BOIL.

J.O.: You haven't succeeded with The Captain. I'm afraid that will work against you in the final score, Treelander. We'll continue. Macadamia nut?

Horace: I guess. Okay.

J.O.: Mr. Treelander now sounds less enthusiastic. Note it in the record, Captain.

Captain: NOT WRITING DOWN ANYMORE MACADAMIA NUTS SO YOU CAN FUCKING STOP BRINGING IT UP.

J.O.: Why?

Captain: NOT PART OF THE INVESTIGATION. PERSONAL PUD-PULLING JERK-OFF CRAP IS WHY.

J.O.: It's part of the testing, Captain, and you're to record the testing.

Captain: NO. NO. FUCKIN' NO MORE "MACADAMIA NUTS."

J.O.: You've soured him, I'm afraid, Treelander. The Captain no longer wishes to play.

Horace: Look, neither do I. If this is about playing, I'm not interested in playing. I came because I believed in the work. I need to work. My mother used to say "if you can't sleep, work. If you can't eat, work. If you can't–"

J.O.: I get it, Treelander.

Horace: Right.

J.O.: All of our mothers are full of worldly wisdom. It's not a distinguishing factor.

Horace: Right.

J.O.:   Did you care before you were recruited?

Horace: About the mission?

J.O.:   About anything.

Horace: No, absolutely not... I wanted to care again,
         though that's why the therapy. I chose that and
         your ad... It stirred me up. But I definitely didn't
         care on my own.

J.O.:   Bravo, bravo, you get fiercer as the day
         progresses, Mr. Treelander.

Horace: Is there someplace to wash? I need someplace
         to wash. Soap and water. I need that.

J.O.:   What did you say?

Horace: I'm sweating with the tension and the exercise.

J.O.:   Captain.

Captain: RATPUKE. *(Jumps up and slaps HORACE hard)*

Horace: Hey, man... What's the... that's not cool man...

Captain: COOL? NO, ITS NOT COOL, MAN.
         ITS FUCKING HOT AS HELL.

Horace: Don't do it again, or I'll—

Captain: MULE SCUM. *(Slaps him again)*

Horace: God damn it, man... I'll...

Captain: YOU'LL WHAT.

Horace: I'll...

Captain: WHAT.

Horace: I'll...

Captain: WHAT.

Horace: I'll...

Captain: WHAT. *(Slap)* WHAT! *(Slap)* YOU'LL NOTHING.

Horace: Jesus, man... Mr. Breeze, look, I didn't come to get beat up. Get away from me you fuckin' animal. Get away...

J.O.: Captain.

(CAPTAIN pushes him into his chair)

Horace: *(Near hysteria)* Stay away...

J.O.: You see how it is with the Captain, Treelander. In all fairness, Treelander, you just lost points here. You'd already lost points in our most recent volley, for "limiting your cheese" and being huffy about "normal guys food," you'd regained points for your dazzling descriptions of "ripping the heart out of your fuckin' chest." But now the mercury drops and plunges below zero for hard-heartedness towards the Captain.

Horace: Wait. Is this fair? This doesn't seem fair.
Who decides this points system?

J.O.: The Judges. J.O. Breeze and the Captain.

Horace: The Captain. But he's...

J.O.: The typist. The typist always decides the value and weight of the truth. At least as it appears on the written page. Capital letters, punctuation, proper spacing, notes on the flow of the interview, all carry tremendous weight when it comes to the record, what goes into the file. It's external, really. The hard-disk, inflexible and unforgiving.

Horace: Then I've lost, there's no point in continuing.
I answer an ad only a loser would answer
and I still lose. It's amazing.

J.O.: Despair is rarely a point giver here.

Horace: I'm in the negative zone.
I can't win and you know it. I expected this.

J.O.: Its true, you've performed badly here today.
Perhaps you're just a bad person and the negative zone suits you...

Horace: Perhaps.

J.O.:   Is this some crack of light or some false modesty, this "perhaps" of yours.

Horace: I don't know. My ego is like a balloon. I go out of my way to let all the air out, and then I go out of my way to pump it back up.

J.O.:   *(Pause)* What about the eight women?

Horace: They were all very lovely, good women. I liked them all. Beautiful and warm women. They were very good to me and beautiful.

J.O.:   And they found you, what, Quasimodo?

Horace: Well, no.

J.O.:   What?

Horace: Women think I'm beautiful.

J.O.:   Really. How lovely for them. And they leave you, in spite of that.

Horace: I'm too much, I guess. Too emotional and sensitive.

J.O.:   Sensitive.

Horace: Yes.

J.O.:   Blush at the smell of body odor?

Horace: No, no. I take on other people's stuff so much, and I fuse out.

J.O.:   "Fuse out." In bed?

Horace: No, no, I'm good there.

J.O.:   Good. How.

Horace: *(Cautious)* How?

J.O.:   How good.

Horace: I know how to give pleasure, and I'm kind,
          and I'm, well, well endowed, ha ha.

J.O.:   A big dick?

Horace: *(Embarrassed)* Right.

J.O.:   The Captain has one, too. A dick like a redwood.
          He's not too kind with his, I'm afraid. *(pause)*
          Well, aren't you going to ask me?

 Horace: Ask you what?

J.O.:   About my own equipment. That would be proper,
          you've had your moment. I've acknowledged the
          Captains monstrosity. We're talking like men about
          manly things. Go ahead.

Horace: I'd rather not. That's your business.
          I'm not interested in that... kind of men-talk.
          It embarasses me, I guess.

J.O.:   "Like men about manly things." Unless you don't
          consider me manly enough to have a dick?

Horace: Of course I don't think that.

J.O.: The truth is, I'm not. No dick at all. Oh, there's a pee-hole, this flaccid little toe of a digit that rides the balls like a team of ponies without direction. Your feelings on that, Treelander?

Horace: It must be... hard...
(Realizing he's said the wrong thing)

J.O.: No, it's soft. Flaccid. Eternally flaccid like an overcooked baby noodle. No erection. No ejaculation. No pleasure at all. Neuter.

Horace: I'm... sorry.

J.O.: Can you imagine what it's like to fall in love, to want a woman, with a hump on your back and a blank for genitalia?

Horace: I'm... sorry.

J.O.: The heart that you would give away so repeatedly, can you imagine that heart without hope, beating, pulsing, breaking. Engorged but disconnected.

Horace: I am sorry.

J.O.: Yes, I believe you are, and you'll get points for it, still, women find you beautiful. In other words, it is difficult for me to wish you well in this area. You understand that.

Horace: I think so.

J.O.:   How could you, though. Your troubles are
           not physical. I am outside.

Horace: I have compassion and imagination.
           I'm sensitive that way.

J.O.:   A compassionate imagination.
           You can imagine yourself dwarfish. Freakish.

Horace: (Quietly) No. Longing and hurt, always.

J.O.:   Sub-human.

Horace: Please don't twist this. My compassion for you
           is genuine. Please, I'm asking you.

J.O.:   Compassion for me. You'll get points for that.

Horace: Fuck the points, I'm sorry your life has been...
           so difficult.

J.O.:   Macadamia nut?

Horace: Sure.

J.O.:   Compassion for me. Bravo.

Horace: Thanks.

J.O.:   And the Captain. Has the Captain's stock risen
           with mine own?

Horace: No. I don't think so.

J.O.: His difficulty exceeds my own. His pleasure mixing with pain, shit with Chanel No. 5, an ounce of cum with a pint of blood, are not attractive for most potential love partners. What's it like. Captain.

Captain: (*Begrudgingly*) LIKE FINDING A COMPLETELY BLIND, LEFT-HANDED TENNIS PLAYER FOR DOUBLES WHO PARTICULARLY ENJOYS LOSING.

J.O.: That was well said. Bravo for the Captain, who is rarely forthcoming. Treelander?

Horace: I don't want to think about this. Your Captain crosses the line. I don't want to cross the line.

J.O.: A difficult love search, for the Captain. No one sympathizes with the brute. With his longing for the flinching buttocks and the beseeching, small-animal-falling-out-of-a-tree-look in his eyes.

Horace: He's a hideous man. In all ways hideous.

J.O.: Perhaps so, perhaps not. Your compassion and imagination could balloon and expand enough to include him. Call him "the suffering survivor," our Captain. A man who is sliding backwards into the ethical primeval swamp because of poor luck or genetics. He could have been used horribly as a child, tortured or worse, used as a human douche bag or living ashtray.

Horace: Was he?

J.O.: He could have been, Treelander.

Horace: You're asking me to make a big leap to... embrace him despite his clear violence, his being awful, without information? I can't do that.

J.O.: *(Wagging his finger)* "There but for fortune."

Horace: No. A sinner has to ask for forgiveness before being forgiven. No, I won't do it. Your "Captain" deserves everything bad.

J.O.: You're sure of yourself.

Horace: Yes.

J.O.: No wishy-washy-waffling.

Horace: Fuck him.

J.O.: Well, I did offer you a number of opportunities, Treelander. Let the record note it. Captain?

Captain: "FUCK HIM" IN THE MARGIN.

J.O.: Good, good. At least we're clear here.

Captain: ALL OVER THE MARGIN.

J.O.: That will do, Captain. Your last "marriage?"

Horace: I was deeply and irrevocably in love, wasn't I? Of course it was a marriage.

J.O.: *(Consults clipboard)* Eight times.

Horace: That's right.

Captain: BUM FUCK

Horace: What?

Captain: LOUSY LAY

J.O.: Gentleman, I've already seen the manly slap-a-thon, and you, Treelander, lost points last time.

Horace: Why. He was the savage.

J.O.: He is a savage. That's his job. You, on the other hand, are being interviewed for the future.
Have you forgotten why you're here, Treelander?

Horace: "The future of all mankind," I remember.

J.O.: Good, good. You don't get points for remembering the purpose of this interview, Treelander. It is such a huge, headline purpose, it would be hard to forget it. You would do well to proceed with a certain gravity. It would earn you much needed points.

Horace: How does it work, exactly, this future of all mankind business.

J.O.: You'll learn that when and if you pass the interview. Tell me about the "marriage."

Horace: Sparky.

J.O.:   What's that?

Horace: Sparky. That was her name.

J.O.:   Her parents named her that?

Horace: No, I did. Because she–

Captain: WALKED WITH A LEASH AND CHASED RABBITS.

Horace: No. She was energized, she could spark a room.
         Any... situation seemed better with Sparky in it.
         She was a good person, very beautiful. I really
         wanted her to like me.

J.O.:   Did she, as you say, like you?

Horace: She wanted me.

J.O.:   Yes. The well endowed thing.
         That's already in the notes, isn't it Captain?

Captain: "HUNG LIKE A MOOSE."

Horace: I didn't say that.

J.O.:   No, that's much too straight ahead for you,
         Treelander.

Horace: But it's in the notes.

J.O.:   The typist's prerogative. Don't worry, Treelander,
         it can't hurt you, being hung like a moose.
         My employer is interested in procreation,

in extending the species. You're not saying that
your relationship was based on your skill as a
stickman, are you?

Horace: What? No.

J.O.: Of course you're not. You're a nice man, a good
guy, an attentive-to-the-needs-of-my-woman-both-
mental-and-physical fella, aren't you?

Horace: Yes. Yes I am.

J.O.: She wanted you, but she didn't like you.
Is that the story you tell yourself, Treelander,
late at night, all alone, and whining.

Horace: That's what happened.

J.O.: We'll need convincing details.

Horace: I don't know how.

Captain: WIFE DUMPED YA.

Horace: She did. Yes.

J.O.: She didn't, as you say, like you.

Horace: Enough. She didn't like me enough
when it got hard.

J.O.: Good... Good Good... You're pinpointing the point
in time when the marriage failed.

Horace: You like that.

J.O.:   Like? Like? No, Treelander, I don't like it.

Horace: Sorry. It seemed like you liked it.

J.O.:   Need. I need it. Accuracy. Specifics. That's how I
          form an opinion enough to make a judgement.
          It's my job, Treelander.

Horace: Do I get points?

J.O.:   No, you don't get points, because you're
          a smug little prick.

Horace: Jesus, I'm just trying to relax.

J.O.:   You take can my advice and relax later, Treelander,
          if you are successful, for now, take my advice and
          cut to the chase.

Horace: I didn't do anything wrong, J.O.

J.O.:   I'm tiring of you, Treelander, very rapidly.
          Call me sir.

Horace: *(Very sarcastically)* Yes, sir.

J.O.:   We're almost through here, Treelander. The
          Captain would love to finish with you early, and
          frankly, I'm beginning to share his feelings. You're
          conceited, narcissistic, cowardly, and a waffler.

Horace: Wishy-washy equivocator.

J.O.: What?

Horace: You forgot wishy-washy equivocator, sir.

J.O.: Don't.

Horace: I—

J.O.: Do not.

Horace: Fine.

J.O.: Why did the marriage fail, Treelander.

Horace: It was my fault.

J.O.: Of course it was your fault. What did you do?

Horace: I was a conceited narcissist, cowardly,
and a waffler.

J.O.: What. Did. You. Do.

Horace: I became frightened of how close we'd become.
I didn't trust it. It was so fast.

J.O.: "It."

Horace: Intimacy. Family feeling. I withdrew.

J.O.: How?

Horace: Rolled away in bed. "Giving me your back"
Sparky called it. Hugged absentmindedly.
I'd get impatient, verbally, and I would pile it on.

J.O.: It hadn't been that way between
the two of you at the start?

Horace: No. Never.

J.O.: Nasty?

Horace: Sometimes. Nasty.
I always seem to know how to be nasty...

J.O.: Violent?

Horace: Never violent. Just touchy, argumentative.
I'd been through it before. I was scared, I guess.

J.O.: Of what?

Horace: Of what?

J.O.: Scared of what? And I don't appreciate your
chosen denseness when it comes to answering
these direct questions, Treelander.

Horace: I'm just slow sometimes. It's a defense mechanism,
I guess. A failsafe system within my emotional
makeup. It just kicks in. Slow, go slow.

J.O.: Pick it up now.

Horace: What?

J.O.: Scared. Scared of...

Horace: Scared I'd fail with her. Not be a good partner.
That's what had happened before. I'd get just so
close to a woman and then a wall would grow
between us. Or a hedge. More like a hedge. I
could still hear her on the other side of it, but I
couldn't find her eyes. Couldn't touch her heart.
After a while, I stopped trying.

J.O.: How did she feel, Miss Sparky.

Horace: I don't know, honestly. She looked panicky.
Her face drawn and anxious, and I'd seen that
face before. I'd had that face before on my own
head. I should have been more sympathetic to it,
that face.

J.O.: What happened, between you.

Horace: Something went dry between us.

J.O.: Something. Went. Dry. Note it, Captain.
By "dry" you mean what, Treelander.

Horace: We couldn't... make love.

J.O.: Make . . . love.

Captain: YOUR DICK WILTED UP INSIDE HER?

Horace: I mean make love. You know how when you're in
love with someone precious, your skin jangles and
your brain gives off little exploding flywheel blasts

that rock your heart constantly, like fire bombing a lily pad with the frogs still on it. Except the bombs are small and constant and the frog is thin skinned and prone to weeping. When you're in love you're so hepped up that making love, the fucking, seems like gravy, like dessert... That had stopped.

J.O.: What are you talking about, Treelander?

Captain: THE FUCKING IS OVER.
SHE WOULDN'T FUCK HIM ANYMORE.

J.O.: Is that it, Treelander? No fuckee-wuckee?

Horace: What.

J.O.: You've gotten off, Treelander. Sloppy description, endless metaphor. Was the sex over, is that what you're trying to say?

Horace: It was over but that wasn't what I was trying to say. I was talking about making love, being in love.

J.O.: So the fucking wasn't important to the making, the being in love?

Horace: Of course it was important, but that's like saying Darwin isn't important to the history of science. He is important to the history of science, but he isn't it.

J.O.: Are you a superior being, Treelander?

Horace: *(On guard)* No. Not at all.
I'm kind of a worm, actually.

J.O.:   I find myself in agreement with you,
           Treelander, you are a worm.

Horace: But I have some good qualities.

J.O.:   Do you think I'll stumble on them, eventually?

Horace: Well... I hope so... why did you ask about the
           superior being thing? I didn't get that.

J.O.:   I assumed since you were lecturing me about
           the nature of love making you thought yourself
           superior to the Captain and I.

Horace: No, not at all.

J.O.:   Why Darwin, then?

Horace: Well, science, the monkey man,
           that's what I was thinking.

J.O.:   Beast on the first rung of the evolutionary ladder,
           us, the angel at the top, you. Ape to intellect, you
           to the Captain and myself, that was the inference.

Horace: Not consciously.

J.O.:   Sub consciously, then.

Horace: I wasn't aware of it, no.

J.O.:   I will tell you, although near dickless since my
           buggy days, I have made love.

Horace: I'm sure you have.

J.O.:   In my fashion. Can you imagine?

Horace: *(confused)* I'm sure you... have, Mr. Breeze.

J.O.:   In my fashion. And the Captain has had his humps, too. Imagine a mongrel dog with an ugly red boner at a French poodle brothel.
That's the Captain.

Captain: LIKE A HUNK A TAIL

J.O.:   We all know something of humping, Treelander, and speaking for myself, I've plummeted the emotional depths of the human heart with many a fine woman, and been awestruck by what we both found there, despite my personal difficulties in the dick department.

Horace: I'm glad for you. I was telling you my feelings.

J.O.:   What about Sparky? The last love of your life? Sparky.

Horace: What about her.

J.O.:   You haven't told us about Sparky.

Captain: CUNT LIKE A RARE STEAK
ALL HOT AND MESSY?

Horace: I object, Mr. Breeze. I'm trying to answer your questions truthfully. I really object to the Captain.

J.O.:   Stuff it, Captain.

Horace: He really is a creep, your Captain.

J.O.:   Creep comes in many colors, Treelander.
            Continue the story.

Horace: It was the chicken.

J.O.:   Which "it"?

Horace: The thing that happened was chicken, kind of.

J.O.:   Hello Horace! Come back to the dock.
            Out of the fog. Solid land over here.

Captain: GET BACK TO THE FUCKING FUCKIN'

Horace: It wasn't about the fucking anymore.

Captain: IT'S ALL ABOUT FUCKING.

Horace: No, man, it was communication. We couldn't
            anymore. She'd say pink, I'd hear blue.
            It was really more of a mauve between us,
            you know.

J.O.:   Note the use of color imagery, Captain.

Captain: POINTS?

J.O.:   Debits. Continue, Treelander.

Horace: Sparky grew up in a poor family, never enough food on the table, and her dad was a nearsighted veterinarian who eventually lost his sight entirely.

J.O.:   This road leads to chicken, Treelander?

Horace: Sparky had this terrible fear of going hungry and she would hoard food. We had two refrigerators and a stand up freezer. Sparky liked to buy things in bulk—a crate of oranges, a barrel of pickles. There was something in her that was always hungry, she said. A hole. She got a case of Bisquick and put it on the bookshelf in the bedroom. She would stare at it when we were making love and feel guilty that she was hoarding all this food. While I was sleeping, she would sneak out to the kitchen and make some Bisquick pancakes and drown them in Aunt Jemima's. Sugar dough. How can anyone eat like that? I would never.

J.O.:   Of course. You limit your cheese.

Horace: Right. I do. She never gained weight, though. She must have puked up the Bisquick and Aunt Jemima's, although I never noticed that.

J.O.:   Really? Treelander. Surprise surprise.

Horace: I was in therapy doing inner child work. I had just gotten this whole deck of inner child playing cards. I was thinking about auras, too. A lot. Later I thought Sparky must have had a very hungry inner child with a sad purple aura. That's when I moved out and found all our plates in the shoe closet caked with sticky Bisquick. I had never noticed.

J.O.: Cluck cluck, Treelander.

Horace: What?

J.O.: Back to the henhouse, Treelander.

Horace: The henhouse?

J.O.: The chicken.

Horace: Sparky ordered a case of chicken. A hundred pounds in ice. It came on a Saturday, which is my therapy day. It came on a Saturday and I was ready to leave, but there was no way she could carry it to the basement freezer, open the box and bag all that chicken on her own. It was heavy and the ice had started to melt, very bloody. When Sparky was a kid, Dad, the blind veterinarian, he lost his eyesight slowly. Plus they were poor, and he was a proud man. He couldn't see after a while to operate on the poor dogs and cats. He taught Sparky when she was eleven to do the cutting. Dogs and cats are full of blood. Sparky can't stand the sight of blood, and now with the bloody chicken, her face was drawn and anxious...
I knew what was wrong because she told me about the blood and the animals, Sparky loved animals, but I was late for therapy.

J.O.: So you did what?

Horace: I got impatient. Loud. Condescending, I guess. How could she be so strange in her thinking to buy all this chicken? We didn't need it, she didn't need it, and to have it come on a Saturday...

Now I was late, and she was selfish, self-centered.
The whole time I was flicking these dead chickens
into ziplock bags, they were slippery and greasy,
and the blood was flying off them. The madder
I got, the faster I went, and the more the blood
flew. I looked up at Sparky and she was pissed,
her eyes filled with black, flooding with India ink.
She started grabbing the bags of chicken and
throwing them at my head, side arm and hysterical
at first, but then she started getting accurate,
hitting me in the head, the chest... Splat. Splat.
Chicken splat. When the chicken was all over me
and the floor, she stormed out in a rage.
She didn't like me anymore.

J.O.:   You figured that out for yourself, Treelander?

Horace: I felt stupid. And then I felt I didn't like her either.
          I was going to therapy because I liked me,
          me was interested in me. I thought about Sparky
          and the others, how they distracted me away from
          my... internals.

J.O.:   The eight marriages?

Horace: None of them were as interested in me as I was,
          and then I thought, I don't love. Them. Her.
          I don't. And yet, I still want, want someone
          to love me for what I am. I felt pathetic.

J.O.:   That's a word.

Horace: Then I saw your ad in the
          Christian Science Monitor.

J.O.: The Christian Science Monitor? That's funny.

Horace: Yes. Ha ha.

J.O.: Ha ha.

Captain: I TOLD YOU!

Horace: It seemed to be about me,
and I didn't want to be here anymore.

J.O.: What about Sparky?

Horace: What about Sparky?

J.O.: You told us a lot of things about how you felt.
Once the thumb came out of the reluctance dike,
you just gushed on the subject of your feelings.

Horace: That's what you asked for.

J.O.: Yes. Yes. Big bravo, you'll get your points on that,
Treelander. Still, where is Sparky?

Horace: I don't know where she is. She wouldn't see me
anymore. The last time I went to her house
it was raining.

J.O.: In the story. In the story, where was Sparky.

Horace: I told you. She was horrified.

J.O.: About you, yes, yes. What about her without you? Did she vote liberal democrat? Wear a St. Christopher's medal? Keep a journal? Dream in color? Use a rinse? How old was she? Was she–

Horace: Thirty. Thirty-one. She was Irish, I think, Norwegian.

J.O.: Speak Spanish? Collect Liberace records?

Horace: I don't know that stuff. I told you about her dad, and the bloody chicken.

J.O.: Was she pregnant when you left her? Suicidal?

Horace: I was paying attention to my own feelings, I was in therapy, that's what you're supposed to do in therapy. I cared about her, I just couldn't do better.

J.O. Maybe, Treelander, maybe that was what it was.

Horace: What else could it be?

J.O.: You're a selfish person? A bad husband? A lousy friend who is so sickeningly self-involved that the world is puking to have you walk on it, and we'd be doing us all a favor to have you no longer sharing our atmosphere? Captain, take him to the waiting room.

Horace: Wait. I'm a flawed person, but I'm not that bad. I need to do this.

J.O.: I've other interviews today, Treelander.

Horace: How badly did I do?

J.O.: Badly. Very badly.

Horace: Did I pass?

J.O.: You're a human being,
       you'll get some points for that.

Horace: I'm glad we went through this, though.
         I found it very therapeutic.

J.O.: I'm sure you did. You wait now, Treelander,
       we'll let you know.

Horace: I didn't say what I really wanted to say,
         could I try again tomorrow?

J.O .: No. Now go.

Horace: Anymore questions? One more for good luck? Sir?
         Just one.

J.O.: Go. Now.

Horace: Can I have another nut?

J.O.: We're out.

— END ACT 1 —
*(INTERMISSION, long enough to
breathe, piss, smoke, have a coffee.)*

SCENE: ACT 2 ENTER DORIS
She moves very purposefully to the table.
Takes the right seat.

Doris: I'm not early. No. I'm on time.

J.O.:   *(Checking clipboard)* Miss...Do-Hanky...
Do-Hiskey... What?

Doris: Doheny. Just a good old Irish name.

J.O.:   A good Old Irish Name...
Did you get the name, Captain?

Captain: DOHENY.

Doris: That's right! You got it right.

J.O.:   A Mick Moniker... Eh Captain?

Captain: TOO BAD, SISTER.
WE AIN'T GOOD OLD IRISH... NOPE.
NOT AT ALL. WE AIN'T GOOD, SISTER

J.O.:   Miss *(Checks clipboard)* Due-any.
Did you eat anything.

Doris: What. No?

J.O.:   Macadamia Nut? *(Holds out bag of nuts)*
Fresh Macadamia Nuts?

Captain: I HATE FUCKIN POTATO BARKING DIRT SNIFFIN
MICKS, SISTER.

Doris: I... You shouldn't talk to me like that.

J.O.:   No, you shouldn't, Captain. Have a nut.
          You really should eat miss... Due-annie.

Captain: WE'VE NOTHING IN COMMON SISTER.
          NOTHING-AT-ALL.

J.O.:   Well, Captain. We're not worrying over her. We're
          not worrying over you, Miss Due-Hanky... You're
          good. Law abiding... *(Looks closely)* Most of the
          time. It's your... friends that seem like trouble, in
          other words, someone died. Is that what this says?

Doris: What? Who? I don't know what it says.

J.O.:   Your roommate, sure. That's a word. Roommate.

Doris: Spider, you're after Spider?

J.O.:   No. No, Now don't move in fear, now, Miss...
          (Looking) Do-Hauser! Don't fret. No.
          We're not after anyone. You came here.
          On your own, I assume.

Doris: I needed the job, the money.

J.O.:   Of course. How's the nut? *(Pause)*
          The Macadamia nut? You ate it.

Doris: Good.

J.O.:   Have another. You'll need your strength.

Doris: Thanks

J.O.:   You'll need your strength to stay clear here. Miss
            (Checks clipboard) Do-hepi. Tell me about Spider.
            In your own worlds now... Mis *(checks clipboard)*
            Due-Hickey.

Doris: Look. Doris is fine. Call me Doris.
            I seem to be missing this, what is it you're asking?

J.O.:   Standing up for yourself. Redirecting the interview.
            Introducing the first name basis. Good.
            That's points. Note it in the record, Captain.

Captain: *(Savagely)* IN THE MARGIN?

J.O.:   That's fine.

Captain: KNOWS HER NAME.

J.O.:   Good. Good. We're going to be friends you and I.
            I like that. Doris and J.O. Breeze. J.O. and Doris.
            "What great friends they are."
            You can call me J.O.

Doris: J.O. Hello. *(Offers hand)*

J.O.:   Hello! *(Shakes hand)* Bravo! Note it Captain, in
            the record. (*Warm. Courteous. Yet Doris remains
            unbowed and decides to respond for herself. The
            Captain types away.)* Good.

Doris: J.O. Breeze. You're what. A Detective.

J.O.: I do some detecting, yes. Peephole observations, psychiatric provacateuring, relationship counseling, that's my special talent.

Doris: Big Cases.

J.O.: Oh, the biggest.

Captain: *(Yelling)* YOU LIKE BOYS, MEN.

Doris: "Like them..." What do you mean?

Captain: Cock Cunt—Tongue. Rub-a-dub.

Doris: I don't have to listen to this,
do I have to listen to this, J.O.?

J.O.: What he's asking in his own indelicate brutish way, is how you feel about romance. Dates. Sex.

Doris: Dancing, I like. Close up, sweeping the floor with a long gown... Being held and swept in someone's arms, soft but taken. I like that.
(Sarcastic) You asking me out, Captain?

Captain: I DON'T DATE SPICS.

J.O.: She's Irish, Captain "A good-old-Irish-Name."
You should have put that in the record.
Is it there, Captain?

Captain: IT'S THERE.

J.O.: Read it to me.

Captain: GET BIT.

J.O.:   I should apologize, Doris, for the Captain.
          I myself don't feel responsible for him, but I do
          choose to continue to work with him and there's
          some responsability in that choice. The Captain is
          all things male, exaggerated and distorting in that
          exaggeration; rude, crude, lewd and yet he serves
          the organization. The mission. His is a difficult role
          to fill. Part menial, part enforcer. It's a rare bird who
          can do both things. The Captain is a rare bird and
          like a vulture or a pterodactyl, he is often unseemly
          in public. *(Deciding)* I apologize, Doris, on behalf
          of the organization, for any discomfort caused by
          the Captain's discourtesy.

Doris: No. It's not your fault.

J.O.:   I feel some culpability.

Doris: They should just fire him,
          if he's everything you say he is.

J.O.:   But where would he go? And more importantly,
          who would replace him? No. The Captain stays,
          I'm afraid, Doris.

Doris: As long as he doesn't touch me.

J.O.:   If he should touch you?

Doris: *(Smiling)* I'll mace him.
          (Takes can of mace out of purse)

J.O.:   Have you maced before?

Doris: Yes. I have. Men on the street, usually.

J.O.:   Usually? How many "men on the street?"

Doris: Twelve. It's happened twelve times.

J.O.:   Really Doris? Twelve times.
          That seems like a lot of times. Do you think it is a
          lot of times to have maced someone?

Doris: A lot of times to have maced someone?

J.O.:   Yes.

Doris: It's very hostile on the street now, J.O. Some men
          follow you, licking their lips and growling, too.
          Like jungle animals.

J.O.:   Growling, Doris? Really? These men really growl?

Doris: It sounds like growling. They're thinking they're
          saying something, the men, but it sounds like
          growling. Arggghh. Arghhh. Growling. Like that.
          "Cock cunt suck-rub-a-dub" like your Captain.

J.O.:   Do you know what they want Doris?

Doris: Everybody knows what they want, J.O. Who cares?
          They can't have it and if they can't have it, and
          with me they can't. They'll bruise, batter, rip, sneer
          just to get something. If they can't love a woman,
          they'll hurt a woman. Men are like that.

J.O.:   "With you they can't have it?"

Doris: I'm not frigid, or a prude J.O. I just think some
           things are precious, we are human and we carry
           in us treasure. Special gifts and between men and
           women, what's intimate, the power of it, should be
           treasured and special. That's what I think, I know
           it's square, but I don't care. I just think debasement
           gets a lot of attention these days and purity very
           little. Purity is met with embarrassment and scorn
           ... Loosen up, baby. Loosen up! Well, when I
           loosen up, I get the mace out. *(Smiles)*

J.O.:   Do they touch you, these men,
           abuse you physically.

Doris: No. I don't let them touch me... usually.

J.O.:   So it's all verbal. Hostile lascivious taunting...

Doris: It's just, I see it coming, I know where it's heading,
           embarrassment, helplessness, rage. Sometimes
           I get right to the rage part, cutting to the chase.
           I mace 'em in the eyes while "the Pussy-Bitch" is
           still coming out of their mouths. Spray! The look
           on their faces! It's great. "Pussy-Spray ACKK"

J.O.:   What is the look on their faces?

Doris: Boys. Little boys.

J.O.:   "Boys," what?

Doris: Like little boys, after a favorite dog has turned and
           snapped at them. Or a loving parent whacks them
           across the face for talking with their mouth full.
           Young and bewildered and frightened.

J.O.:   You like to see the frightened faces
          of small children.

Doris: On adults. These men are adults. Aggressive
          adults. They ask for it and I let them have it...
          Their intention is to frighten and bully me and
          I won't stand for that.

J.O.:   This happened 12 different times.

Doris: No. 10, 11 and 12 were the same guy.

J.O.:   You maced this guy 3 times.

Doris: On different occasions, different nights.
          He kept coming back.

J.O.:   Why?

Doris: He liked it.

Captain: WHAT'S HIS PHONE NUMBER!

J.O.:   Down. Captain, down. Tell us that story, Doris.

Doris: Well, he lived in my building. Usually, they were
          just guys on the street, but he lived on the first
          floor, near the elevator. I live on the sixth. I work,
          you know, at night. Sometimes– I had to, for
          awhile before Spider... went away. He was sick with
          these terrible migraines, he couldn't work at night.
          This guy...

J.O.:   Did he have a name, this Guy?

Doris: Ceanhead.

J.O.: Ceanhead?

Doris: That was his name. Carlos Ceanhead.

J.O.: Was it a street name?

Doris: No. No. You mean like gangs kids.

J.O.: Yes.

Doris: No that's what it said on his mailbox. Ceanhead. Why do you ask J.O.?

J.O.: It's strange. Ceanhead. A very strange name.

Doris: Well, he was a very strange man.
Carlos Ceanhead.

J.O.: Apparently so.

Doris: At first, it was just watching. He'd hear me come through the foyer, the key in the lock... and he'd come to his door, open it all the way and stand half in it. Watching as I walked by. You can feel them, the eyes, on your body, roving. You know what I mean, J.O.

J.O.: I understand what you're saying, yes.

Doris: He did it obvious, too. Shameless and gawking so he was sure I knew he was doing it.

J.O.:   You didn't mace him then.

Doris: For the gawking? No.

J.O.:   You don't find "gawking" a mace-a-ble offense.

Doris: Then I didn't. Now, I might.

J.O.:   You've progressed. In your use of mace.

Doris: I make faster decisions now. I was worried about
         Spider then. Plus I had him in my life, and I would
         think about him in Mace situations.

J.O.:   You felt—sympathy for other men,
         their aggressive side, because of Spider?

Doris: No. Not sympathy. I felt protected—supported by
         Spider. If I needed him he would appear. I could
         count on Spider. Plus, I didn't notice men as much.
         As loudly, I guess.

J.O.:   We'll get back to Spider, I'm very interested in
         Spider, but first we need to finish off
         Carlos Ceanhead.

Doris: (Laughing) Oh, I'd love to finish him off.

J.O.:   Yes. I can see that.

Doris: After a week of this staring, I began to rush
         through the foyer, put the key in the lock, hope
         the elevator is on the first floor... He would still
         open his door but usually he would only catch a

glimpse of me. I live in a modern building, the elevator door opens and closes quickly. Finally one night, I came home. He was standing in front of the elevator, talking low, like purring in his throat. I maced him. Right away. I'd promised myself I would. *(Long pause)* Aren't you going to ask me. How it felt? To mace him?

J.O.:   No. I was more interested in how he felt being maced.

Captain: ME, TOO.

Doris: Who?

J.O.:   Ceanhead. Carlos Ceanhead.

Doris: You want to know how Ceanhead felt?

J.O.:   I do. Yes.

Doris: Who cares how he felt. He isn't even human.

J.O.:   Ah Ha. Here I would walk softly, Doris.

Doris: Because you're a man you sympathize with him?

J.O.:   No. Although I do appreciate the nod of recognition, I am, as you say, a man. Freakish, hardly recognizable as such, but a man none-the-less.

Doris: You're not horrible looking. J.O. Unusual, but not horrible looking.

J.O.: Good. Good. Your kindness precedes you
 like the first blush of spring.

Doris: It's not kindness. I've seen ugly. You're not ugly.

J.O.: Bravo! A pretty compliment and worth some points.
 And it's points your beginning to need, Doris.

Doris: Why? I thought I was doing well?

J.O.: Yes. Yes. You've done well, better than most, actually.
 Still. I would be careful. Compassion counts for
 much here. It is the basis of the structure of our
 judgement. One of them any way, in other words...

Doris: And the others? I need to know.

J.O.: Well, perhaps I give you unfair advantage here,
 Doris.

Doris: I deserve to win.

J.O.: *(Deciding)* Warmth and courtesy, personal appeals,
 firm sense of self, aggression without doltishness,
 zest. But first and foremost. Compassion.

Doris: *(Nodding her head)* They're all important.

J.O.: Yes. I proposition that Ceanhead is human,
 in other words, has feelings, some of them
 are recognizable.

Doris: HIs mother loved him? He's kind to animals,
 especially dogs. Tips the fat waitresses excessively
 out of pity, that kind of thing?

J.O.: Yes. That kind of thing . . .

Doris: It's bullshit. Liberal-Love-The-Troubled-Bullshit.
Ceanhead was a terrorist. Plain and simple and
deserved to have his dick cut off.
I only maced him.

J.O.: Really, Doris. You're that sure?

Doris: Yes. Yes. Yes.

J.O.: And when you maced him a second time?

Doris: The next night after the first macing, the foyer was
empty when I came through it, his door stayed
closed and I felt triumphant the macing had
crushed him, burned his guts out as surely as it
had burned his eyes. I stomped to the elevator,
I whistled as I pushed that button... The doors
flew open, I live in a modern building and there he
was. The triumph in my eyes was battered by the
rage in his. I felt myself falling backwards, faint and
almost will-less in the shock of him being there
and now coming at me, not growling or purring
this time, his eyes doing all the talking, as he fell
forward meaning to fall on top of me and pin me
to the floor, I rolled away at the last instant, one
of his hands grabbing and yanking my hair, as his
unprotected head slapped the floor. He was a
clumsy jerk, Carlos Ceanhead... and as he sobbed
from the force of his head against the linoleum
floor, he twisted my hair until it burst, burning at
the scalp, I found the mace in my pocket book and
let him have it. He screamed this time as the mace
hit his eyes and I fired again at his open mouth
and he gulped it in. Sucking the gas deep into his

lungs. And I was up and flying into the elevator. Two nights went by. Three. I went to work as usual, I didn't tell Spider, I didn't tell anyone. I just waited. On the fourth night, I was grabbed by fear on the way home... When I rounded the corner and saw my own building, my stomach turned into a lurching hole. Poisonous and burning. He would be there. I entered the foyer. Nothing. Past his door a deep breath and I pushed the elevator button, the door swung open immediately, I live in a modern building. The elevator, empty, I rode to the 6th floor and when the door opened I stepped out spraying, holding the can of mace in front of me, at arms length, like a lantern in the darkness, I felt him fall rather than saw it. I was moving through the cloud of mace myself and my eyes were burning, too. I kicked at him, instinctively, hoping to mash his crotch, but maybe he had curled up in to a fetal position, to protect himself, because my foot connected with his shin bone instead... In a minute I was through my door and home with Spider... I waited for some weeks, expecting to see Carlos Ceanhead again.

J.O.: Did you know?

Doris: What?

J.O.: That it was him? In the hall. Carlos Ceanhead.

Doris: What.

J.O.: Read it Captain.

Captain: "THE DOOR OPENED... STEPPED OUT SPRAYING" BLAH

J.O.: You didn't mention seeing him.
Did you see him? Find his image on the
recognition lenses of your eyeball.

Doris: I didn't have to see him. I knew it was him.
He was waiting.

J.O.: So you expected.
You maced based on expectation.

Doris: I knew it was him.

J.O.: How?

Doris: Who else could it be?

J.O.: The drunken janitor, a door-to-door religious
zealot. The grandfather from the 7th floor, having
gotten off at the wrong stop, the elusive Spider.

Doris: No. No. No. It was Ceanhead. I knew it was.

J.O.: You sensed it was.

Doris: I knew it was. I trust my instincts.

J.O.: Apparently. Man in the hall... you sprayed away,
regardless of who was there

Doris: No. I sprayed because I knew.

J.O.: Reckless, Doris.

Doris: What?

J.O.: I'll call it recklessness and you'll lose points for it.

Doris: You bastard. I was in danger.

J.O.: Possibly, yes, possibly no. My position is, you didn't know for sure. You acted out of cockiness. Aggression. You enjoyed it Doris.

Doris: I...

J.O.: You enjoyed it, Doris.

Doris: No, I won't say that. I thought it was necessary. That's a fact.

J.O.: As a fact, it's a point-loser. Captain, make sure it's noticed as a point-loser.

Captain: LITTLE STARS IN THE MARGIN, LITTLE BLACK STARS IN THE MARGIN.

J.O.: That will be fine. I'd like to get back to Spider *(Pointing to the mace)* You could put this away now.

Doris: The mace?

J.O.: Before we continue, yes. The mace.

Doris: No. I'll keep it here.

J.O.: You won't need it, Doris. It's an old habit.

Doris: I'll keep it here, J.O.

J.O.:   Old habits are like snakes, Doris. They tend to eat
            themselves, in other words, as a snake handler, this
            macing is dangerous for you.

Doris: It's my mace. I'll decide when to put it away.

J.O.:   You're losing points here, Doris.
            I'm trying to be fair.

Captain: SLAP THE BITCH AND JUNK THE MACE.

Doris: Your captain gives weight to my stance on the
            mace question, J.O. I'll keep the mace, if my
            position makes sense it's because people like
            your captain make the rules in the world.
            Captain, would you like to take it away from me?

Captain: CUNT BITCH WHORE.

Doris: *(Macing him)* Pig-On-Two-Feet.

Captain: *(Crying and coughing)* AH FUCK FUCK FUCK...

J.O.:   A bold move, a strong move, Doris.

Doris: Necessary and inevitable.

Captain: FUCK FUCK FUCK

J.O.:   Captain, come with me. We'll find some water and
            rinse you clean...

            (J.O. leads the CAPTAIN out...
            J.O. exits for the first time in the play
            and DORIS is left alone.)

(After a long uncomfortable pause J.O. returns and Doris offers him a macadamia nut.)

Doris: *(to J.O.)* Macadamia nut?

J.O.:   Good, Good. I think we can continue, just the two of us. We'll talk of Spider.

Doris: I'm not sure I should talk about it. It's private. My own... Story. No. I'm sure I shouldn't talk about it.

J.O,:   It's required, if you are to pass the audition.

Doris: Why, the dirty old may gossip column I thought that was the Captain's department.

J.O.:   Required and I needn't supply you with a reason that you find acceptable Miss *(consults clipboard)* Du-Henry.

Doris: I'm still Doris, J.O. please, don't be ridiculous.

J.O.:   We are deteriorating at a rapid pace, Miss *(getting it)* Doheny. We're going to hell in a handbag. We've gone below points at this point. Indeed, points seem outside your reach. I am conducting this interview and I find you wanting in some very areas, in other words, tell me about Spider. It is required by me, by my employer, that you tell me about Spider. Now.

Doris: You can't talk to me like that. I won't be bullied. I'm not desperate for this position, you know. J.O.

J.O.:   Pompous Bravado.

Doris: I'm leaving.

J.O.:   You have no place to go or you wouldn't still be here, Miss Doheny. You are fooling no one.

Doris: I withdraw my application.

J.O.:   You are desperate. Desperate enough to answer an ad in some newspaper.

Doris: I'm not desperate. It was in the "Nation." "The Nation."

J.O.:   Well, La-dee-dah. Aren't you the little Mother Courage. "The Nation."

Doris: I wouldn't come from some newspaper ad.

J.O.:   An ad that promises untold wealth if you agree to give up your life on this planet, to travel through space with a mate of our choice. You who find such things as romance and marriage such treasures. To found a new world in the name of some rich old crackpot! In other words, you apply to play Adam and Eve for the rest of your life and you tell me you're not desperate? What are you, a lunatic?… a new rising sun will rise out of the exploding earth as we are hurtled towards Jupiter, how could you believe such crap, unless you were desperate?

Doris: I'm confused. Is it real? The spaceship.

J.O.:   Tell me about Spider, his death.

Doris: I was in love with Spider.

J.O.:   I don't doubt that. Now tell me.

Doris: I'd had men. Not a lot, but far too many men and
         each time it, the romance came apart, a piece
         of me went with it. This boy took my sweetness
         along with his ugly sweaters and clumsy humping.
         This one carved off a huge hunk of my freshness
         and joy like it was beefsteak and he the butcher.
         This one got my secret names for things, another
         my baby daydreams. When I met Spider after all
         the protrusions, buttocks, breasts, noses, gave way
         into each other, soft, Spider's hands were roving
         brushes of cotton after a hundred washings, soft,
         and mine were little electric bolt producers that
         provoked all sorts of *ohs* and *oohs* from him and
         many nights we held each other naked, giggling,
         and whispering, like children who have first
         become aware of their own beauty and are caught
         by it. I loved him and counted him as a blessing,
         as the blessing of my life, and with him all the
         wounds in me seemed to peel away, like when a
         snake loses its old skin, dry scales, and cracked
         silver in favor of the tender new skin. I liked myself
         with Spider. In those hours... sometimes awake
         and engaged with him, sometimes drifting in near
         sleep but with his touch still on me connecting us
         like a web connects two spiders. I... felt his soul.
         I'm embarrassed to say it.

J.O.:   Embarrassed? Why?

Doris: It's not something most people feel... the soul...
          I'm not sure you could get what I'm saying.

J.O.:   Ah, ha. You're embarrassed for me. For J.O. the
          hunchback freak who's never had a soul–to–soul
          experience.

Doris: No. No. No. That's not what I mean, J.O.

J.O.:   What do you mean?
          Say what you mean Miss Doheny.

Doris: I'm not... what you said would be condescending.

J.O.:   Yes, It would "Condescending." That's a word.
          Good use of the word, too, worth a Bravo or so,
          but not a warm or kind thing to say. Again, Doris,
          you earn points for clarity, boldness and wipe them
          out with your coldness and lack of compassion.

Doris: Look, J.O, I have plenty of compassion for you.
          I like you and up to this point in this conversation,
          I have had no problems with you. You seem fair...
          sensitive. Please don't make me out to be the
          queen bitch. I think it would be horrible for you
          if you had never experienced the soul in another
          person. It's beyond delightful. To experience that.

J.O.:   But what if I had. What if I, too, have looked
          into the eyes of another, a special another, like
          your Spider, Doris, and we have connected,
          had recognition, past the point of a heartbeat,
          tumbling together thru a bottomless pit. That kind
          of love. What if, Doris?

Doris: I'm so happy for you. I had no idea.

J.O.:   And "What if" that "special another" is
            my dear friend "the Captain."

Doris: What?

J.O.:   The Captain.

Doris: No. no. no.

J.O.:   Why not the Captain. He is human, assumedly,
            and therefore possessed of a human soul.

Doris: He is an evil man, a bug.
            This is twisted of you, J.O.

J.O.:   Really–

Doris: A twisted joke and I don't like it.

J.O.:   You are correct and you were correct earlier.
            In your condescension, I have never had a
            soul–to–soul experience with another.
            I don't believe I ever will.

Doris: Don't say that. You just haven't met
            the right person J.O.

J.O.:   Shall I stay open to it?

Doris: Yes. Yes. Yes.

J.O.:   Wanted woman with the brains of an angel, the
         sex of a Devil, and the patience of St. Francis who
         carries a picture of Quasimodo in her secret heart.
         Something like that?

Doris: I... yes.

J.O.:   Would you answer such an ad?

Doris: No.

J.O.:   Well, there you have it.

Doris: But it's not about the body, that's so...

J.O.:   Perhaps in the next life, Doris.
         We were talking about Spider.

Doris: You shouldn't give up.

J.O.:   Spider... you were mining each others souls, the
         last we checked and since that is outside of my
         comprehension, we need to get more mundane.
         Did you get along, enjoy each others company?

Doris: Yes. We had a lot of common ground.

J.O.:   Good. Such as.

Doris: He was a good person. Very excitable.
         He giggled with excitement. My Spider.

J.O.:   Really.

Doris: I liked Debussy, he loved Debussy. I read Virginia
          Woolf. He devoured Virginia Woolf.

J.O.:   His work, his job.

Doris: He was a writer and a goofball.

J.O.:   You learned to eat sparingly on dates?

Doris: I didn't care about that.

J.O.:   No. Of course not.

Doris: He had this goat tuft on his chin that he used to
          tickle my belly, my face. He had goats eyes and a
          goat's smell, ruttish, like smoke and wood resins
          smashed with patchouli oil...

J.O.:   Charming.

Doris: Oh, it was. That smell hung on the room when
          he sweated and he always sweated and farted
          and burped, not like a man farts, noxious and
          deliberate, but absentmindedly and kind of doofy,
          like a big baby who squirms and fusses until the
          bilious gas is out of him, and then charges on
          in its pursuit of the nipple or the rubber bug,
          wherever his real attention might be. I loved him
          and counted on him as a blessing in my life. All
          the wounds in me seemed to peel away like when
          a snake loses its old skin, dry scales and cracked
          silver, in favor of something tender and new. I like
          myself with Spider, too, he made it all seem easy.

J.O.:   What all.

Doris: The man and woman things… The need, the want, the have, the swings and psychic jousting.

J.O.:   "Psychic jousting?"

Doris: Yes, men and women do that to each other.

J.O.:   I'll have to remember.

Doris: You're being sarcastic.

J.O.:   Not at all.

Doris: Yes. You are.

J.O.:   Perhaps a bit. It's only that I long to be like you and Spider.

Doris: Really.

J.O.:   *(Very sarcastically)* Absolutely.
        I absolutely long to be like you and Spider.

Doris: You should stop doing that. It's mean and it's cheap of you, J.O. and you're suffering from it.

J.O.:   Really. What are the signs of this suffering?

Doris: I see it in you.

J.O.:   My face?

Doris: Your soul.

J.O.:   Ah ha. You can see my soul?

Doris: Just glimpses.

J.O.:   Really? *(Looking all over his body)* I can't find it
          at all and here you are able to get glimpses.

Doris: You are better than you act, deeper, cleaner.

J.O.:   I had no idea you were so powerful, Miss Doheny.

Doris: There's a shadow on you, J.O....
          I'm worried for you.

J.O.:   No idea at all. I thought you were just a loser
          whose lover killed himself giving you the big
          "fuck you" message and leaving you looking
          for a way out.

Doris: That's not how it happened.

J.O.:   How did it happen?

Doris: I had completely fallen headlong into this...
          picture of our future. Baby Flora if it was a girl.
          Beckett if it was a boy...

J.O.:   Beckett?

Doris: Spider was an existentialist.

J.O.:   Really? You surprise me, Miss Doheny.

Doris: Why?

J.O.:   Hopelessness. Godlessness.
         How would that effect your soul-to-soul?

Doris: Enlightened Existentialism? Ha ha.

J.O.:   That's funny?

Doris: He had a dark, romantic edge. My Spider. A poetic
         presence. The Beckett thing was part of that.

J.O.:   It didn't alarm you?

Doris: No. No. I was intrigued. Plus I knew we'd found
         each other. We'd change together.

J.O.:   I see.

Doris: It was a place to go. To expand. Together.

J.O.:   All right. You would go to work and
         he would do... what?

Doris: He had to stay home.

J.O.:   The migraines. I remember.

Doris: He wasn't well, then. But he would recover later.

J.O.:   What would he do? During that time?

Doris: Write. Most of the time. He was a wonderful writer.

J.O.:   Yes, he would be. "Most of the time?"

Doris: What?

J.O.:   What would he do the rest of the time?

Doris: I don't know, really. He was private about it.
         Sometimes I would come home and he would be
         weeping. Crying about us. How beautiful it all was,
         he said. But he didn't seem happy then. At those
         times. It worried me.

J.O.:   Yes. That's good.

Doris: Good. Why?

J.O.:   You were paying attention.

Doris: Have you ever wanted a child, J.O?

J.O.:   Prove to the world that it is possible for me
         to reproduce. A charming little Quasimodo,
         fashioned by my own likeness, just waiting
         in the wings?

Doris: It is sad, J.O.

J.O.:   What is sad?

Doris: How much you hate, loathe yourself, J.O.

J.O.:   We're not talking about me, Miss Doheny.
         You yourself wanted a child, I assume that's
         why you brought the subject up.

Doris: Yes. yes I did. But only when I was alone could
            I see it. I had pictures in my head of babies,
            children. I was in those pictures and I was always
            happy. Serene. But, in reality, I never was with a
            man who even knew how to approach that picture,
            let alone enter it. Until Spider. That boy had babies
            in his eyes...

J.O.   He wanted them to?

Doris: I thought he did. One morning I was pregnant.
            That's how it happens J.O.
            One day you're empty as... as a well gone dry or
            worse, never having known water and the next day
            full and flowing bursting with presence. That's how
            it happened. I felt a little soul nudge, nudge me.
            I was changed and would never be the same.
            I told Spider. He trembled and held me, trembling.
            What do you think it was, J.O.

J.O.:   You tell me.

Doris: You could guess.

J.O.:   "Psychic jousting."

Doris: I thought it was joy. I'd hoped it was joy.

J.O.:   You doubted it.

Doris: Yes.

J.O.:   This weeping of Spider's, it continued?

Doris: It increased. Spider would burst into tears.
           He became insomniac, tossing and turning.
           I finally had to ask him to sleep on the couch.
           I couldn't sleep it wasn't fair really, my body was
           going through tremendous changes, I was the
           one who was sick. Puking everyday. I had to stop
           drinking coffee. Couldn't stand the smell of garlic.
           Spider stank of garlic. Spider stank. I only asked
           him to sleep on the couch.

J.O.:   How was it for Spider, on the couch?

Doris: He felt bad, rejected, hurt. He said he felt hurt.
           I mean, I was the one having the baby.
           We started to argue, every day. I was leaving
           for work, unsettled. Coming home, unsettled.

J.O.:   He did what, while you were gone?
           Continued the weeping?

Doris: Yes. Yes. Yes. I would call on the phone and he
           would weep into the phone. Very anguished.
           I felt for him, I really did, but he started smoking.
           Oh not in the house, he wasn't insensitive, just
           out of control I thought he was out of control.

J.O.:   You thought, "he was out of control." But he...

Doris: He didn't think so. He was frightened and needy.
           Sleeping on the couch freaked him out, he said.
           He said all of this loudly, harshly, not like Spider at
           all. Spider had always smelled goatish, now he was
           rank, like a sewer. He looked seedier, too.

J.O.:   How did you respond.

Doris: Well, I was reading the books, all the books
          I could and they all said the same thing.
          That the first months were hard and all of
          this uncomfortableness, this puking, this over
          sensitivity to the mate, the man's smell was
          nature's way "Protecting the fetus from the male
          by urging the female to keep her distance."
          He hated that, all of that. I knew it would pass.
          I urged Spider to read the books.

J.O.:   And did he?

Doris: Yes. He did. It seemed to calm him.
          I thought we would get through it.
          We should have gotten through it.

J.O.:   Woulda– Shoulda– Coulda.

Doris: I can't believe you said that. Therapists always
          say that. Why would you say that, J.O.?

J.O.:   It seemed to apply, Doris.

Doris: I hate that.

J.O.:   I'm sorry.

Doris: I expect you to be, if not compassionate,
          original, J.O.

J.O.:   I am sorry, Doris, It's been a long decade.

Doris: *(Laughs)* That's better. Isn't that better, J.O.?

J.O.:   Yes. It's better, Doris. Macadamia Nut?

Doris: Sure. *(They both chew, somewhat solemnly)*
        I was at work, working and I started cramping,
        like menstrual cramping but harder like my inner
        body was gripped by a massive squeezing muscle.
        I felt the little soul nudging me in panic. Panic. I
        left work. Took a cab. The cab driver was smoking
        one of those little black cigars, foreign and crappy,
        it made me want to puke. I had to insist that he
        throw it out. He was jerky about it, too. Scowling
        and peeling around the corner.

J.O.:   "Foreign and crappy."

Doris: What?

J.O.:   You said the cab driver was foreign and crappy.

Doris: Not the driver. The cigar.

J.O.:   The Driver. Was he black?

Doris: No. No. No.

J.O.:   Was he swarthy?

Doris: No. No. No. I'm not a racist, J.O.

J.O.:   I'm pleased for you.

Doris: It's a stupid line of questioning.

J.O.:   We're thorough. Contempt is everywhere.

Doris: I'm talking about the most important things that
           ever happened.

J.O.:   To you. It's the most important to you.

Doris: Of course, to me... I'm not sure I want to tell you
           anything if you're going to be dense.

J.O.:   What?

Doris: Dense. Dense. This is my life. You're playing
           around with my life.

J.O.:   *(Long pause—considering)* Again. I'm sorry.
           You're right again. Doris. This is rare for me.

Doris: That you're wrong?

J.O.:   That someone else is right, Doris.
           You've done it twice. I'm impressed.

Doris: I need the points.

J.O.:   Yes. Well. Bravo. I'd like it if you'd continue, Doris.

Doris: Can I count on you, J.O. to play it straight.

J.O.:   Yes. Yes, you can.

Doris: I was in the cab.

J.O.:   Yes, in the cab.

Doris: The driver had slowed down. I told him I was pregnant, scowled but he slowed down. The cab pulled into the stoplight and I saw Spider, my Spider. He had gotten seedier, his hair standing up in all directions, wearing these terrible clothes that he kept sleeping in... It was Spider but he wasn't alone… He was walking with a man. The man a step ahead of him, on his right side, Spider's right hand resting on the shoulder ahead of him. The gesture relaxed. Intimate, as if they'd walked that way dozens of times before. I was surprised. Spider didn't have many friends. None that he would touch that I had ever met. I rolled down the window to call to him. I was relieved, I wanted to tell him about the cramping. The man turned his head, to say something to Spider and I looked him right in the eyes. It was Carlos Ceanhead. He didn't seem to know me, but I knew him. Carlos Ceanhead. My brain bucked and twisted, Carlos Ceanhead.

J.O.: Good. Thank you, Miss Doheny... for your time. If you would be so kind as to wait in the waiting room while we tally up the score.

Doris: What?

J.O.: We'll let you know. Shortly.

Doris: That's not the end.

J.O.: No. It wouldn't be. Still, it is enough. It will serve. For our purpose.

Doris: You insisted that I tell the story.

J.O.:   Yes. Bravo. You've told it well, with flair, and an eye
          for the dramatic. Not worth points, per se, still, an
          eye for the dramatic, well told, and we'll note it.
          That way. The waiting room is out that door and
          to the right.

Doris: You gouged me for details.

J.O.:   To which you responded like Mount Vesuvius
          at lava time. Really, Miss Doheny, despite your
          supposed privacy concerns, it doesn't take much
          to provoke a gusher out of you.

Doris: Spider isn't dead yet.

J.O.:   Denial and nonsense.
          Must we produce the death notice?

Doris: In the story. I haven't reached his death.
          It's the climax of the story.

J.O.:   Perhaps you can climax in the waiting room.
          For now, this interview is terminated.

Doris: I won't go.

J.O.:   Shall I ring for the Captain? Good old #13?

Doris: Why are you doing this? You complain of my lack
          of compassion for Ceanhead, of my coldness
          toward the Captain, but you are... in my most
          sensitive moment... a brute.

J.O.:   Brute? Certainly not a brute. A troll.
          A goblin. But never—

Doris: Why do that?

J.O.:   Why do you suppose, Miss Doheny? *(Warmer)*
           I've done my job. I know what i need to know.

Doris: But you don't want to know what happened
           between us? It was terrible. Don't you want to
           understand it?

J.O.:   I understand it. Now I'd like you to leave.

Doris: *(Going for the mace and holding it out)*
           You're not going anywhere.

J.O.:   Really, Miss Doheny. And we were doing so well.

Doris: Ask me what happened to Spider.

J.O.:   I'll do better, I'll tell you. We are at the moment
           when your eyes locked with Carlos Ceanhead.
           You know him, he does not know you. The cab
           driver is scowling, foreign, and impatient.

Doris: I remember. What do I do?

J.O.:   You tell your driver to drive on to the park,
           or better yet, the lake, the shoreline.
           Your mind is leaping like a school of dolphins.
           Spider and Ceanhead. Ceanhead and Spider.
           Spider! Ceanhead! If your life were a page
           you'd be jumping off of it. You drive along
           the shore for hours.

Doris: I don't have much money.

J.O.:   You get out, then.
         And walk along the shoreline for hours.

Doris: Right.

J.O.:   The cramping has stopped.

Doris: It continues.

J.O.:   But you have to walk.

Doris: The walking helps.

J.O.:   Helps the body. But the mind is still jumping.

Doris: Yes.

J.O.:   You imagine scenes so vividly that you stagger
         from their weight. Spider and Ceanhead locked
         in fellatio. Their mouths and cocks heathen and
         writhing. Spider and Ceanhead snorting crack and
         knocking over hardware stores. Ceanhead and
         Spider surrounded by their witch's coven, stalking
         down young women who live in modern buildings.
         Finally you can't stand what's in your head and you
         rush home, determined to have it out with Spider.
         He's there, he's dumbfounded, shocked at being
         found out... he becomes enraged, beating you
         about the head and stomach.

Doris: No. No, no. He would never hit me. Spider.
         He was a very gentle man, always.

J.O.:   Really? I would have thought beating, but...

Of course! He weeps, curls at your feet, whining like a baby... He admits everything.

Doris: No, no, no. He admits nothing. Nothing at all. He won't explain Ceanhead, he just cries.

J.O.: You insist. For hours this little scene goes on. For hours, his weeping, you insisting. Until, finally, he rushes out into the rain. You follow, slipping and falling on the stoop, the horrible stoop, then the blood. You cry out for help and Spider is halfway across the street, he turns, sees you, fallen and bloody, and is hit by a red Jeep. Thrown six feet. As you are rushed to the hospital, you feel his soul gasp and plunge toward heaven.

Doris: It was a bus. Not a Jeep.

J.O.: Really? A bus. Hard to avoid, a bus.

Doris: It didn't happen that night, either. Several weeks went by. That night, I just asked him to go. He was impossible about Ceanhead. And I was worried about the baby. Several weeks went by.

J.O.: He just went?

Doris: He looked all collapsed, panicky, around the mouth and eyes.

J.O.: You sent him away.

Doris: Yes...

J.O.: You were in the director's chair.

Doris: Yes. At first he called three or four times a day.
            Whining on the phone machine at first, and then
            angry, abusive. He said I was unfit for motherhood,
            should have an abortion. It was his child, too,
            he had rights, too.

J.O.:   You were alone during this time?
            In other words, isolated?

Doris: I stayed at home, because of the cramping.
            Friends brought gifts for the baby, a spotted
            leopard, so small, an ugly high chair, lovely flowers
            that I had to throw away after everyone left. I slept
            a little hugging the leopard, daydreaming my little
            girl, her trips to the library, her graduate school.
            The cramping continued.

J.O.:   Your friends talked to you?

Doris: What?

Doris: About Spider and Ceanhead,
            they offered advice, insights, opinions?

Doris: Yes, they were helpful.

J.O.:   One was happily married now, after his fourth
            attempt. He understood about relationships,
            what a man is supposed to do to make a real
            commitment. In other words, the Ceanhead
            incident was unforgivable without explanation.
            Spider offered no explanation, thus Spider
            should remain unforgiven, and he continued
            to be uncommitted.

Doris: That's right.

J.O.:   Another was a therapist, a professional, she was a working mother and a feminist. She too, was a success at marriage. As a therapist and a woman, she would find Spider, his crying, his secrecy, his demands, unacceptable. Spider must hate women and impregnate them out of hostility, that must be what it was.

Doris: Yes, That's right.

J.O.:   All the others, the healthy friend who thought Spider's stinking and migraines a sure sign of cancer, the gay male friend who was appalled for both of you and thought you just needed some quality time, the mailman who found Spider's abandonment of you the actions of a man who had the ethics of dog food...

Doris: He was the plumber.

J.O.:   Really. You talk openly to the plumber.

Doris: I've known him for years. How did you get my friends to talk to you? You must really want me for the mission.

J.O.:   An assumption.
           Your friends are an assumption on my part.

Doris: I don't understand how you could.

J.O.:   Oh, you were difficult to get at first, Doris, but I cracked you, and now I can read you like the proverbial book.

Doris: You're lying. Its all in your notes.

J.O.:   Oh, no... not much to begin with. Spider's death.
          Your desperation in wanting to join us. You're a
          type, Doris. A post-sixties-strong-solid-woman-
          with-grit-and-tunnel-vision-caught-in-a-Hard-Copy-
          generation-melodrama type.

Doris: I am not.

J.O.:   You are. Surprising at times, worthy of respect,
          but of course, that type would be.

Doris: I hate that.

J.O.:   No doubt you do. Put away the mace. You don't
          need it with me. The testing is over and you did
          fine. Now it's just a question of compatibility.

Doris: My story isn't over.

J.O.:   No, I can't imagine it stretching on adnauseum,
          like the human race you will soon represent.

Doris: Spider hasn't died yet. Spider deserves to die.

J.O.:   Do I deserve to hear? The poor fucker was
          doomed from the moment you laid eyes on
          Ceanhead. Let's leave Spider pushing up daisies
          and get on with the task at hand.

Doris: You'll think less of me once you know all, J.O.

J.O.:   I couldn't think less of you, Doris. Let it lie.

Doris: I could lose points.

J.O.:   No. No. Some flaws give points. Its your humanity
          we've been testing. At their best, human beings
          resemble Swiss cheese. You're simply that; a swiss
          cheese human being.

Doris: Several weeks went by and Spider stopped calling.

J.O.:   Bravo for him. He was busy talking to his friends
          about how self-righteous and unforgiving you were.

Doris: I guess that's right. The cramping continued and I
          was always afraid, afraid of losing the baby, J.O.

J.O.:   (Sadly) Yes.

Doris: Finally, one morning I woke up to blood gushing
          everywehre. The baby was gone, just like that.
          I felt the little soul go. Felt it leave me.

J.O.:   Yes.

Doris: I went to the hospital. There was no heartbeat.
          I waited for hours and finally, they removed things...
          I called Spider. I called Spider, his phone machine.
          "I am at the hospital and I don't know how to speak
          to your face. Our baby is dead." He didn't come
          and find me at the hospital.

J.O.:   No.

Doris: I always thought he would. But he didn't even come.
          He called me the next day and I hung up on him.

He got through to the machine, though...
a number of times and said how sorry, sorry, sorry.
I did not answer. He had betrayed me, my Spider.

J.O.: That's how you saw it.

Doris: Several weeks went by...

J.O.: I can't give you absolution, Doris.

Doris: My body was going through these swings.
I was enraged, manic.

J.O.: I'm not a priest, Doris.
My soul has a shadow over it, you saw that.

Doris: I started calling Spider and speaking to his phone
machine, accusing. He wasn't a man. He wasn't a
real man. He was a small bird, helpless, grasping
with his brainless little beak, waiting... heart,
without sympathy, without value...

J.O.: Several weeks went by.

Doris: I called him that day. I raged and railed. It was
pouring rain. Terrible buckets full. Spider was
walking with an umbrella. He was always a
klutz with mechanical things. He never used an
umbrella. It was raining, sheets of rain, he
couldn't see. He got hit by a bus.

J.O.: Thrown six feet. Dead on arrival.

Doris: Yes, I didn't feel his soul go. I tried to, but I didn't feel it. There was too much wrong between us. No one loved each other anymore.

J.O.:   "No one loved each other anymore." I'll write that down. An existential ending after all, Doris.

Doris: What do you think, J.O.?

J.O.:   You lost a few points.

Doris: No. What do you think of me?

J.O.:   You're a normal person.

Doris: And... and?

J.O.:   I won't judge you, Doris, that's not my job.

Doris: There's something horrible and cruel about being a normal person, isn't there, J.O.?

J.O.:   I don't know. *(Gestures towards self)* I'm outside.

Doris: Yes, but what do you think?

J.O.:   Comme çi, comme ça. Que sera sera. You should go now.

Doris: *(Sprays mace and nothing comes out)* Aw. It's empty.

J.O.:   You knew it was empty all along, Doris.

Doris: I used it up on the Captain.
           I would never spray you, J.O. We're friends.

J.O.:   How kind of you to retain that, Doris.

Doris: *(Starting to go, turns)* Macadamia nut?

J.O.:   We're out. All out of macadamia nuts.

Doris: That's a shame. I have a real craving for one, J.O.

J.O.:   We'll call you, Doris.

— *THE END* —

THE THIRD DEGREES OF J.O. BREEZE >>

Bryn Magnus and Paul Tamney, 1995 Chicago production

Beau O'Reilly

Ira Glass

Eddie: A Man In His Skin

Premiered May 9, 1997
This American Life - broadcast episode #63
PRX / WBEZ Chicago Public Radio

written and read by:

Beau O'Reilly

THE
PLAYS

INTRO

This is as close to telling a true story as I will ever get...

In the ten years I knew Eddie he told me a lot of it in bits and pieces, I witnessed some of it and the end was told to me second hand... the hearsay seems right... there are a handful of beings who have affected the way I write; the characters from Godot, Dylan Thomas and Bob Dylan, Jenny Magnus and Eddie Collins!

I wrote it for the stage ten years after I last saw Eddie, Ira Glass asked me to do it for THIS AMERICAN LIFE, and god bless him, barely touched it. He let me record it as written.

I did it at Lunar Cabaret, Colm gave me a soundtrack of 'Eddie' reading from "Catcher in the Rye..." Paul Leisen played cello-bass live.

More people have heard this piece, on the radio and onstage, than anything I have ever done.

SYNOPSIS

A mostly true tale, told in the third person, about Edward Hickock Collins, the "nude run" messiah and beast of revelations. Eddie, legendary nude public speaker, stages an unsuccessful run against Ronald Regan for president on a 'Nudity Now' platform arena, all as reported by the writer who was a witness to most of it.

Eddie Hickock Collins taught high school English in Baldwin, Long Island. Remedial readers whose attention spans kept them far away from Herman Melville or Nathaniel Hawthorne. Holden Caulfield and *Catcher in the Rye*, those seemed just right to Eddie, despite the fact that *Catcher in the Rye* was on the banned bookshelf of the school library. The library didn't like the use of the F-word on page 201 of *Catcher in the Rye*, but page 201 was Eddie Collins's favorite page. And he figured his remedial readers would love it too.

His young hooligans who all wanted and needed to get naked and needed page 201, thought Eddie. The school soon gave notice though: under no circumstances was Eddie to teach that dirty *Catcher in the Rye*. The F-word, the love word on page 201—they were deemed questionable and inappropriate. Eddie began reading the book aloud to his remedial class that day. And the remedial readers all took notice, they nodded and they grunted at all the good parts, running their long adolescent fingers over and over through their greasy pompadours as good old Holden Caulfield rolled along. And cheering and chanting out the F-word when Eddie tore into page 201.

Edward Hickock Collins was fired from teaching English in Baldwin, Long Island. And he spent the rest of that year

pacing in front of the fireplace at his mother's house.
It was a cold winter, but Eddie was already heated up from
his recent battle with censorship, so Eddie pulled off more
and more of his clothes—his shirt, his shoes, his pants. And
he flung them in all directions. Eddie built up the fire and he
sweated aloud. If he couldn't teach the F-word how could
he live free? That, he demanded of himself. The F-word, the
sex act—that had to be naked and lovely. That felt right, and
right felt natural, and why hide that? Eddie thought. And
that's when he first thought it: he would never dress again.

You know how an idea catches and grabs ahold of you?
Maybe you've had that. An idea that speaks to your
most private imaginings and your deepest hurt feelings,
your most secret strange joys. And that idea says here
I am, change everything, because I'm here, I'm perfect.
I'm enlightened by sexuality, I'm the new laughing cure
for cancer, I am my body in shape and in perfect yoga
pose. And these ideas feel so crucial that the axis of your
world turns to embrace them. Eddie's idea felt like that.
And Eddie's idea was naked, and it was obvious. It was
without guilt or second thought. Nudity. Nudity now.

Eddie ran naked all the way to the high school. It was his
first nude run. His body was flapping like a ship that has
come free of its moorings and is now spinning and reckless
in the surf. And at the high school, all his former students,
the remedial readers, were playing manic playground
basketball. And Eddie happily ran out onto the court. He
wanted to dunk a few in the glorious springtime. Dunk a few
and then tell his smart guys of his new vision of freedom.
And Eddie yelled in his joy as he hit the court, but his

remedial readers weren't glad to see him. They turned away, laughing, embarrassed by Eddie's nakedness, and they refused to pass him the ball. And when Eddie persisted, he leaped at each of the boys in turn, one of them grabbed the ball and smacked it into Eddie's face hard. So hard that both lips stung and bled and Eddie's eyes filled with tears. Eddie was lost then. The remedial readers surrounded and hounded him home. They flipped popsicle sticks and clods of dirt at his exposed penis and his poor backside. And Eddie slammed the door of his mother's house. He was crying and he was shaking. And all the remedial readers, they gathered in a pack outside. They were flushed and they talked themselves into a deeper hatred. And one of them grabbed a brick and threw it through Eddie's mother's picture window and shattered it. And then there was such a roar of rage and hurt and it just ripped through Eddie's brain, and he grabbed the same brick and he threw it back through the same window, the remaining glass just flying, and then Eddie jumped through the now open window, falling and gashing his poor hands and his poor feet. The remedial readers running in all directions, Eddie landing on a lawn of glass. And when he looked up in the sky, written in huge letters of flaming black and red, six feet high, were the words:

"Why? Don't ask why—live."

And right then, something deep exploded in Eddie.
And his face and his heart, his whole being, flushed with joy.

Shock treatments are serious and they're undermining and in Eddie they led him to a decade of quiet years. Years in which he memorized D.H. Lawrence's *Women in Love* from cover to cover, but his body, his naked body, lay in waiting, impatient for the day when the clothes could come off and his body could go public again.

Eddie Hickock Collins came to De Kalb, Illinois to work on the railroad. And he grew a huge red beard that shouted out a fanfare wherever he went. *The Palace* was our vegetarian restaurant theatre and coffee house. It was work, and it was home, for we young, anti-war hippies. It was a workshop for our ideas on how to change the troubled world that we'd been given by our parents. But it was also a refuge and a magnet, a magnet for people who were obsessed with one idea, and for the odd. If your father was a mason and now you'd lost your chi and you were doomed to wander the five-room universe of *the Palace* looking for it, if you were hopelessly shy and allergic to the twentieth century and everything that made it tick, if you were a closet arsonist who just needed a place to rest and battle the flames inside you, if you were a bottom-pincher who drank too much Schnapps and read only 17th Century literature, you were welcome at *the Palace*. You could bring your dogs and your books and your bare feet. And as long as you didn't drink Coca-Cola there and at least considered not paying your war taxes, you were welcome. And we would never call the police.

Eddie set up outside the Palace. Smiling and silent at first, and he offered his own newsletter, *"The Beast of Revelation,"* a passionate journalistic manor? that proclaims the beauty of the human body. "The penis is glorious.

And the vagina is magical. They have to be seen to be believed," argued *The Beast of Revelations*. And after Eddie had figured most of us, the hippie community of *the Palace*, had a grasp of his basic message, Eddie came in off the sidewalk and he began to talk to us. He was a public speaker, could he speak there?

Eddie had a voice, and his eyes were wide awake, and the title of his first talk was, "Nudity. Nudity Now." He quoted liberally from D.H. Lawrence's *Women in Love*. "Lawrence is big, oh he's big: nudity and orgasm equals freedom. That's what D.H. Lawrence sees. And Lawrence sees me, Eddie, Lawrence agrees with Collins. Nudity, sexuality, they form a square knot of human perfection. Until the Catholic Church and public education get a hold of you. Oh, they'll twist you and they'll shame you. And that's bad, it's bad. Read Lawrence, he knows, he's big. Nudity. Nudity now." We all laughed, not knowing why. And at the end of each performance, we followed Eddie out onto the sidewalk, Eddie tossing his clothes in all directions before running off naked into the night.

De Kalb is a small place but by the next week there was a real crowd that followed him outside for his personal unveiling. Edward Hickock Collins blossomed with nudity and attention. And by the fourth week, with the crowd urging him on, the clothes came off onstage and Eddie became the Nude Public Speaker.

"Speaking out but speaking nude!" he shouted.

Eddie now began his talks naked, and he hung around naked. He could be found at *the Palace* at all hours, naked. Sometimes we'd politely asked him to dress for an occasion, like when someone's parents came to town, and then Eddie would put on his kilt—a kilt he had made out of a pair of cutoff jeans slashed free at the legs.

Once my mom came to visit me at the Palace, and I don't know what Mom expected but what she got was Eddie— naked and relaxed Eddie reading the *New York Times Book Review* section. It made me very nervous when Eddie sat down with my mother, but my mom loved the *New York Times Book Reviews*, and Eddie must have sensed that because he offered it to her. And the two of them were soon chatting about books they would never have time to read. And quickly they seemed comfortable together. And that was amazing to me. My mother fully clothed and Eddie not clothed at all. It was only when Eddie leaned over and asked something so private that my mother never told me what it was, that my mom flushed and stormed away from the table. And that's the thing about Eddie. As much as he could win you over, and I liked him, he always found a way to just push things too far. As if any boundary or border was a foreign thing and it was to be disposed of and gotten through, no matter how you felt about it.

Eddie moved into our house and invited some of the Palace women to sleep with him. And some of them were happy to do it until the most private details of their intimacy started showing up in his speeches, surrounded by big blinking exclamation points: "Look at this!"

The police came two months into Eddie's talks. Eddie was arrested. And soon now, this nude Messiah would stand trial. And he felt that—messianic and rune—and filled with a vision of the world where the pants come down in simultaneous synchronization, and whole nations freed from the shackles of clothing, walk freely and hang out in peace. And Eddie spent the weeks prior to his trial alternating between phone calls to Brezhnev and the Kremlin, and Jimmy Carter's White House. Eddie made his calls from the corner laundromat, urging long distance operators to support his new strategy.

"International Nudity Day, July 4th. Disarm now. The pants come off in simultaneous synchronization for world peace. That's the hook! If you're naked, how can you take yourself seriously holding a tank or fondling a nuclear warhead? You'd have to set them down."

Soon the Kremlin actually answered one of Eddie's calls. And Eddie just poured it on over the phone, his whole platform, but at the White House they just put him on hold and left him there. Eddie hardly noticed. His campaign was heating up.

There was a large crowd at Eddie's trial for indecent exposure. When the judge walked solemnly in and the clerk called out, "All please rise," Eddie slipped out of his kilt and his T-shirt, and he did rise. The judge found him in contempt and the cops dragged him, handcuffed and kilted from the courtroom—Eddie meaning to go willingly—but the crowd was too good to waste, so Eddie shouted over his shoulder, pulling away from the cops, to urge them to join him for

International Nudity Day. And the cops moved Edward Hickock Collins from the county jail to the county hospital. Now Eddie was a lamb at the hospital. He was polite and he was cooperative. He'd had shock treatments before and he didn't wish to have them again. He needed his mind. But the doctors gave him Nembutals and Thorazine—large amounts—and his tongue thickened and his bright eyes grew heavily lidded. And he stumbled over his quotations of good old page 201. And after some weeks, all Eddie was really sure of was that the world would be better off naked and he was the man to strip it bare. He hung on to that. Eddie got out one deep blue day and he wept because it was June and he was free, with International Nudity Day just round the corner. Over the month, Eddie's plans spread and took wing.

"International Nudity Day, that's only a beginning. It's a great beginning, it's a campaign-launcher. The Republican convention that's set for Kansas City mere months away. The Republicans need to disarm now. The pants come down in simultaneous synchronization candidate. A nude-run messiah. That's the perfect choice for Kansas City. I'm running, and I'm running nude." And on the Fourth of July, two hundred of us gathered in the center of downtown. It was a place marked by the crossing of two lines of railroad tracks. Eddie arrived late, running up in his kilt and T-shirt and shaking hands and passing out campaign literature. Someone pulled a baby out of the crowd for Eddie to kiss and the crowd cheered. And Eddie spoke, and he was poignant in his wonder at the human body, and then in simultaneous synchronization, the pants came down. I was there and it was great.

We all pulled off our clothes. Really only about thirty of us did it, but we were all standing at the front so it felt like a crowd, a naked crowd. And Eddie was ecstatic, he beamed with joy and, leaping about, his own clothes flew in all directions with an extra zip that day. The police moved in with paddy wagons, arresting the naked crowd, but they saved Eddie till last. And before they could reach him, a long freight train raced up the tracks, just as the cops were moving toward Eddie. He timed it perfectly, waving and nodding, he jumped over the tracks, right in front of the engine, leaving the cops on the other side. And by the time the freight train had already passed, Eddie was gone. He was running, and he was running nude.

Eddie ran all the way to Kansas City, mostly at night, and *Playboy magazine* picked up on his story and sent a reporter and a photographer to follow him. The pictures were all of Eddie naked, eating banana splits with a bunch of old farmboys at a Stuckey's, or posed on the seat of a big hog Harley at a rest stop, surrounded by big hairy biker guys, naked except for a MacDonald's cap, giving out free French fries and Nudity Now buttons under the shadow of the golden arches. *Playboy magazine* bailed him out each time he was arrested.

But when he got to Kansas City, Eddie got cagey. This was the big time. And he covered himself, his nude body, his kilt, and his T-shirt, in a black three-piece suit he bought at the Salvation Army. He borrowed the Playboy writer's press I.D. and Eddie boldly moved behind Republican lines, making it to the front steps of the convention center. That was close enough. And the next day Eddie found a fruit crate and he wrote "Soap" all over it in black magic marker and he returned to the convention steps, standing up high on the soapbox above the crowd, his whole being overwhelmed with the moment, the power of his big idea; blurting out verbiage and joy, his clothes flying and hysterical in all directions. And there were brief looks of childlike wonder across Republican faces in the crowd. But then they were replaced with this all-too-adult frown of disgust and censor. The Kansas City cops, hard men who had been put on kook alert, knocked him from the soapbox and they slammed him into the cement steps, and they dragged him bodily away. Eddie's anxious cry of "Nudity now!" drowned out by police radios and the charging march of police boots. And Eddie stayed in jail for the rest of the convention. His name would never appear on the Republican list of nominees that year. And like so many presidential candidates—Jesse Jackson, Gary Hart, Paul Tsongas, Ross Perot—the early days of his campaign would prove to be the most memorable. Edward Hickock Collins had peaked too soon.

He returned home to the Palace. But he was never quite the same. Eddie's confidence dropped after Kansas City. He had other big moments, like attending his Yale class reunion football game and dropping his pants, dashing along the sidelines when Yale scored against Harvard. But this episode led to jail and more hospital, where a stream of Nembutals and shock treatments left Eddie struggling to keep a hold on his mind. It's strange when you think about it. That nudity would exact this kind of retribution from our society—nudity. But Eddie stuck to his vision of the world, his one big idea: that a naked man is a free man, and should be allowed to be free.

The last I heard of him, he had moved back home to Baldwin, Long Island. He'd begun liberating the neighborhood cats and dogs of their leashes, their choke chains, and their flea collars. Eddie ended up reading to his cats and dogs, good old page 201, *Catcher in the Rye*. The dogs and cats listened, they were animals, they had no problem with the F-word. Nudity came naturally to them.

— THE END —

Beau O'Reilly as **Edward Hickock Collins**
for **EDDIE: A MAN IN HIS SKIN**, 1997

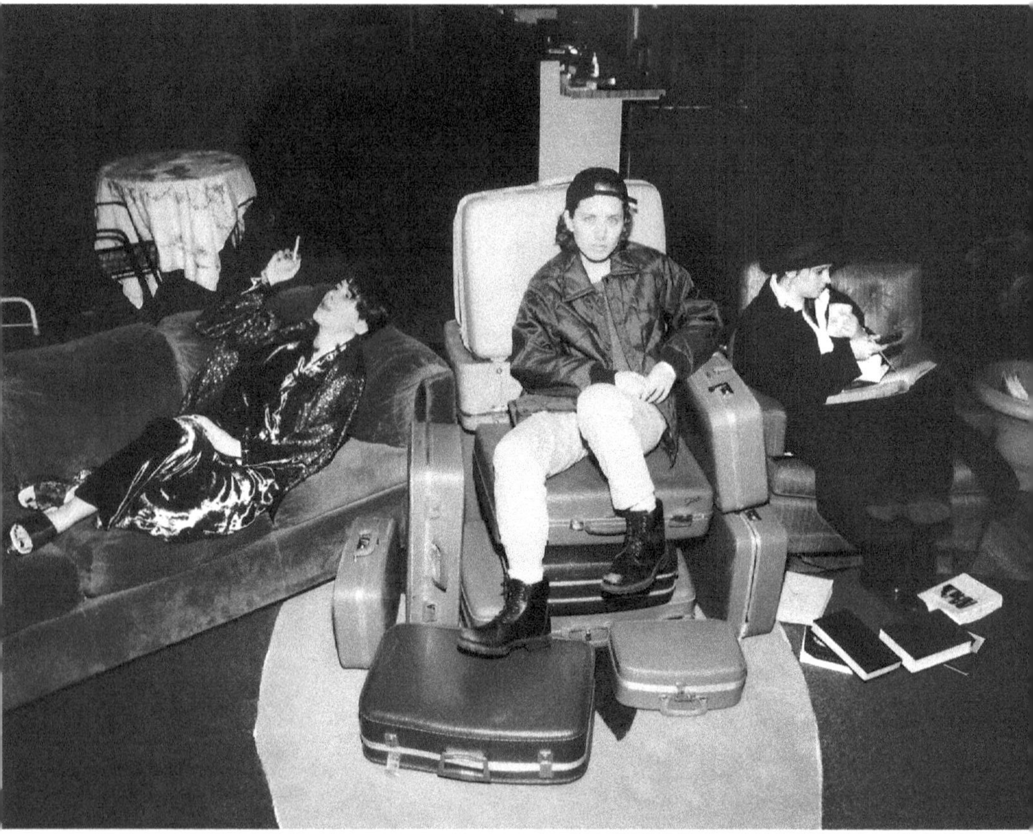

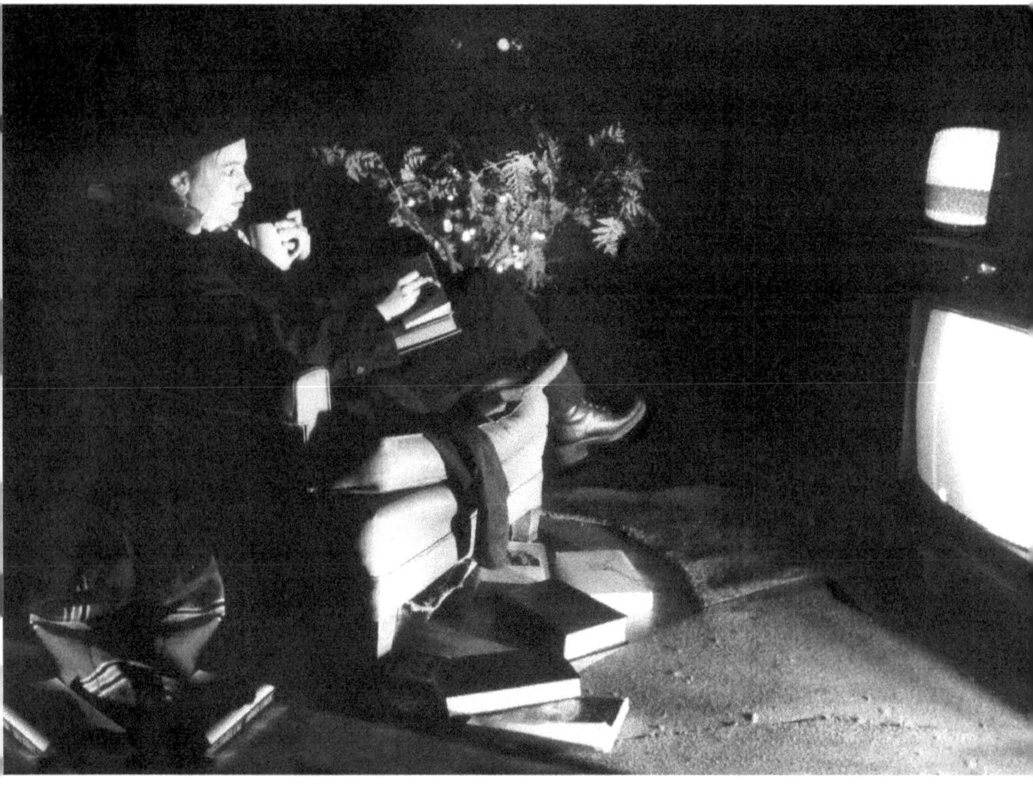

Talking About Godard

Premiered November 1999
The Lunar Cabaret Theater
Chicago, IL

performed by:

Anne Fogarty
Paul Leisen
Jennny Magnus
Beau O'Reilly
Vicki Walden
Eric Ziegenhagen

INTRO

My friend David Isaacson did a performance, an homage, to Godard at the Lunar Cabaret where Curious did our shows...

It was smart, funny, over my head, and it spun me into this play... I wrote it fast, I was on a roll at that time... I had barely ever watched Godard but I didn't let that stop me... the Luftmensch joke I must have heard somewhere but I stretched it out and upped the fable quality...

Jenny wanted to play Helen right away... she was sharp and focused throughout, driving both the rehearsals and the performances... Vicki and me and Jenny were fans of each others' work... Vicki's comic timing, now so crucial to so many Curious shows, was already in full force... She played Mary Barnes like there was nothing loopy about Mary, exquisite, is my memory, it was our first show together... Anne Fogarty we didn't know but she had chops and was well recommended. Our show was very low buck compared to what she was used to but she was a trooper. When I read it back now her version of Crissy is exactly the performance I wanted. Paul Leisen was a Curious stalwart and he probably built the set while fixing the electricity and shoring up the plumbing at Lunar while also playing Leon like he had known him all his life, 'on accounta'... I asked David to write the faux Godard scenes, Hallie Gordon directed the short movie that David wrote... David reminds me now that we showed the piece as its own work before the play started, I think we all really wanted those scenes to be seen... Jenny and Anne played the filmic roles... Eric we knew from Barrie Cole's work and he is always funny on stage... I directed the play... people came.

SYNOPSIS

Two thirty-something women are living in New York at the end of the 90's. CRISSY is in love with HELEN, who knows that but finds it funny. She prefers to have sex with a variety of men, sometimes in their home, rather then give in to CRISSY'S amour

MARY BARNES is HELEN'S friend, she is obsessed with the films of GODARD but doesn't own a VCR. She spends all her time on HELEN'S couch. This drives CRISSY crazy.

LEON is a local Brooklyn boy, with a passion for stealing suitcases and bringing them over to CRISSY'S house. Something too ridiculous to be scary occurs when a french minor gangster appears, drunk with a lust for all the women. The women team up to frustrate and then de-pants him! Godard runs in with a super 8 camera to film it all! There are exclamation points everywhere!

SETTING

THE STREET IN FRONT OF HELEN'S HOUSE can be skeletal, implied through light and sound; its transition into an apartment should take no time.

THE APARTMENT should be lived in. With CRISSY'S stuff (suitcases especially) everywhere. MARY BARNES' TV should not dominate the scene, but be in clear view of the audience. Or video monitors are a possibility, as long as the audience sees what is watched.

CAST OF CHARACTERS:

CRISSY

HELEN

MARY BARNES

LEON

PAUL-JEAN

GODARD

NOTES: THE GODARD PIECES

There is no specific way in which to display the seven Godard pieces. One possibility is to take excerpts from Godard films and play them. Another is to take dialogue from Godard and have the actresses playing Crissy and Helen act them out in real time on stage; or on film (in wigs)—this last option was employed in the original production by Curious Theatre Branch in Chicago to great effect. The playwrght, David Isaacson, re-worked Godard scenes into 2-person dialogues and we filmed them in a faux Godard style with Godard's shadow and camera in evidence. Other methods can be explored and developed for this presence.

SCENE: ACT I

On the street in front of HELEN'S house

Leon: So. Where you been?

Cris: None of your motherfuckin' business and don't
          touch me again, Leon Diaz, or I'll tell your mother.

Leon: She was asking for you just the other day, on
          accounta she says she enjoyed having you to
          Sunday food that time. Remember? Me'n you
          and Uncle Louie and Mom's steak fettuccine.

Cris: What time? I was in eighth grade that time.

Leon: She remembers it fondly, she said to tell you...
          I waited all night, I was worrying big time on
          accounta Uncle Louie got me tailin' these
          French guys, gangster guys...

Cris: You thought I was out fuckin', is that it?

Leon: No, I...I didn't wanna think--

Cris: Are you a pimp, Leon?

Leon: No...no... I'm a tough guy, one'a Louie's thugs.
          Pimps are low-lifers, you know, bottom feeders;
          me'n Louie's boys, we got real class... these French
          gangster guys, they're low-lifers on accounta...

Cris: You act like a pimp, Leon.

Leon: No... I don't... I'm likin' you,
         since the seventh grade...

Cris: I don't get it, Leon. I never kissed you, I never
         fucked you... I never will... *(As if to a child)*
         Never ever kiss. Never ever fuck.
         I think you're ugly.

Leon: I'm not, I'm fuckin' John Travolta,
         I'm the vanilla Charles Barkley.

Cris: You're ugly and that's it.

Leon: That's it? That's not it.
         *(He moves on her. Slaps her. She slaps back.
         LEON slaps again.)*

Cris: Stay away from me you motherfucker.
         We're not doing this anymore.

Leon: I'm not lettin' go here, on accounta I feel it,
         it's like poison ivy all over a swollen tongue i
         n my heart! In my heart! But I feel it for you.

Cris: Leon Diaz, go away, very far away.

Leon: Europe. You'n me. After I do this job
         on these French guys...

Cris: Go to where you go when you go away.

Leon: What's in your heart? A big empty bucket.
          A garbage can you can beat on, I love you on
          accounta—

Cris: Okay. Okay. I'll go away. *(She does.)*

          (SCENE SHIFTS TO INSIDE THE HOUSE)

Helen: Crissy. Hello. I'm cookin'.

Cris: Smells awful. *(She tastes it)*

Helen: Awful?

Cris: Well. Is it supposed to be burnt?

Helen: Mary Barnes liked it. Didn't you like it,
          Mary Barnes?

Mary: I did. It tasted smoky. Very barbecue, like chicory,
          I thought... smoky.

Cris: Chicory? Mary Barnes, that's not what chicory
          tastes like. Chicory tastes like—

Helen: Dead licorice.

Cris: Really?

Helen: After you let it set, and the sugar seeps out?

Cris: God, you're right. Chicory does taste like that.
          That's awful, really.

Helen: I would think it would have to be.
Mary Barnes liked it, though.

Cris: It doesn't taste like chicory, Mary Barnes.

Mary: I thought it did.

Cris: It tastes burnt. Fried.

Mary: Well, I liked it. Burnt.

Helen: I have to start over. *(She throws it out)*
It's turning into goo, anyway.

Cris: What's it for?

Helen: Dinner.

Cris: Just us?

Helen: Guests and Mary Barnes.
Mary, are you staying for dinner?

Mary: If we can watch Godard.

Cris: Is it for class, Mary?

Mary: It's "King Lear." Woody Allen's in it, Cris.

Cris: Is it for class or not, Mary?

Mary: It's very... *(Spooky voice)* EXPERIMENTAL!
I really love Godard and I wrote him a letter.

A kind of fan letter. But not really a fan letter, actually. More like a nod of recognition letter. He's mature, Godard, and I would like him to think me mature in my love of Godard.

Cris: Mary Barnes. Answer the question.
          Is it for class or not?

Mary: Not!

Cris: Then we're not watching it.

Mary: It's Godard! Cris! "King Lear!" Woody Allen!
          It's a triple excellent quality thing. Helen?

Cris: Don't give us the quality line, Mary. That's crap.

Helen: I've seen it, Mary. I enjoyed it.

Cris: Molly Ringwald's in it, for God's sake.
          Helen, how could you enjoy it?

Mary: She's great. Have you even seen it, Cris?

Cris: Yes, Mary Barnes, I've seen it. Three times.
          You watch it here, all the time.

Mary: That's not true, actually, Cris. I just watch a lot
          of Godard, so maybe you think–

Cris: How many times have you watched it, Mary?

Mary: You mean here, or in general?

Cris: In general? In general? How many times, Mary?

Mary: Seven... seven times.

Cris: Seven times. Don't you think that's enough times?

Mary: Well, no. I don't, actually. Not if you want to get it... Godard's a genius, Cris... maybe you just—

Cris: What? What? Do I just—

Mary: ...Don't get it? *(Pause)*
          Maybe? I mean, he is a genius.

Cris: Maybe... *(Very sarcastic)* I got it the first time.

Mary: Oh, that couldn't be.

Cris: It couldn't, huh?

Mary: It's Godard, Crissy. I mean, I'm sorry, but—

Cris: Why don't you go home and watch it, then?
          Watch it over and over again! What is it?
          Two hours?

Mary: Two hours and forty-seven minutes, and Godard thought that was too short for such an epic.

Cris: *(Raging)* There are fourteen hours till dawn Mary, you can watch it six times!

Mary: Five, actually, I think.
          You wouldn't have time for six.

Cris: Then skip work and keep watchin' all day!
          Twelve times! You don't have to sleep, do you,
          Mary? Not with the great genius Godard feeding
          you. Go home, Mary Barnes, and watch.

Helen: You're so mean, Cris. Stop it now.
          Mary Barnes, you stay for dinner and
          just find something else to watch.

Mary: *(Sighing)* I'd better watch it now then.

Cris: God! God! God! Helen, I can't stand it.

Helen: It's just a movie.

Cris: I liked it better when she was stuck on Monroe
          and Greta Garbo... that was something to watch...
          Godard is so messy. And the best thing about men
          is the rational part, and... and...

Helen: What's that?

Cris: The rational part. Blocks and men.
          Men and blocks. That's kinda fascinating.

Helen: It can be.

Cris: Godard is just chaos. Like taking a Chinese meat
          chopper knife and whacking away at a perfectly
          usable tic-tac-toe board.

Helen: Oh yeah... just like that.

Cris: Chaotic men are worse than women who smoke.

Helen: (*Lighting up*) On that, we do...agree.

Cris: I hate women who smoke.

Helen: Uh-huh.

Cris: Don't smoke!

Mary: Who's coming? Who are the guests, Helen?

Helen: Two very orderly, fertile men.

Cris: In the house.

Mary: We could watch "Fellini's Satyricon."

Cris: And break the Godard spell?

Mary: Men like Fellini.

Helen: Something with Marlon Brando.

Mary: Ugggh. Mickey Rourke.

Cris: Ugggh.

Helen: No.

Mary: No.

Helen: Crispin Glover!

Cris: Well, maybe...he's pretty squirrely.

Mary: Actually, he's got presence. What would it be?

Helen: David Lynch. "Hotel Room."

Mary: I'm cautious. Lynch has style. But his films
          are reactionary, aren't they?

Cris: He's a fetishist.

Helen: (Lighting another cigarette) Oh, yeah.

Mary: "Satyricon." It's a better choice.
          Don't you think so, Cris?

Cris: I think so... Helen, what is this supposed to be?

Helen: Pasta.

Cris: You boil the water first, Helen.
          You don't just dump it in. It'll just starch
          and stick together like that. A big lump.

Helen: Oh, fuck. I'll start again. (Throws it out)

Cris: You want me to?

Helen: I wish you would, Cris.

Cris: God! All right! What's left?

Helen: Eggs. And cheese.

Cris: I could make omelettes. Any vegetables, Helen?

Helen: Mary Barnes.

Mary: Two onions and some red peppers. In my bag.

Cris: Could you set it out?

Mary: I'm trying to watch "King Lear," Cris.

Cris: God! *(CRISSY gets the vegetables. Pause. Cooking and movie plays.)*

<GODARD #1 BEGINS>

Helen: *(Noticing)* You scratched your face, Cris. Are you all right?

Cris: It was Leon. That motherfucker.

Helen: That motherfucker?

Cris: Can I just tell you?

Helen: You've told me. Tell Mary Barnes.

Cris: I don't want to tell Mary Barnes.

Helen: I'm going to be firm, Cris... I've listened carefully to your tales of Mister Leon Diaz...

Cris: Just let me tell you.

Helen: Was it different? This time?

Cris: I got mad.

Helen: You always get mad, Cris.

Cris: He hit me, and broke...

Helen: He always hits you, and that's a sick thing.
          What's sicker is, you let him.

Cris: I don't let him.

Helen: What did he break? Your heart?

Cris: Shut up.

Helen: Your cherry?
          (She giggles. MARY BARNES giggles, too)

Cris: Shut up! *(She giggles)*

Helen: Are you hurt? Seriously injured?

Cris: No, but...

Helen: Hurt physically at all?

Cris: Not really.

Helen: Then you can't tell me.

Cris: *(Raging)* HELEN!

Helen: No, Crissy. No. We made an agreement...
          it's a pattern. Pattern talk. No.

Cris: I need your advice.

Helen: I gave you advice. Have Leon arrested.

Cris: We've been friends since the seventh grade.

Helen: Then give him a good fucking and get over it.

Cris: *(Yelling)* Ugh! Ugggh!

Helen: Passion gone rancid! Boom you hit him, he hits you... it's not healthy, Crissy... just fuck the man.

Cris: I don't like him.

Helen: Don't even talk to me about it.

Cris: He hit me and it hurt!

Helen: Tell Mary Barnes. Mary Barnes, Crissy wants to talk to you about Leon Diaz.

Mary: I can't do it, Crissy... I'm watchin' Godard.

Cris: Well, can't we talk and watch at the same time, Mary Barnes? You've only seen it seventeen motherfuckin'—

Mary: I'm watchin' the edits.

Cris: I'm in an abusive non-sexual relationship, Mary Barnes, and I need support.

Mary: It's a shame, Crissy. You should get out of it.

Cris: That's what you always say.

Mary: It's not, actually. Usually I don't say anything.

Cris: You're fat, Mary.

Mary: Condescending? Obnoxious? Mean? No. Actually, you're a slimeball. Now shut up so I can watch Godard or I'm going home.

Cris: Go home. Go home. Go—home—!

Mary: Helen, make her shut up.

Cris: Make me. Make me.

Helen: Crissy, shut up. Mary Barnes is very right. You've been a cad to her, and you don't deserve her support.

Cris: A cad? A cad!

Helen: Oh yeah. (Lights cigarette) A cad.

Cris: That's not the proper use of the word 'cad.'

Helen: Oh, I think it is. Mary Barnes?

Mary: Completely proper usage, dictionary wise, actually. Crissy.

Helen: Mary Barnes and I agree.

Cris: 'Cad' is male. It has to be male.

Helen: What?

Cris: Only men are cads.

Helen: This is really irritating.

Mary: English words don't have a gender... or do they?

Cris: They do. All words.

Helen: Just shut up now, Crissy.

Cris: Helen.

Helen: Shut up, Crissy.

Cris: All right, I will.

Mary: Hallelujah. *(There's much clanging of pots, followed by a long silence. MARY BARNES turns on Godard #2)*

<GODARD #2 BEGINS>

(MARY BARNES begins to speak, as if to herself, but maybe she never gets excited.)

Mary: With everything I'm learning I could write a paper... or make a film. I'm almost an expert on Godard, actually. Or an amateur expert, anyway. But what does an amateur expert on Godard do? If I write a paper I get a degree, in Godard... if I write more papers, I get more degrees, in Godard... but then, what do I do? I could teach others to write papers about Godard. I could write cool, poppy asides on Godard for film zines, or scholastically insightful epiphanies for ivy covered old academic reviews... but that's still writing papers on Godard. One paper leads to more papers leads to more papers... all on Godard. Or I could make a film... buy a man a meal and he'll be hungry by morning, but teach a man to fish and he'll eat trout daily... is that how it goes?

I'm not sure, actually, but the principle feels right... I write about Godard and I'll just write on and on and on...but make a film about Godard, and others will write papers about me... it will take me years, because if I don't write that paper on Godard I won't graduate and my parents won't give me any money, and no one will bankroll my project because I don't have a film degree. Now if I had a film degree it would be on Godard, but I still wouldn't have a degree that says I could make a film as good as Godard. So they wouldn't bankroll me, anyway... no degree, no bankroll, no film... now if I write a good enough paper, get the degree in film criticism, and then go into film school...well, I'd be starting from scratch... but I'd know a lot...about Godard, which I already do... know... my parents...

Cris: God! God! God! Helen!

Helen: Yes, Crissy?

Cris: Make her stop. If you love me, make her stop.

Helen: Mary Barnes, would you like my advice?

Mary: I've been hoping for it, actually.

Helen: Make a bright and vivacious film about a charming
          and vital film criticism student overwhelmed by her
          knowledge of Godard, her quandaries, her crises,
          her epiphanies! Use a number of splashy Godard
          cuts and edits, but keep the writing special and
          your own. If you do that, your film will be special
          and undeniable. You will succeed.

Mary: And the bankroll?

Helen: Write a great paper on Godard, get your degree,
          and extend your student loan. Your parents...

Mary: Can it be in Super-8?

Helen: I'm sure.

Mary: I love Godard in Super-8.

Helen: Then that's how it will be.

Mary: But I don't have a Super-8.

Helen: Crissy will lend you one.

Mary: I don't know how to use it. I've never shot a film.

Helen: Crissy will show you.

Mary: Crissy?

Cris: What?

Mary: Will you?

Cris: If you promise to shut the fuck up about Godard for the rest of the evening.

Mary: It's a deal. Thank you, Helen.

Helen: Okay.

Mary: I'll go rent "Fellini's Satyricon."
(MARY BARNES leaves.)

Cris: Thank you, Helen.

Helen: Okay.

Cris: I fuckin' hate Fellini.

Helen: I'm sure. *(She lights cigarette)* You know how, when you sleep, you get a restless leg?

Cris: What?

Helen: You know, how, like, when you go to bed your leg flops around like a hopeless beheaded chicken anxious to go to ground, but just unable to stay put? You know.

Cris: If by 'you' you mean me, and if you mean do I know from experience, you know I know because... I've been in bed with you when you're doing it.

Helen: Oh yeah... well, that's a syndrome.

Cris: What syndrome?

Helen: Restless Leg Syndrome.

Cris: God! Did you think I'd forget?

Helen: Forget?

Cris: That in sleep your legs are like pythons!
          You'd squeeze.

Helen: I didn't forget, Crissy, I just didn't think about it.

Cris: You didn't think about how we fucked?

Helen: *(Irritated)* It was a long time ago, Crissy.

Cris: Two years...!

Helen: Right! A fucking long time ago.

Cris: Not to me.

Helen: It was me who was doing the thinking
          and the forgetting, not you.

Cris: How did it feel to you?

Helen: What?

Cris: When WE DID IT. How did it feel to you?

Helen: This is really irritating, Crissy.
          Do you want to hear about this, or not?

Cris: What?

Helen: The women with the varicose veins.

Cris: *(Letting it go with an effort)* Tell me.

Helen: You're really a terrible person to spend
          any time with, Crissy. You know that?

Cris: Tell me. What were her veins like?

Helen: Swollen and awful.

Cris: And her arms. What were her arms like?

Helen: Ditto.

Cris: Swollen and awful?

Helen: Right.

Cris: Do you know her?

Helen: No, I didn't know her. Before, you mean?

Cris: Where did you see her? On the bus?

Helen: No. In the desert. It was very brown, like fine-
          blown brown glass. All sharded into tiny—

Cris: What desert? I thought yesterday... didn't you say
          yesterday, Helen? This is the Village. New York.

Helen: At Jacques'. His room. His hotel.

Cris: You really have to help me, Helen.
           You know what this does to me?
           It makes me feel disassociated! I'm disassociated!

Helen: Oh... yeah. *(Lights cigarette)*

Cris: Who is Jacques?

Helen: I met him last night. Jacques. Like a kiss. I think
           I wanted to fuck him. He's a French gangster.
           I think that's what he said. I've never fucked
           a French gangster.

Cris: *(Scared)* But you didn't do it.

Helen: We drank too much. Red, red, burgundy wine.
           I got very warm, flushed and hot; I felt like all my
           shapely parts were stuffed into my clothes...
           my breasts and ass swollen and bursty, like I had
           to get out of there. Out of my clothes and then
           my skin... 'cause my skin was too tight. I might
           have seemed wild; I pulled off everything and got
           down to my panties. He said I was very brassy and
           that we should go slow and get to know...
           and I said, Why? Why care about that?
           I want to fuck you right now... let's just do it...

Cris: What about the woman?

Helen: What? What woman? I was the woman, Crissy...
           he put his fingers...

Cris: The woman with the swollen veins and arms.

Helen: Just the tips... barely touching, just skimming my stomach and flicking around the tight crotch of my panties, like a millipede working the honey cup with its dozen lacy insect feet.

Cris: What about the swollen woman with the arms and veins? Where was she, Helen? Tell me. Was she watching? Was she there?

Helen: Of course she wasn't there. That was later, after I fell asleep... are you even paying attention?

Cris: She was in your dream? You were dreaming, Helen, goddammit.

Helen: We didn't fuck, I guess. I was ready, but... he didn't.

Cris: You're always ready, Helen, or so you tell me.

Helen: I'm not always ready, Cris. I'm not ready now.

Cris: You're nasty. That's nasty. Do you know how I feel? Do you even know, Helen?

Helen: I know because you tell me. Over and over, Crissy. You are relentless and relentless and relentless about what other people don't get.

Cris: You think?

Helen: I think. (Lights cigarette)

Cris: I guess I'm sorry.

Helen: You guess.

Cris: I'm just doing what I—

Helen: Right! Right! And so am I. Now if you don't want to hear about this... *(Pause.)*

Cris: Okay goddammit. Okay goddammit. Tell me.

Helen: I fell asleep, and he was very sweet and very polite.

Cris: You passed out.

Helen: The millipede stayed though... I could feel him on the panties; root around my cunt, slipping and seeking and searching for a honey home. The man had sweet fingers.

Cris: I should really hate hearing this. I really should.

Helen: He was polite, but...to be honest, Crissy, I wasn't so passed out that I couldn't feel him humping the pillow once he though I was asleep. I could still taste that dead-animal look on his face; you know the look, like when all the sperm has been pulled out of a man and he's suddenly empty... and shocked by it. *(Laughs)* I like that.

Cris: It's grotesque.

Helen: Right. *(Lights cigarette)*

Cris: That's number ten.

Helen: What?

Cris: Since I've been home.
          You're chain-smoking, Helen.

Helen: Only at home, Crissy.

Cris: Around me?

Helen: Right.

Cris: Don't smoke.

Helen: Okay. *(Does)* He was polite, old Jacques,
          but not too polite to come when he thought no
          one was watching. *(Laughs)* I could fuck him.
          I think it would be good.

Cris: I shouldn't listen to this.

Helen: Did you enjoy the story, Crissy?

Cris: I wanted to hear about the lady with the arms.

Helen: You don't like stories about—

Cris: I can't have sex, Helen.

Helen: Can't Chant! Can't Chant! Can't Chant!

Cris: I can't.

Helen: You don't.

Cris: I can't.

Helen: Very weird, Crissy, very weird.

Cris: It's not weird. It's because I love—
          (MARY BARNES returns.)

Mary: They didn't have Fellini, so I got double chocolate
          mocha fudge and Jolt cola, I gotta lot. I figured if
          men aren't watching maybe they'll talk, and that
          might be interesting, at least.

Cris: Wait! Wait! You didn't get a film, Mary Barnes?

Helen: Is that really true, Mary Barnes?

Mary: Well... sugar makes them talk.

Cris: Don't tell me you got more Godard, Mary Barnes!

Mary: No, actually. I didn't do that
          because I agreed not to.

Cris: Good, Mary Barnes. I would've knocked—

Mary: I agreed not to for tonight... but—

Helen: What are you hiding, Mary Barnes?

Mary: They had "Fellini's Satyricon" and I had it in my
          hand and was reaching for my video rental card
          and I just froze. I couldn't do it. It seemed wrong...

Cris: God! God!

Mary: ...to rent anything that wasn't...

Helen: Godard?

Mary: Exactly. I felt sick at the idea, actually.

Cris: I am not weird, Helen, Mary Barnes is weird.

Mary: I figured why watch anything if you can't watch
         what you actually have a real passion for.
         Do you agree with me, Helen?

Helen: I sure do, Mary Barnes.

Mary: See, Crissy? Helen and I agree exactly about this.

Cris: Well, that's just great, Mary Barnes.

Mary: So. We'll talk about something. *(Pause. She hums)*
         Well. I'm tapped out. I'm gonna watch...
         (Mouths it) Godard.

Cris: No, no, no...

<GODARD #3 BEGINS>

Mary: What were you talking about, Helen,
         when I came in?

Cris: *(Reckless)* Sex. She was talking about who she
         almost had sex with.

Mary: Oh. Who was it?

Helen: Our dinner guests, Mary Barnes.

Mary: Oh. Our dinner guests are going to have sex here?

Cris: Sure. All over the place.

Mary: I think you should teach me how to use that
          Super-8 now, Crissy, in that case.

Cris: Sure. Let's get it down. On celluloid.

Mary: Because footage like that we'll use.
          Do you think the guests will mind, Helen?...
          I mean, if they're coming to have sex at dinner...
          anyway, it's already public.

Helen: Only one of them is coming to have sex,
          and he's going to have it with me.
          Afterwards. At least I hope he is.

Mary: Oh. So I suppose we won't be watching?

Helen: I don't think so, Mary Barnes. It'll be late.

Mary: I don't mind staying up late for that.
          It won't be a problem, especially
          after the double mocha fudge.

Helen: He'll be shy. At least I think he will.

Mary: I'm disappointed, actually. We could use the
          footage. It would be gorgeous, you're a doll,
          Helen, and the camera will eat you up.
          Unless he's a troll.

Helen: *(Laughs)* Well, he is. Sorta.
           More like a goblin, I would say.

Mary: That's very interesting. What about the other one?

Helen: What?

Mary: The other guest. Will you be having sex with him?

Helen: No, I don't think so. He'll have to find someone
           else to have sex with.

Mary: Crissy, maybe you could.

Cris: Don't even talk to me, Mary Barnes. God. God...

Mary: It was just an idea, actually, Crissy.
           (She returns to humming)

Cris: Mary Barnes. Are you going to keep humming
           like that?

Mary: Until something interesting happens, I am, to take
           my mind off—

Cris: I want you to stop. Right now.

Mary: Well, I'm sure you do, Crissy... but I think I'll
           continue, actually, until...

Cris: STOP IT, YOU ANNOYING MOTHERFUCKER.

Mary: All right, Crissy. *(Pause)* Is this better?

Cris: I should motherfucking think so.

Helen: I had a good dream, Mary Barnes.

Mary: Just now?

Helen: Well, early this morning.

Cris: After she didn't have sex.

Mary: Oh. Did you watch her not have it?
          I thought we had to miss it, later.

Cris: What?

Helen: I would like to tell this dream to somebody.

Cris: Tell it, tell it.

Mary: Do you mind if I take notes? For the movie.

Cris: Tell the motherfucker.

Helen: Lady on a blue bus. The seats, a checkered
          tablecloth pattern, blue-black and red.
          The bus was bulbous—

Cris: Bulbous?

Helen: Like a pregnant llama looked at sidewise.

Cris: God.

Helen: She was very swollen and carrying these
          big shopping bags; the bus shuddered
          when she rolled onto it.

Mary: I'm sorry, I'm just not following this.
          The woman was bulbous and the bus was–

Cris: Swollen. The woman was swollen, Mary,
          and the bus was bulbous.

Helen: That's right, Mary Barnes. Now, try to keep up
          and I'll take questions afterwards.

Mary: *(Deciding)* I'll just keep a separate list of questions.

Helen: That's a good plan. *(Lights cigarette)* Aaaah...

Cris: Tell it.

Helen: She was carrying these big shopping bags, paper.
          Heavy red bags filled with meat rolls of veal and
          lamb and young calves' hearts, choked and gutted
          with string, blood dripping and squeezed into
          the white butcher paper that loosely wrapped
          each hunk of meat... the bus was going very
          slowly, slowly enough that each desert view had
          time to be memorized, burned into my eyes. The
          desert wind was pushing at the bus so hard that
          the vehicle was barely moving at all, a slow bug
          crawl... like a caterpillar on its last legs. *(Laughs)*
          Oh, that's funny! The wind was whipping this
          white-white sand around, up and up and around
          the bus... the ivory-colored shopping bag, like a
          Jewel bag but nicer, first staining an animal red
          and then, sodden and dripping. The swollen arms

319

holding the bag straight and steady; her sore legs, all fried looking, blue and red varicose veins. Placed straight out in front of her, the sodden drip forming a pool at her feet and she, staring and muttering straight ahead and resolute, didn't notice it. So I leaned over...

Cris: You're not surprising me at all with this.
          Helen, it's obvious. Menstrual...

Mary: Questions after, Crissy!

Helen: I said, Hey Lady, there's a lot of blood, and she said, "Oh no, dear, I'm way past the babies. My children are all grown, with babies of their own." And I said, No ma'am. The meat. Like she was deaf or in a trance. But she wasn't; she was sharp, so she sharply said, "There's plenty of meat to go around and you'll get yours in time to get it in your oven and cook it up. But my man, he likes it raw in July," and she laughed. *(She laughs)* Well, it was funny. Do you think so, Crissy?

Cris: No. I don't think it's funny.
          Why did you tell me this, Helen?

Helen: Amusement? The communal need to share?

Mary: Now it's question-and-answer. And I don't get one thing—was the bag white or ivory?

Cris: Christ! It was ivory. Who cares?

Mary: And what makes it ivory as opposed to white?

Helen: Ivory is classy. Classier.

Mary: *(Writing it down)* It was a classy bag.

Cris: It was a Jewel bag, for God's—

Mary: *(Writes it down)* A classy Jewel bag.

Helen: Right. *(Laughs)* A classy Jewel bag.
         (Lights cigarette) That's good, Mary Barnes.

Mary: I have another question, it came up earlier, but
         I wrote it down second because we weren't—

Cris: Shut up, Mary Barnes. You had your question.
         It's my turn.

Mary: Oh, is that right? I didn't know we were taking
         turns. If I would have known I wouldn't have
         wasted my first question on the bag; there are
         more important details than the bag.

Cris: Up-shut, Mary! Or I'll put my fist through your skull
         so hard and fast that your brain will explode like
         an amoeba under intense radiation treatment,
         first multiplying and splitting and feeding off
         itself, becoming a manic grotesque inbred in-
         breeding with itself, each little amoeba tail caught
         copulating again and again until it thins and blats
         out in a frenzy of forced growth, leaving a spray of
         thinned liver pate' brain matter all over that wall
         behind your head.

Helen: What?

Cris: That's what amoebas do, under intense radiation.
          They multiply, spread, and thin.

Helen: How do you know that?

Cris: Everybody knows that.

Helen: What bullshit... still, a great image.
          You are really quite amazing and bright, Crissy.
          Don't you think so, Mary Barnes?

Mary: I do, actually. Amazing and bright, but...

Cris: "But" what?

Mary: But... well, I shouldn't say.

Cris: Say! Say! God! Mary B—

Mary: Prone to hysterical imagery.

Cris: What are you saying?

Mary: A lot of adjectives and invectives, carried by
          a whipped-up rage that is impressive in your
          consistent use of it. But if you crafted—

Helen: Huh. You're right, Mary Barnes, very perceptive
          of you. Prone to hysterica—

Cris: What? You agree?

Helen: Very perceptive.

Mary: Godard... a great master knows when to reign it in, when to spit it out. Actually, a lot of hysteria goes a long way, dramatically speaking.

Cris: I wasn't dramatically speaking, I was screaming at you. I want to punch your fuckin'... head... it wasn't art. Everything is not...

Mary: Well, perhaps there lies the rubber in the woodpile. Is that right?

Cris: No. Absolutely not. God, is it wrong.

Mary: Well, I'll look it up. The problem is an artist should always be paying attention to the craft of the art. A wordsmith, like yourself.

Cris: I am not an artist. I'm a baggage counter. At the airport.

Helen: Wrong. You're wrong. You're an artist first.

Mary: I agree.

Helen: You should listen to Mary Barnes, Crissy, she's very smart about this.

Mary: Helen and I agree— *(CRISSY screams and hits MARY BARNES hard, knocking her down. Surprised silence.)*

Helen: Crissy. What the fuck. You hit Mary Barnes.

Cris: I know.

Helen: You can't just hit Mary Barnes.

Cris: I know.

Helen: But you did it. Mary Barnes... *(Helping her up)* Are you all right?

Mary: I'm shaken and disappointed, actually.

Helen: I should say so.

Mary: Maybe I should just... go home.

Helen: Well, maybe you should. *(Long pause, HELEN lights up. Finally, disgusted.)* CRISSY.

Cris: I'm sorry, Mary Barnes.

Helen: I'm not sure that's enough. Is it, Mary Barnes?

Mary: Actually... no, it is not.

Cris: You're driving me crazy, Mary Barnes. You keep driving me crazy... I asked you to shut up and go home. You just wouldn't... I wanted to talk to Helen. You won't let me. I was upset about Leon Diaz and neither of you would talk to me.

Helen: That was an agreement. We had an agreement.

Cris: You keep lining up with Helen. Helen and I agree, Helen and I agree, and you know how I feel about Helen. It's mean. It's like you want to take up the whole page with her and you know how I feel about her.

Mary: Actually, Crissy, I don't.

Cris: I LOVE HER.

Mary: Oh, my. Actually real actual love?

Cris: Yes.

Mary: This is very interesting.
         And Helen, how do you feel? The same, or...

Helen: Not the same.

Mary: You don't love Crissy.

Helen: Not like a fuckin' wife. No, I don't.

Mary: In some other way, perhaps.

Helen: As a friend.

Cris: Right! A pal, a buddy, a goof-partner.

Helen: Right. *(Lights cigarette)*

Mary: Has this been going on... for awhile?

Cris: Forever.

Helen: Two years ago, we slept together.

Mary: Once or...

Helen: For a few weeks.

Mary: Excuse me. But how many times?

Helen: I don't remember.

Cris: God! GOD!

Helen: It doesn't matter.

Mary: Well, it might, Helen, if we want to get it right.
          Do you mind if I take notes?

Cris: We don't want to get it right. And yes, I do mind if
          you take fuckin' notes. This is not a project... this is
          me. You leech... you bloodsucking little spy...

Mary: Crissy, I know you're upset about the Helen
          situation and the men coming over to have sex
          with her after dinner, but I am trying to accept your
          apology, and if we want to make this movie...
          well, we need to keep the details straight.

Cris: God. *(Goes to hit her)*

Helen: Crissy!

Mary: Now. Where was I?

Helen: What?

Mary: When you two coupled up?

Helen: I think it was during the Marilyn Monroe period.

Cris: Then she was here. Watching *"The Seven-Year Itch"* over and over on our VCR. If I ever have to see that white dress blow up again, I'll—

Mary: The library. That was a hard project.
I had to read all that Arthur Miller.

Cris: God!

Mary: And Norman Mailer. Truman Capote. It was rough.

Cris: I just want to talk to Helen sometimes
without you here.

Helen: I like Mary Barnes to be here.

Cris: Then can she just not talk. For a few minutes.
Can you just not talk, Mary Barnes?

Mary: I'm not sure that's fair, Crissy.

Cris: I'll kill you if you don't do what I want.

Mary: This is a graceless apology, Crissy.

Cris: I know.

Helen: You really sound like a selfish jerk, Crissy.
You know that, right?

Cris: I know.

Mary: I'd like to take notes, Crissy. For the movie.

Cris: All right.

Mary: If I can take notes, I'll be all right not talking.

Cris: All right.

Helen: So. Mary Barnes. What do you think?

Mary: I'll accept your apology, Crissy.

Cris: Thanks a lot.

Mary: And if you hit me again, I'll rip your face off
          and throw it in the trash.

Cris: Good.

Mary: So go ahead and ask your question. *(Long pause.)*

Cris: I'm dog tired.

Helen: For God's sake. Just ask.

Cris: Why did you really tell me that dream?

Helen: You understand a lot... and I thought you could
          see her. My woman with the varicose veins.

Cris: Your mother. She reminded me of your mother.
          The way you described her.

Helen: Ding-dong. You're wrong.

Cris: Really. I thought so.

Helen: My mother the swollen lady? My mother was not a swollen lady, Crissy.

Cris: But she had all those babies, and you said she had varicose veins, pains in her feet. You said.

Helen: She wasn't large, my mother.
She was a small person.

Cris: Not always. She had arthritis, you said.

Helen: She was MY mother, Crissy, and nothing like the woman in the dream at all.

Cris: I knew her.

Helen: You met her.

Cris: I knew her. We went there, and while you were sleeping your mother taught me to play pinochle. She warned me, too. About you.

Helen: That's what Jacques and his brother want.

Cris: What? Who?

Helen: Jacques and his brother.
They want to play pinochle. After dinner.

Cris: Why?

Helen: They're pinochle players. I told them we were very
           good, and we would beat them handily.

Cris: Beat them handily? Is that supposed to be
           sexy or something?

Helen: God, no... *(Lights cigarette)* Never that.

Cris: God, you... but who cares. I don't care about that.
           Your mother warned me...

Helen: About me. I heard you. And is this going to be
           when you dis and rag on me?

Cris: She said you were bad to love. Especially for girls.
           That you didn't want it, really. That you just wanted
           girls to want you. That got you up for men...

Helen: My mother told you that?

Cris: She did. Yes, she did.

Helen: That's very strange. Even for my mother.
           Don't you think so, Mary Barnes?

Mary: *(Writing)* Hmmm...?

Helen: Very strange.

Mary: Hmmmm...

Helen: She's keeping her silence, Mary Barnes is.

Cris: I thought is was very strange, and it really
          scared me, what she said. Because I felt it
          was real and true.

Helen: My mother was blowin' smoke in your ear.

Cris: It scared me because I love—

Helen: Blowin' smoke until the wax heats up and drips out.
          She used to do that when we were kids. My mother
          worried a lot about waxy build-up in the inner ear...
          she said it was genetic, and we would lose our
          balance and walk like Looney Tunes, heads at a
          ninety-degree angle to our feet, ramming into
          walls until we bled and cried and ran around in
          circles... bleating in Band-Aids. She couldn't
          afford ear doctors, so she'd line us up and blow
          into our ears until the wax dripped. I grew up
          believing Camel cigarettes were a medical tool
          for early health... did you win?

Cris: What?

Helen: Beat my mother at pinochle.

Cris: No... I... no.

Helen: That's why she told you, she hates to lose,
          at pinochle.

Cris: You tell me about this sex. To make me feel bad.

Helen: We didn't fuck, Jacques and I. Last night.

Cris: Last night! But you told Mary Barnes you will.
           Tonight.

Helen: Well, I might.

Cris: You told Mary Barnes. That you WOULD.

Mary: *(Looking through her notes, finds it)* Hmmm.
          HMMMM... *(Frantically waving the notes at
          CRISSY)*

Helen: Well... *(Lights cigarette)* I MIGHT.

Cris: But that's not what you said.

Mary: Hmm! Hmm!

Cris: What, Mary Barnes?! Say it, or so help me I'll
           get a fly swatter, a rolled-up newspaper, and
           mash the bejesus out of you.

Helen: She's keeping her silence, a silence
          you insisted on.

Cris: God God God you are annoying, Mary Barnes...
           say what you have.

Mary: HM! HM! *(Thrusts paper)*

Cris: All right... *(Reads)* "Only one of them is coming
           to have sex and he's having it with me. ME."
           Meaning you. There. You said it.

Helen: There. *(Lights cigarette)* I said it.

Cris: Thank you, Mary Barnes.

Helen: So we all agree about what I said and what my intentions are. When Jacques gets here I'm gonna roll him like his back ain't got no bone.
(Laughs) We'll fuck that boy silly. Won't we, ladies?

Cris: We! WE! I'm not in this, this... Mary Barnes is not.

Helen: She is too... with her note-taking and her camera angles. It's a great opportunity: Godard's "Obsession" meets Monroe's blowing skirt. Mary Barnes wouldn't miss it.

Mary: Hmm! Hmmm!

Helen: Don't say anything, Mary Barnes.

Mary: Hmm!

Helen: *(Laughing)* Your position is clearl
(MARY BARNES turns on Godard #4)

<GODARD #4 BEGINS>

Cris: I'm not in on this! I hate it. It makes me feel...

Helen: Mary Barnes' movie will give us a clue as to how she feels about the sex I'm about to have. But you, Crissy. You're clear. There's a fuck a'comin' between me and another animal, and you want in on it! No matter what.

Cris: No... I... no. I'm scared of—

Helen: So scared your nostrils flare! You picture...

Cris: It will hurt.

Helen: Sure it will. Like when Leon smacks you and you
         smack him back. Smacks of pure desire. I could
         just smack... you, I suppose; orgasm, and skip the
         main dish. Is that what you want?

Cris: No... I...

Helen: You want to watch. He's not much to look at,
         short and kinda scuzzy. But a lovely ass.
         An ass like a melon doing push ups,
         muscular and humpy... his dick...

Cris: I don't wanna know that.
         I don't care about Jacques.

Helen: Neither do I, really. But I care about me, Crissy,
         and, believe it or not, I care about you.

Cris: Then why make me go through this? Helen.

Helen: I don't make you, Crissy. You just insist on
         knowing. Who am I fucking and who am
         I not fucking? Do I ever and will I never?
         You never shut up about it.
         You are the antagonist. Provoking.

Cris: You rub it in my face.

Helen: I answer your questions, you hate it. I don't answer
         your questions, you hate it... provoking...

Cris: I'm fucked up.

Helen: Right! *(Lights cigarette)* Fucked up.

Cris: I don't want him here.

Helen: Then spare yourself and leave. You talk about
         Mary Barnes overstaying. Mary Barnes is
         comfortable with what I do in my home.
         If you're so uncomfortable, leave. Go.

Cris: I live here.

Helen: The streets are empty. Almost. Plenty of room for a
         woman of your woes. Go, and suffer full-time.

Cris: No! You want I should be a bag lady? No!

Mary: Hmmm... *(Scribbling)*

Helen: Mary Barnes likes it. It's a better character for
         the antagonist. Instead of a baggage handler
         now you're a broken, babbling bag lady.
         That's a better character. Isn't it, Mary Barnes?

Mary: Hmm. Hmm.

Helen: You're becoming quite the artist, Mary Barnes.
         Searching for tragedy in the commonplace.

Mary: Hmmm.

Helen: Good for you, Mary Barnes.

Cris: This is... godawful nonsense. It's not what I want.
          I just want you to fuck me, love me.

Helen: But I did. Two years ago.

Cris: And it was great.

Helen: No. It wasn't great.

Cris: You said you didn't remember. Mary Barnes...?
          You wrote... *(MARY BARNES begins searching
          her notes.)*

Helen: Never mind, Mary Barnes. I remember what I said.
          I lied, Crissy.

Cris: How can I take you seriously if you—

Helen: Listen to what I say.

Cris: I... what?

Helen: Listen, now.

Cris: All right!

Helen: We were friends. Good and fun friends.
          You were smart and charming... you had a
          different way about you than my other women
          friends. Abrupt. Confrontational. Quick to
          state your feelings. Very funny.

Cris: That's right. That's the way I... was.

Helen: You had a weird job, handling baggage, and when I went to your house you had handled a lot of that baggage. Stole it, I figured out. Stacks and stacks of square leather containers of other people's property—

Cris: Abandoned, mostly.

Helen: Stolen. Ripped off.

Cris: Well, sometimes.

Helen: Dozens of sometimes. Hundreds of sometimes. You were a thief.

Cris: God! God!

Helen: You were.

Cris: I guess.

Helen: And are. Still.

Cris: I guess.

Helen: I didn't mind... it interested me... at first. You took the stuff out and sold it.

Cris: I kept the lingerie.

Helen: Drawers after drawers. Which you never wore.

Cris: But you did.

Helen: Very beautiful stuff, tight black straps and
flimsy red silkies. They felt delicious.

Cris: Gorgeous, on you. On me, ridiculous. I looked
like a truck driver at the debutante ball.

(CRISSY poses, all hip and bicep)

Helen: (Grinning) You tried them on?

Cris: When no one was around. In the mirror.

Helen: I would have liked to have seen that.

Cris: You would have liked to have seen that?
You would have liked to have seen that?
How can you tell me that now? Do you
know what you're saying to me, Helen?

Helen: I never hid out about it, Crissy.
You got what you were after.

Cris: You came and you stayed.

Helen: And you smothered yourself against me.

Cris: That's what we wanted.

Helen: That's what you wanted...
I wanted to dress up, have some fun.

Cris: You liked me turned on. I turned on. You liked that.

Helen: Well, somewhat...
Mostly I wanted to turn myself on.

Cris: Just like your mother said.

Helen: Right... *(Lights cigarette)* But so what? It didn't
          hurt you. You got yours, and then I moved on...

Cris: But you didn't. You stayed.

Helen: Why should I go? I'm happy here.

Cris: It's selfish. You're selfish. You hook people and
          leave them dangling... just out of the water,
          unable to reach...

Helen: Like a trout. You feel like a trout, Crissy.

Cris: I do, yes. A scaly, suffocating trout who's got
          the hook in deep and is bleeding at the hole.
          Bleeding to goddamn motherfucking death.

Helen: So... go.

Cris: I... can't. I don't want to.

Helen: Right... *(Lights cigarette)* You can't.
          And you don't want to. And there's the rub.

Cris: It's so easy for you, you could just—

Helen: Lay down and fuck you so you could
          get it out of your system.

Cris: Not like that! No. Be kind.

Helen: I am kind. I like you. I talk to you.
          I listen to your feelings.

Cris: Not about Leon, you wouldn't.

Helen: Except about Leon because you're sick
           and weird about him, and he's endlessly assholic.
           I talk to you about every—

Cris: You sleep with total strangers.

Helen: "And I won't sleep with you." Blah! Blah! Blah!
           Crissy. I pray to God every day that you can speak
           with insight, add new dimensions to the dynamic
           here, because you're boring me. Blaw raw.
           I'm blah-raw towards you.

Cris: But you won't sleep—

Helen: Because I'll have to pay for it for years with you...
           you'll talk and reprimand, equate and rationalize,
           and that's no fun... Crissy, I want to have fun...

Cris: Okay. Okay.

Helen: You can be a power babe.
           Crissy, be a power babe now, and—

Cris: Power babe?

Helen: Mary Barnes thinks you're a power babe.
           Don't you, Mary Barnes?

Mary: *(Scribbling all the while)* Hmmmm...

Helen: Right... Mary Barnes and I agree.

Cris: Okay, okay. *(Long pause)* The Luftmensch goes to the house of the renowned industrialist, Mister Rothschild, and rings the bell. Mister Rothschild comes, in a very busy mood. "What? What do you want?," he says. "Just ten dollars," says the Luftmensch. "I'm busy, I'm busy. I've just lost ten-million in American pork bellies. "Go away," says Mister Rothschild, and slams the door. The next day, same time, the Luftmensch comes back, knocks on the door. Mister Rothschild comes, in a very busy mood... "What? What? What do you want?" he says. "Ten rubles, please," says the Luftmensch. "I'm busy, I'm busy, I've just lost eight-thousand dollars in African wheat! Go away!"says Mister Rothschild. Slams the door. The very next day, bright and early, the Luftmensch knocks on the door of the renowned Rothschild with the same request, and the same thing occurs. Wednesday it's Italian carburetor parts and a three million dollar loss... Thursday, Spanish olives and four hundred-thousand dollars. Finally on Friday, bright and early, the Luftmensch knocks on the door of the renowned philanthropist and Mister Rothschild, very busy, opens the door... "Here. Here. Yours. Ten rubles. But I have to say, you have really annoyed me all week, and I considered giving you nothing at all." To which the Luftmensch very politely responded, "My dear Mister Rothschild, I don't tell you how to invest. Don't tell me how to beg." *(Everybody laughs.)*

Helen: That was funny, Crissy. You're great when—

Cris: Don't tell me how to beg.

Helen: Look! *(Lights cigarette)* Why don't you just leave, okay? Take all these fuckin' suitcases and load all your whiny neurotic little protestations to the contrary and go... I've got a date and I don't care.

Cris: All you'd have to do.

Helen: I don't care anymore. *(HELEN leaves.)*

Cris: All right! All right! I'm going!

(CRISSY begins to pull down the piles of suitcases, randomly throwing things into them. It's chaos, and she goes faster and faster. Perhaps she packs the meal she's cooked last... this could be funny. Finally, she sits on a pile of suitcases and weeps, or laughs, digs her fingernails into her cheeks or hands...)

Mary: Mmm. Mmm. Mmm.

Cris: Shut up, Mary Barnes. You can talk.

Mary: Don't hurt yourself like that, please.

Cris: Like this? *(She bites into her palm)*

Mary: Stop it, please... Crissy.

Cris: *(Smacking head)* Or this! *(Smacks again)*

Mary: I want you to stop it, Crissy.

Cris: Like I really care what you want, Mary Barnes. *(She hits herself repeatedly)* This doesn't even hurt. It's like hitting a big, empty, foul smelling volleyball. Every time you hit it you unleash another foul-smelling piss puke on the air around you...

(MARY BARNES grabs CRISSY by the wrists and forces her to the ground. It is surprising and abrupt, they end facing downstage. In the tussle one of them steps on the remote, turning on Godard #5.)

<GODARD #5 BEGINS>

Cris: Hey!

Mary: Can you stop this now, Crissy? I wonder actually... you make Helen feel like a deer in the headlights, frozen, exposed... unable to back away.

Cris: She backs away.

Mary: Not really. Not out of the picture. It's very difficult to be the object of desire, apparently. Godard thinks so... a perfectly lush, lush dripping lily on a fine field of ivory... "The role is an intoxication... the center of the frame." That's very powerful. And Helen is a power babe... like Marilyn Monroe, the room lights up.

Cris: She doesn't suffer... it... I...

Mary: *(Pressuring the wrists)* The object of desire always suffers, until she can come out of the center of the picture. That's what I think, actually. With you, Helen is always the center of the picture... you'll have to let her go, I think... now is as good a time as the next time... but I won't have you hurt yourself about it...

Cris: What's it to you? I hate you.

Mary: I don't like you, Crissy... I think you're actually spoiled. Selfish. Emotionally irresponsible... actually. And you're usually mean and dismissive of me. Usually... but I could use your help on the film about Helen and Godard. It's going to be a major work, and a major work needs an artist. I am not an artist, but a graduate student in the great film school of Godard; Helen could be an artist, but for now she is the object of desire... and that's a heavy load... you're our gal, when it comes to the artist department.

Cris: "Spoiled. Selfish. Emotionally irresponsible."
            You want that.

Mary: The artistic raw material. You have it in abundance. Will you do it?

Cris: No! God! No! I hate—

Mary: You should do it... imagine this: the emotional catharsis you could achieve by throwing yourself into a project that focuses unblinkingly on your object of desire...

Cris: I'm done with—

Mary: No, Crissy. Please. Let's minimize the flim-flam between us; it's important if we're going to make a great work on Godard and the object of desire. You are not done with her. She is not done with you. And the movie is barely started—

Cris: She's done with me.

Mary: You don't know that.

Cris: I do... I'm miserable and wretched.

Mary: Then it's time to transform those terrible feelings into transcendent art. I think I'm letting you up.

Cris: *(Rubbing wrists)* God! That was some move. Where did you learn that?

Mary: My mother was a marine.

Cris: Do you know any more?

Mary: Hit me, hit you, find out. *(A knock at the door.)*

Mary: It's the date! Crissy, get the door... and I'll get the camera... coming! Stall them at the door, please... we need this on film... it's a crucial moment. *(MARY BARNES goes.)*

Cris: Coming! *(She pauses, waits. Knocking continues. Some bellowing.)* Hello! Hello! *(She opens the door. PAUL-JEAN is drunk and sweaty, barely upright.)*

Paul-Jean: I'm going to charm the living love juice out of you ma cheri. My cock is beautiful. My cocks...

Cris: What?

Paul-Jean: I'm the irresistible force with a cock like a divining rod, pointing straight to that luscious place between your thighs.

Cris: Helen! Helen? Your date's here.

Paul-Jean: I've already lost my heart, baby. Let's lie down. I am Paul-Jean.

Cris: *(Freaking)* Helen? Helen!

Paul-Jean: I am French, irresistibly French. I am Paul-Jean. You won't resist. You can't resist me. I am French.

Cris: Helen will be down in a minute...

Paul-Jean: You'll be the rabbit to my snake, the object of my desire.

Cris: What? Helen–

Mary: *(Re-entering)* Crissy, this is terrific! Get him to say it again.

Cris: Shut up, Mary Barnes. Helen!

Paul-Jean: I've lost it. My heart, my pulsing heart to you. I'm the balloon to your sweet tornado. Fuck Helen. Who's Helen?

Cris: Helen. The woman you met last night. You're here–

Paul-Jean: I met no woman last night... but if I had,
            your face would have blotted her out of my heart
            forever. Today, I know no woman but you.
            Who ARE you?

Cris: Jacques. You're Jacques.

Paul-Jean: I am Paul-Jean, French and irresistible.

Cris: Oh, I see. I thought–

Paul-Jean: I'd touch you now, but when I do one of us is
            bound to explode...

Cris: God! God! Mary Barnes, get Helen.

Paul-Jean: I won't touch you yet, I'll let the come build
            inside until the pressure is so great that I'll drench
            you. Your breasts, your mouth, your eyes, your all
            will be soaked with the come of Paul-Jean. You'll
            be sticky... wet.

Cris: Yuck! Yuck! Yuck!

Paul-Jean: *(He drinks)* You gettin' this down?
            (To the camera) ...profile all right?

Mary: I'm not sure about the light.

Paul-Jean: Well, did you check it? Do a meter reading!

Mary: Well, no. Actually, I don't know how.
            Crissy, could you...?

Cris: No. Absolutely no.

Paul-Jean: We'll be making romantic history. You and Paul-
        Jean. Paul-Jean and you.

Cris: No! NO! More NO! Get out!

Paul-Jean: I mean you no harm, sweetheart. I only ask that
        you let the touch and sperm of a man, this man,
        change you forever.

Cris: Out! Now!

Paul-Jean: You've got nothing to fear from me unless stark
        naked sexual obsessiveness makes you nervous...

Cris: I've got a gun...

Mary: *(Who's been shooting all along)* What?

Paul-Jean: Now you're surprising me, ma cheri.
        News of a gun from your lips like a cow pussy.

Cris: Right here! *(Puts hand in pocket)* I'll take out your
        navel with one... twitch of my trigger finger...

Helen: *(Coming in)* Crissy. Stop it. I really hate it when
        you threaten my dinner guests. It's obnoxious...

Cris: He's really awful, Helen. Everything he...

Helen: To you, Crissy. Because he's a man,
        you think all men...

Mary: "Lips like a cow pussy..."

Helen: What, Mary Barnes?

Mary: That was the last thing he said, Helen, actually.

Cris: He's awful.

Mary: Crissy's right, actually... Helen.

Helen: You think so?

Mary: I think so...

Helen: You're agreeing with Crissy, Mary Barnes?
            You stun me... Mary Barnes.

Mary: We have a pact, Helen, Crissy and I.

Helen: I was only gone for ten minutes!
            You must be Paul-Jean.

Paul-Jean: You're Jacques' girl.

Helen: Right. (Lights cigarette) Jacques told me so much.

Paul-Jean: You just met him last night... is it so?

Helen: That's right.

Paul-Jean: Was he boring, Brother Jacques?

Helen: Oh no, I quite liked him...

Paul-Jean: And yet, he talked of Paul-Jean.
            It is true I am a magnificent subject.
            But a lovely woman and a French man.

Helen: We talked until late into the night.

Paul-Jean: About me? The whole time?

Helen: Not the whole time... *(Grinning)*
            ...we were otherwise occupied.

Paul-Jean: In a not-boring way?

Helen: Not at all.

Paul-Jean: Jacques ravaged you.

Helen: I was drunk... and he...

Paul-Jean: He was a gentleman.

Helen: Right...

Paul-Jean: Jacques is a pathetic French man.

Helen: He was... nice and I was drunk.

Paul-Jean: Yes drunk but willing and able to be ravaged.
            I would have ravaged you.

Helen: Really, Paul-Jean, on a first date...?
            How manly of you...unless it's all talk.

Paul-Jean: You drunk now? We could just...

Cris: Out! Out! Now! *(Moves toward him with the 'gun')*

Helen: Crissy, please... he's not...

Cris: Out or I'll blow your face off.

(CRISSY moves up on PAUL-JEAN, who suddenly and forcefully removes the 'gun' from her pocket. But it is not a gun at all and PAUL-JEAN holds it up for all to see.)

Paul-Jean: This! It's not a gun! This! Is a comb! Now this– *(He takes out his own Colt .45 from a side pocket)* –is a gun!

Cris: He seemed bluffable, I thought.

Helen: He seems like a drunk and dangerous man, to me, and you threaten him with a...

Cris: All right. All right. But at least I didn't flirt... with him.

Helen: I know his brother.

Cris: So fuckin' what?

Paul-Jean: This is a big gun.

Helen: Yes, it is. A little old and rusty, though, isn't it? I mean, to use on people.

(PAUL-JEAN fires a shot.)

Helen: But effective... I think, Paul-Jean, very impressive...

Paul-Jean: It was my father's gun.

Helen: It's great... a great gun. Do you mind if I... hold it?

Paul-Jean: Who's drinkin' with me?

Helen: Right. *(Lights cigarette)* I am.
           Crissy get some glasses.

Cris: No. No. No. I am not going to drink with this
           sexual Cro Magnon... and let him paw me or
           worse yet, watch him paw.

Helen: *(Very loud)* Bad time!

Cris: What?

Helen: Bad time to be precise and proper protective
           lesbian feminist power babe, Crissy.

Cris: I am not a lesbian feminist power babe, Helen,
           I just happen to be in love with you.

Helen: Who cares? The man has a gun which you
           prompted him into showing us...

Cris: That's fine but I am not a lesbian...

Helen: Crissy. This is irritating. You are irritating.
           The man has a—

Paul-Jean: Let's drink and fuck... shall we *mes ami*?

Cris: What a charming style he has...

Helen: Crissy... shut up... Paul-Jean... I wanna wait for
            Jacques. He was looking forward—

Paul-Jean: Jacques is a mouse when it comes to the mounds
            of love... he is a Frenchy but hung
            like a rodent.

Helen: Really. That's surprising in a nice man. It's the jerks
            that are usually carrying toothpicks.

Cris: You didn't notice that?

Helen: I didn't see his dick, Crissy, I told... you that.

Cris: So the fact that he has small equipment,
            does that change how you lust?

Helen: Crissy, don't even talk to me.

Cris: Why...

Helen: This man has a gun and you're still talkin'... about...

Cris: I just want to know.

Helen: You're a pathetic obsessive succubus. Know that.
            Crissy, and if he doesn't shoot you I'm not never
            going to talk to you again.

Cris: Never ever. Shut up.

Helen: Never ever. You shut up.

Paul-Jean: I would really appreciate it if you would both shut
            up and have a drink.

Helen: She is really irritating...

Cris: Yeah, well she's–

Paul-Jean: All this talking. This quibble.
            Don't you want to be ravaged?

            *(MARY BARNES has been filming away and now
            she approaches the group, filming as she comes.)*

Mary: Excuse me, sir. I've been filming you discreetly,
          I hope...

Paul-Jean: Sure.

Mary: So as not to affect your natural man stance...

Paul-Jean: Great... film away. You drinking?

Mary: Your natural man stance is impressive,
          may I say sir... you are savage and filling
          the frame and your profile...

Paul-Jean: John Barrymore...?

Mary: Your profile reminds me very much of the great
          character actor Jack Palance.

Paul-Jean: The desperado... Shane... Boom! Bang!
            In France we love the western.

Mary: The producer in the great French filmmaker
          Godard's "Obsession," that was the Jack Palance
          I was thinking of... actually.

Paul-Jean: Whichever Jack Palance, yes. Yes! Paul-Jean.
          I am liquid. I am love. I am liquid love. My tongue
          is a hundred proof aphrodisiac and I am waiting to
          ravage you all.

          (PAUL-JEAN falls drunken to the floor.)

Mary: Your date has fallen on the floor, actually, Helen...

Helen: Uh-oh.

Paul-Jean: But I will rise again. My penis is a divining rod and
          I am rising to ravage you all.

          *(PAUL-JEAN moves to stand, and as he does
          MARY BARNES grabs him by both wrists, forcing
          him down to his knees, as she did previously with
          CRISSY. On the way down she head butts him,
          knocking him out and takes the gun away. He falls
          on the remote, turning on Godard #6.)*

          <GODARD #6 BEGINS>

Cris: *(Pause)* We should deal with the man on the floor.

Mary: *(Checking)* Clearly breathing, actually.

Helen: Mash-ode. But still cute...

Mary: *(Makes note)* Facial features, altered...
          the wild man.

Helen: (*Checking*) Bumped and stinking.

Mary: I think we should film him first...
placing the gun on the floor.

Helen: Really? Why?

Mary: It's a strong image, actually. Helen, you lie down
next to him. The gun between you.

Helen: Plus, with men, we expect guns.

Mary: In film, certainly.

Helen: Right. (*Lights cigarette*) But putting the gun
on the floor, isn't it only one small remove
away from returning the gun to him?

Mary: That's a significant problem, actually. I'd hate to
give up the shot but perhaps safety dictates.

Cris: God! God! God! Attach it to a wire or fishline
and if he wakes up, snatch it out of the frame.

Helen: That's good.

Mary: I like it.

Cris: Jesus, I hate you motherfuckers.
(*Knocking on door.*)

Cris: Come in, for God's sake.

(*LEON comes in.*)

Leon: Crissy, look we gotta get you outta here
on accounta...

Helen: Crissy, your boyfriend's here...

Cris: This motherfucker! This motherfuck–!
I told you not to come...

Leon: This is important, Crissy, it's the job...

Cris: Get out! Get out!

Mary: Good evening, Mr. Diaz.

Leon: Hi-ya... Crissy?

Mary: Mary Barnes.

Leon: Sure, I've seen ya. How are ya? Crissy... it's Uncle
Louie's job... I gotta get all the French guys—

Mary: We're setting up an important shot here actually.
For our upcoming triumphant nod to Jean-Luc
Godard, and unless you're willing to be in the
shot... I think we would prefer as a group,
if you'd leave.

Cris: The City! The Country!

Leon: Be in the shot, you mean,
like slo-mo instant replay?

Mary: I think so. Of course if that's a sports thing,
I wouldn't know. I watch Godard, almost
exclusively...

Leon: *(Hopefully)* Soccer player?

Mary: French experimental new wave king of the cinema.

Leon: Huh...

Mary: What do you think, Helen? We could add Mr. Diaz
          to the shot... for the male/female tryptych image,
          he could hold the gun.

Leon: I don't need it, on accounta, I've got my own...
          (Takes out his gun)

Helen: Oh, good. *(Lights cigarette)* This time, Mary
          Barnes, I think you get credit for encouraging a
          dangerous man to take his gun out...

Cris: *(Advancing on LEON)* Get! Out! Get Out Now.

Leon: *(Retreating)* I gotta stay, Crissy. On accounta this
          guy is the guy we want done...
          I already got one of 'em.

Cris: What?

Leon: Uncle Louie's job... these are the guys I'm setting
          up for setting down. That last fuckin' guy, I got him
          outside and now—

Helen: Wait, now... Leon Diaz, you came here to kill
          this guy? And you shot Jacques?

Leon: Sure. And he went down easy too.
          Like a pile'a garbage, he flopped—

Helen: That's not romantic... how romantic is that?
I was going to fuck Jacques.

Leon: Uncle Louie wants it done,
on accounta it gets done.

Cris: *(Shouting)* You loved him, didn't you?!

Helen: Shut up, Crissy. I didn't love. I liked and I was
going to fuck him... Leon, get out of my house.
This is my house and now I'm planning to fuck
this one. You can't have him.

Leon: I gotta.

Helen: Crissy, make him go away.

Cris: GO AWAY GO AWAY GO AWAY—!
(CRISSY hits LEON)

Leon: After the job.

Cris: Didn't work.

Helen: I see that. Mary Barnes, could you please?

Mary: I can, actually... Mr. Diaz. It's really not my business
who you shoot and since I'm not planning to
have sex with anybody... I certainly don't want to
interfere with your work, I just would like for you to
pay attention to my work, as well. That seems fair
to me, does it seem fair to you?

Leon: Sure... as long as it doesn't take all fuckin' day, me and Crissy got a plane to catch, plus I gotta talk to Crissy.

Cris: No. You don't.

Mary: It won't take long at all, Mr. Diaz. Please, just step into the shot...
(She takes him by the arm and does the same move as before, forcing him down by the wrist, head butting him unconscious on the way down.)

Helen: Thank you, Mary Barnes. *(Knocking at the door.)*

Cris: That's the door.

Helen: Someone at it.

Cris: What do we do? What do we do?

Mary: It is a problem. The scene is already crowded, messy with men. I don't suppose it could be a woman. A woman in a state of desire? That would be... *(Goes to door)*

Cris: Shut up, Mary Barnes.
Nobody cares about this fuckin' movie.

Mary: Well, that's not true. I do, actually. Helen does. Godard would if he were here.

Godard: *(Behind the door)* I am here. I am here.

Mary: *(Opening the door)* Godard.

(GODARD's entrance should take very long.)

Godard: Mary Barnes.

Mary: Godard! *(Begins filming him)*

Godard: Mary Barnes. *(Begins filming the corner of the room with own camera)* I received a letter. It was addressed simply to Jean-Luc Godard, Paris. Luckily, the postmaster there is a great film buff. He is particularly a fan of my work from the 60s. He forwards the letters by freight over the Alps to Switzerland, where I live. I brought in the morning's mail. But kept it on the bedside table and did not open it for two weeks. One night I awake from a dream of waves crashing against the shore and saw the letter sitting there in the moonlight. Mary Barnes, Mary Barnes... needs me. I came slowly as I could, savoring the invitation, the imagined crises... Mary Barnes.

Mary: Godard.

Godard: Is this your movie?

Mary: Yes, "The object of desire always suffers until she can come out of the center of the picture." It's in Super-8.

Godard: I shoot only the margins. The lightness, the flexibility of Super-8 seems appropriate to the scene.

Mary: This is fantastique.

Godard: Yes, it is... actually...

Mary: Meet my friends, Helen is the object of desire
          and Godard is the great French filmmaker,
          Godard actually.

Helen: Hello.

Godard: *Cet obscur objet du desir*, could you lend me 500
          francs? I need to shoot the margins.

Mary: *(Panicking)* I'm running out of film! I've got to
          shoot this. "Godard Meets Helen In the Object of
          Desire's House!" I can't stop.

Godard: *(Kindly)* We could switch back and forth.
          It is a combat film. Hand to hand filmmaking.

Mary: That's great. Actually great!

          *(MARY BARNES and GODARD begin tossing the
          cameras back and forth, filming manically back
          and forth.)*

Cris: This is fuckin' art. Oh yeah. Great fuckin' art,
          throwing stuff around with French people.

Godard: And after I've nailed all the margins, perhaps...
          (Flirting) Helen, the object of desire, you and I,
          we could lie down together. I always want the
          object of desire. I am Godard.
          (CRISSY knocks out GODARD.)

Mary: Crissy! This is Godard. You can't hit Godard.

Helen: Right. *(Lights cigarette)* Okay.

Cris: God! God! You drive me crazy, Helen,
         you really do.

Helen: Girls. Women... Dear Friends. We have three men
         unconscious on our floor. This is a rare opportunity.

Cris: To what? A rare opportunity...

Helen: To pants them and measure their wangs.

Cris: Yuck! Yuck!

Mary: It's true, actually.

Cris: Count me out.

Mary: Crissy, it will be good. For the movie.

Cris: For the movie? This movie is losing focus,
         Mary Barnes.

Mary: "The Object of Desire–"

Cris: Is Helen. Not unconscious men on floor.

Mary: I'm sure wangs have something to do with the
         object of desire. Actually.

Helen: Right. *(Lights cigarette)*

Cris: God! God!

Helen: Oh, come on, Crissy, don't be such a prune.
        Let's have some fun.

Cris: All right! All right!
        (Now that they've decided, the women approach
        the men gingerly and with caution.)

Cris: (Whispering) How do you do it?

Mary: Start with the belt buckle and unzip... I suppose.

Cris: Helen?

Helen: Oh for God's sake.
        (She does it and the others join in. Giggling.)
        Elephantine.

Mary: Like a pretzel.

Cris: Where's my magnifying glass?
        (All laughing.)

<GODARD #7>

— THE END —

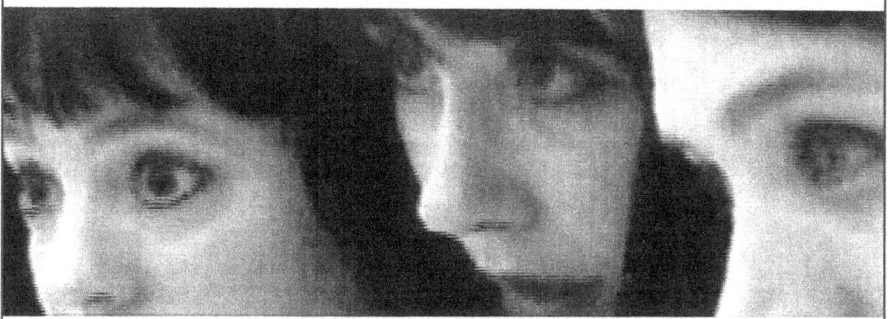

TEXT/IMAGE / / BEAU O'REILLY
MORE TEXT/IMAGE / / DAVID ISAACSON / HALLIE GORDON
SOUND / / JACK THE DOG

CAST / / JENNY MAGNUS / PAUL LEISEN /
VICKI WALDEN / ERIC ZIEGENHAGEN / ANN FOGARTY

BEGIN / FRIDAY   FEBRUARY 12 / / END / MARCH 20
FRIDAYS / SATURDAYS / MONDAYS / / 8 PM

LOCATION / / OLD   LUNAR   CABARET
2827 NORTH LINCOLN AVENUE

PHONE / / 773/327/6666   COST / / $10 / / OR LESS

THE CURIOUS THEATRE BRANCH PRESENTS

TALKING /
ABOUT
/ GODARD

Curious is funded in part by The John D. and Catherine T. MacArthur Foundation, The Brainaus Foundation, The Parky Foundation, WPWR-TV Channel 50 Foundation and The Illinois Arts Council, a State Agency.

11x17 inch poster for **TALKING ABOUT GODARD**, 1999

Whiskey in Blue

Premiered November 2000
The Lunar Cabaret Theater
Chicago, IL

performed by:

Rory Jobst / Paul Leisen
Kat McJimsey
Colm O'Reilly
Kathleen Powers

THE
PLAYS

INTRO

I wrote this out of one fragment that I found in my minds eye: two boys one on wooden crutches, a soup pot, hobo fire... I named the boys and things got rolling, a bit of Huck and Tom Sawyer in there, my childhood self burning garbage in the yard...

MERCY wrote himself and FINGERS was the revelation, she gave me the conflict, plot, story line... We did it the first time with Rory Jobst playing TOMMYO and Kat McJimsey as FARMBOY, Colm O'Reilly as MERCY, Kathleen Powers as FINGERS, we did it with a short play by Rory that first time at the Lunar Cabaret, I think it was the only time Colm, Rory and me were all in the same show. Later we did it at the Storefront Theater downtown, more lights, more seats, Paul Leisen replaced Rory, I directed, the cast was great... When it came time to put it in this book a script could not be found, I had to reconstruct it from notebooks and memory... It was like working with my 40 year old self, what was he thinking and what was the order?... Hard but really interesting to me.

SYNOPSIS

Two teenage boys, one with 2 broken legs and a thirst for whiskey, the other with a loneliness that always leads to saving folks, arrive in a patch of woods during the depression. Along the way they run into a mean bootlegger, his sleepless wife hungry for those relations, a gentle lawman with an always empty stomach, a pack of wolves, and a mysterious scarecrow with something to say... An exploration of love and, maybe, forgiveness.

SETTING

The set should feel continuous, a road, a campsite, a bit of porch, a bit of boxcar, a large old scarecrow, easy to walk from one spot to the next. A few blackouts, shifts in time, lights up and down... the play is mostly at night... a cart that rolls is needed, whiskey bottles, a soup pot, and fire... sounds of animals at nightfall; birds, frogs, wolf howls...The wolf howls will get louder after the pups and James Small are killed.

CAST OF CHARACTERS:

FINGERS

FARMBOY

MERCY

TOMMYO

SCENE ONE:

An old time Depression era clearing, lit only by a fire burnin,' a very large old scarecrow. FARMBOY enters on wooden crutches; both legs broken.

Fingers: *(Is hiding behind the scarecrow)* Crack! Crack!

Farmboy: What's that now, that crackin'?

Fingers: Crack! Crack!

Farmboy: There's a scarecrow in the woodland,
           I heard 'im.

Fingers: Bones break. You know they do, FarmBoy.

Farmboy: You don't have to tell me, no. Don't tell me
           nuthin. Cause I heard it. I heard it and I know.

Fingers: Bones break sharp like the driest old sticks, they
           break like the driest old sticks in the hottest old
           summer. You know that summer, FarmBoy.

Farmboy: Hot summer like the dogs are all dying,
           tripping over their tongues and breaking their
           heads when they fall. Big fat tongue hanging
           down between dog paws, troubling their
           walking and causing that trippin.'

           (FINGERS appears, but in the shadows)

Fingers: Bones break sharp, heat like that.

Farmboy: I know it.

Fingers: Crack. Crack. Like that? Crack. Crack.

Farmboy: I heard it.

Fingers: Crack. Crack. That's how it was. Crack.

Farmboy: Sure. It was.

Fingers: How are them legs, FarmBoy?

Farmboy: Mendin up.

Fingers: Mendin' up good, are they?

Farmboy: Sure they are.

Fingers: How does a Farmboy get two broken legs,
           unless somebodys livin' hard in this world.

Farmboy: Fallin, is what it was, even a good boy can fall,
           and landing hard too. Both legs so broken the
           bones shone through… Stickin' outa the skin.
           That and the goose egg, on my side head,
           that took some time to go down.
           TommyO bandaged me up as best he could.

Fingers: You tell TommyO I'm coming. You tell 'em.
           Just that. TommyO, she's coming. Say it.

Farmboy: TommyO, she's coming.

Fingers: And then you get him and you pull him up close.
            (FINGERS pulls FARMBOY's head to her, in his ear)

Fingers: Crack. Crack. She's a comin.' Just like that.
            You'll do it. Say you'll do it!

Farmboy: I'll do it.

Fingers: "TommyO she's coming." Crack. Crack.
            (FINGERS goes)

Farmboy: Thats that scary, scarecrows talkin'... Me and
            TommyO we are living on the gray side 'a town,
            by the abandoned train yard... That was the place,
            four box cars scattered and busted up, like that big
            wind picked 'em up and dropped 'em willy-nilly...

            Me and TommyO we live in the best one, the door
            still shut and we were most times warmed by the
            sum... Me and TommyO we were living on the
            grey side. Mostly I think, I'm a boy who woulda
            lived on the lonesome side of life if TommyO
            had'na a found me, me lying in that field, crying real
            tears after my momma took the fever and laid
            it all down, her life and soul an' all of it... the air
            just holdin' itself in all around her and in my chest
            too, the wolves, who had been howlin' and looking
            after meat, respecting my crying and hushin' up...

            That's what TommyO found and didn't he start
            digging right away ?

SCENE TWO:

Flash back in time, FARMBOY with two good legs and TommyO: already digging. TommyO is 14,15... thick hands and broad back, digging a hole... FARMBOY is 14,15, skinny, boney, sitting and worn, early morning.

Farmboy: You ever stand up in a swamp.

TommyO: Sure I have.

Farmboy: Was where I did most of my chirpin.'

TommyO: Well I heard you there then.

Farmboy: How many you done like that.

TommyO: What's that?

Farmboy: Laid 'em out like that and put the dirt on down.

TommyO: Dead people? I figure about a dozen,
if I was to count 'em up.

Farmboy: Hard times when a boy got to burying folks.

TommyO: A man will do what a mans gotta do.

Farmboy: Wal', sure but you ain't much older then me,
I figure.

TommyO: Wal,' if you figure to keep that on the shush,
I'm a grateful man.

Farmboy: Nobody know it, brother? Look at you,
        you got that boy face, that boy skin.

TommyO: Shush it now, tho.

Farmboy: You buried my mama, now I figure
        to owe you one.

TommyO: Fever got her then, I guess.

Farmboy: Swept right thru her like a flame in a
        straw hutch... in two weeks she was nothin.'

TommyO: That's hard, you miss her?

Farmboy: Every minute and then some...
        the ghosts ever come up on ya,
        once you finish layin' that dirt?

TommyO: I ain't never seen 'em and I never will.

Farmboy: Well, I think my mama's will... her ghost.

TommyO: I don't think so, I don't.

Farmboy: I'll wait on her, that ghost.

TommyO: Your folks all sick now, you all alone,
        is why I am asking

Farmboy: Fever got 'em,' weren't much, anyway, my papa
        being a hard man, stone hard if I was to tell it
        truly, never spoke, worked sun up, sun down, it
        was me and mama, most ways.

TommyO: Where you figure to go?
          Stay on the farm?

Farmboy: It weren't ours nohow…
          I'll wait on Ma's ghost and figure it later.

TommyO: Wal,' you might try sitting on her grave, then…
          that's likely to get a dead one agitated
          and uncomfortable enough to squeeze
          that ghost out.

Farmboy: You think?

TommyO: If I'm dead and people get to sitting
          on me that will get me moving,
          if anything's gonna do it.

Farmboy: All right then nice… kinda soft, isn't she,
          the good earth.

TommyO: Oh, that she is… you ever drink whiskey?

Farmboy: I never have done that.

TommyO: It will make that good earth jump up and down
          and talk pretty too, all the colors jump up and
          down, if you wanted to try her out.
          (Offers bottle)

Farmboy: Wal,' I could (Drinks and sputters)
          brother that's something, something good.

TommyO: You gotta name now?

Farmboy: Well my pa called me Ezekiel, but maybe he called it too much, cause it seemed like we used it up early and never kept using it later on, mama called me Farm Boy, cause I was.

TommyO: A boy on a farm.

Farmboy: Wal,' sure.

TommyO: That'll do then, Farmboy... I'm TommyO.
(They shake)

Farmboy: Pleased to meet you.

TommyO: Wal,' now that's done.

Farmboy: You got family, TommyO? What's your story.

TommyO: Nothin' to tell... the whiskey's good.

Farmboy: Sure it is.

TommyO: You done with this ghost watching now? 'Cause I'm about done with these dead people and I expect to move on up the road.

Farmboy: Where would you go then?

TommyO: Someplace where the grass is always greener and the stars shout out your name like they knowed you was coming forever and here you are and aren't those stars right glad to see you and aren't they playing up star music on star fiddles and lifting you up for all that star dancing, star women perfect and beautiful, flying around the sky and those star men all so kind grand in their noble faces… a place like that that's where I'm going.

Farmboy: Brother! I'm thinking haven't I got that here… look at everything

TommyO: That's the whiskey talking, Farmboy?
Didn't I tell ya and isn't it something
what that whiskey will do?

Farmboy: Man, it is.

TommyO: So let's go… you ready?

Farmboy: Wal', sure I am.

SCENE THREE:

Further down the road. FINGERS, early middle aged, bone thin and purposeful is walking quietly. MERCY beginning to grey and go soft around the edges, but tougher than he appears and he knows that, is following a few steps behind.

Fingers: I see you…

Mercy: Wal'lll, now, missus, you'd be a walkin' the roads now, and a mercy to a lookin man, too… The Lord God knows that… still, its wild an' lonely out here and at the risk a' steppin' into shoes that ain't mine to wear… Is there some sorta trouble, missus, at home say that a man like me could offer a helpin' hand?

Fingers: Wal' now. If you've seen me you know that I'm married to James Small. That'd be my husband.

Mercy: Wal'lll, I know it.

Fingers: So what kinda trouble could there be, with a husband like mine?

Mercy: Wal', he's a hard man, seems like, tha' James Small.

Fingers: He's a man, you mean, what a man should be.

Mercy: Wal'lll, you say that, still you are out and about an' it makes a man wonder.

Fingers: Not if his minds in order and he's got his own thoughts, no, he would not be.

Mercy: Wal'lll, still. Hard times like these, folks is careful over each other and that's called neighborly…

Fingers: Wal', you're some kind of lawman, tho, which makes you question hard… and how neighborly is that?

Mercy: Wal'lll, I guess I do.

Fingers: My husband, James Small, he's a clean man… If the floor an' table need scrubbin, he'll scrub it. "I donna wait for another man to scrub away that dirt, not when it's my place that's been dirted, no. I get right to it." Farmhands are always dropping mud and spillin' beer.

Mercy: A road house like that James Small's place, sure. Farmhands are always droppin' mud, but you gotta have 'em. Like that chicken to that chicken stew. Farmhands to a roadhouse.

Fingers: That cleaning, it moved from the roadhouse to our place in back, my husband figured to be good at that cleaning all the time… the place would not matter… James Small would clean God's heaven, if God got sloppy and let it go. He was a doer, that man. An' he didn't leave me much to do, little cooking, little washing, I'm a reader, tho, but hard to find enough books on the blue side of town.

Mercy: There's neighbors, now, always a mercy, and church over to the violet side.

Fingers: I'm not much for crops or weather talk, tho, and never did find much a god in those churches. Farmwifes didn't offer much more than that.

Mercy: They'd a keep what there is to keep, hard times like these. Still, it's a wild countryside and quiet too, no one walkin' much.

Fingers: There's the creatures, tho… Frogs that'll rumble the water, blue herons and crazy loons, all wing spread and wolves, like they have already lost their pack and now is the time to call them back, wailing for them. You ever hear them. Ever listen up at all?

Mercy: Wal'lll, sure I have, they do touch your heart, missus… then I'm grateful to 'em…

Fingers: My mind, more like. You watch those creatures long enough you see some things that can get you studying on life, the way it works. You ever see the way a trout will leap six feet straight up outa the water just to catch a blue tail fly?

Mercy: Six feet. The Lord God knows thas' a leap. Six feet, that'd be taller than a lot of men.

Fingers: And more pleasure to look at, too.
All shining and silver, sprayin' the water thru the air. Beautiful.

Mercy: A sight like that it sure would be.

Fingers: Or the way a carp will lay under the mud, for months, sometimes. All reptile cool and just waiting, slow for the pond to fill or… a horsefly just dying to be a carp dinner. You ever see a carp do that, lying in the mud and getting long and ready, and knowing how to lie so slow, you ever watch a carp at all?

Mercy: I'd a guess not, them not being good eatin' and me being after the mercy of a meal. Ate a carp the once tasted 'a garbage and mud.

Fingers: Wal', they are cleaners and they do love that mud. What do you watch? A man's gotta watch something…

Mercy: Wal'lll, people mostly. How a man can set himself up for trouble and a woman, too…
an' how likely that's to happen, hard times.

Fingers: And do you watch it quick, glancing at a man just to get the particulars and draw your conclusions up, or do you take the time an' really look?

Mercy: Wal'lll, now. I'll spot some folks, an' study on those folks for a time. Say a man's roughin' it, some hard times on him an' his face is like a map, all the crops that dried up on him, the cow that soured up and went dry all together. I'll see that, the water hole that used to be so fine and clear goin' bitter and brackish, now, and how his wife just cried out all sick with fever and asked the Lord God to take her in his arms an' tha Lord God showed his mercy and did take her. That man shows her goin', deep around her eyes wearin' wrinkles like tears there, an' how he just about had to give it up then, no choice, leavin' the farm and headin' up the road, not towards anything tho, just movin' cause his feet still worked and his blood still pushed him onto livin'. I'll study on that and know it's a blessin' to do it, too.

Fingers: That's a lot to see.

Mercy: Sure, it is. You ever watch how the farmhands and their wives to be, this'll happen after church, say, or a picnic? Months of courtin', each finding each alive and wantin', the wonder and the sweetness of that? An' how once they've had each some in the hay, some in the bed, some in the woods where they're sure they belong...An' they get their couple lives on their faces and babies in the cradle... They get all steady and hard, hidin' their tenderness. I'll see that in folks around and I'll wonder over studyin' close for a while. But no more than that, 'cause, not having that way of marrying up myself, I'm not likely to understand it even with all that studying an' that studying will make a god-loving man hungry after dumplings, say. Or peach cobbler.

Fingers: You don't think it through then. How a man and a woman made with blood and bone that knows each other, body to body, an' can no more not mate up an' change with that mating then that trout can go flashing after that fly? Cause that fly is his fly an' he's got to have it? How can you not see that? That's like breathing and it is natural.

Mercy: Wal'lll, I dunno bout 'natural' a natural dog'l hump in heat and it don't matter whose waggin' the tail… Horses are happy to husband up the one time and move on down the road… A snake don't give any kind of damn, Lord forgive me them words, whose coilin over the eggs. The chicken ain't got no marrying morals and just goes to chasin' the cock… Seems 'nature' don't know the rules until folks get to puttin 'em there… this marrying up, now, ain't' natural.

Fingers: Swans will marry, tho. Soon as their tail feathers find their length, stay together until one breaks its neck, or gets some old swan sickness and dies, an' the mate will carry on in grief until death quiets her.

Mercy: Swans are strange birds, now and the Lord God knows it, all twisted necks and floating around so. Once you get to eating em, they'll be all stringey and boney, not like a nice chicken say… I donna figure a swan to make no kinda sense.

Fingers: A fox will marry, they say… once that she-fox lifts
up her tail and waves it around, that he-fox is
hooked up for life, if you separate a pair of fox by
even hundreds of miles, they'll come running back
to each other no matter what.

Mercy: Now I'm a curious man as to how you know about
them fox and their long-range habits, missus.

Fingers: Well, books. There is all sorts of books
on fox and other creatures.

Mercy: Now, I donna read those books,
I'd be stickin' to the bible mostly.

Fingers: Noah and the Ark. Everyone in pairs.

Mercy: Thas' so, still everything in there, you got a cruel
and a loving God both, an' 100 year old patriarchs
like your Saul an' your David everywhere and them
fellas know all about marrying up, they'd marry the
one farmers daughter an' marry up her sister, too,
and her cousin, whatever it takes to get it done…

Fingers: Old Testament. That and that harsh,
hard times in the Old Testament.

Mercy: Wal'lll, not much different then what the Lord'd be
givin' us now, and that Old Testament has got a
lot of everything in there and nothing about how
loving them foxes are, foxes got strange minds,
they'd murder up a henhouse without blinkin' no.
A fox is not the animal I would think to go to about
the ways of love.

Fingers: Which one would be then?

Mercy: Wal'lll. A pig, I'd consider on a pig

Fingers: Not much beauty in a pig

Mercy: Still, I'd consider 'em. And you could eat 'em, too, after considerin.'

Fingers: Too tamed up, tho. Docile pigs. Love, even the marryn' kind. Has got to have somethin' wild in it.

Mercy: Wal'lll, that'd be true.

Fingers: You ever see the wolf, say in a pack.

Mercy: Wal'lll, I have. Gray side of town most recent… saw a pack of 'em 5, 6 years ago runnin' right then gray, heads up, eyes bouncing. Wal', they were somethin', ten in all, if your countin' the cubs and they were packed in and safe, like all them adults knew how them cubs had to run, clumsy and bumpin' off of each, but them he and she wolfs they knew them cubs was a blessing, full a joy that the Lord God made them that way. Wolves'll run full out, hair standin'up in the wind. I seen that, course that was before the hard times set in, you see a wolf, now. Wal', you donna see them. Much.

Fingers: Well, I do. And I do go looking to see them, too. Fierce and noble, that's what I want to see in a creature. Wolves, always in pairs, married up and happy too.

Mercy: Do you. Now? See 'em for true.

Fingers: Over by them boxcars. Grey side a town.

Mercy: Sure. It'd still be wild there and safe. A place a safety for that he and she wolf, they layin' in the box cars, you think?

Fingers: Wal', there's pups, young ones, wolfs will love the pups. They are smart and curious, the babies. Everybody plays. Wolfs will mate for life, too, and never worry over that an' they won't cause us no trouble, either, most times, unless you trap'em bad or stare'em down. A wolf bite then. Tear you up.

Mercy: Wal'lll, hard times like these, I'd be careful around 'em, Missus. The Lord God made 'em wild for times like these, thas how I'd figure it.

Fingers: I am. I only watch, and to keep my distance. You know tha' old scarecrow down by those boxcars?

Mercy: Been there sixty years, you know I'd know it… not much left just the head, all bulgcy.

Fingers: Shaped now like the good god a scarecrows squeezed all the brains down around the jaw.

Mercy: Wal'lll, sure, to see if them brains a work better down there, round the teeth and jawbone. Brains not always a mercy.

Fingers: The arms are there still, sitting boney toward the horizons, pointing all them crows to heaven.

Mercy: Wal'lll, I do know tha' scarecrow.

Fingers: I'll hide there, behind, watching the wolves for
           hours, the wolves get something in their faces, a
           kinda grave chuckle that I have never seen on any
           other. I can watch them, too, for hours.

Mercy: Wal', thats a mercy and a blessing, too and good
           to do, hard times like these, missus.

Fingers: You can call me Fingers. That's my name.

Mercy: And where would you get a name like that,
           if you donna mind the asking.

Fingers: My husband, James Small, he gave it to me
           and I liked it enough to keep it.

Mercy: It would have a meaning.
           I'd guess a reason for the naming

Fingers: It would, but a man and a woman the marrying
           kind, they'd get a secret or two, between them an'
           keep-em, too… still you could use the name, you
           see me on the road, us bein' neighbors and all.

Mercy: Fingers it'll be, then and a mercy to know it,
           even without the reason why.

Fingers: It is.
           (Shakes hand)

SCENE FOUR:

Further on up the road.

Farmboy: "You got to cross that lonesome valley. You got to cross it by yourself. Ain't nobody here gonna cross it for you. You gotta cross it by yourself."

TommyO: That's a nice song, and a good one to hear. You make it up?

Farmboy: No, it's an old song. My mama told it to me.

TommyO: Wal', you sing it good

Farmboy: Only cause I'm in a world of hurt, fulla tears like I got slivers of glass in my heart, that cuts me when I get to breathin' and I'm doin' that breathin' and heavin' out sighs both when I think on my mama.

TommyO: Wal', it's a nice song.
I don't a think I ever heard it before.

Farmboy: You can thank my mama then,
most times I sing like a frog.

TommyO: Yeah? How's that frog go now?

Farmboy: *(Singing like a frog)*
"Froggy went a courtin and he did ride a huh,
Froggy went a courtin' and he did ride a huh,
with a bottle of whiskey right by his side."

TommyO: Wal' now it seems like—I heard that one before.

TommyO: *(Sings)* I looked high, I looked low,
I looked everywhere I go!

Farmboy: How long you figure we been walkin,' TommyO?

TommyO: Wal', thirty days thirty miles a day, that's 90 mile.

Farmboy: And we have not got to the blue side yet?

TommyO: We have not done that.

Farmboy: I'd say my feet are pretty sore then, TommyO,
if we was to sit for a while, even a day or so,
them feet would get to feelin' better the next
time we moved along.

TommyO: Wal', that would make some sense.

SCENE FIVE:
> *FINGERS' porch, nighttime.*

Fingers: You here for my husband, James Small.

Mercy: That's so, missus, and it would be a mercy
to find him home...

Fingers: Wal', you'll be waiting on him then, that man is
after being a while... a night like this one here
I don't know where he goes, most daytimes he
is nowhere but that stoop there, made right for
stand-in 'and watching the sky, nights like this
here I ain't expecting him til midnight or later.
You know my husband, James Small, then?

Mercy: Lord God, I do. Hard times like these a man's gonna drink. Drink's a mercy, James Small was as regular as a paycheck used to be. With that James Small there has got to be a story, a woman like yourself missus and the kind of man that James Small appears to be and you are talkin' to a man who loves to hear it all.

Fingers: Now didn't we just talk enough yesternight? Ain't that enough ?

Mercy: Well we might of done some tounge waggin' but I am thinkin' didn't it just make me want all the more? A woman like you telling a story.

Fingers: The story stands on that stoop first. It doesn't go nowhere for a good while.

Mercy: Well, I'm sittin.' I'm a patient man, and that's a mercy.

Fingers: James Small would stand out on that stoop three times a day, just like the weather, blowin in and blowin' out, but always there.

Mercy: Sun up, sun down, sure, and then it's midnight.

Fingers: Right. That's my husbands smoke time…

Mercy: That's when I'd see him, me bein' a smoker, too… He'd stand leanin' against that door jamb.

Fingers: Between the doorjamb and the windowsill, his shoulder rubbin' that old oak planking dark and smooth. It was old wood. Not paint, just old. My husband is a tall man.

Mercy: Over six and a half foot, I'd say. No one could fault
           him there. You don't fault a man for his natural
           gifts. Lord God, no, you don't.

Fingers: At sunup my husband would throw a long shadow
           to the left. At sundown he would throw a long
           shadow to the right. At midnight he'd throw no
           shadow at all. The dark had a thick purple in it.

Mercy: Well, we're living on the blue side of town,
           and at night that deepens up.

Fingers: Not black, exactly. So we called it purple.

Mercy: Lord God, that is some night sky,
           and a mercy to see.

Fingers: My husband smoked these long cigarettes,
           sucking the smoke in through the tip.

Mercy: Slow and greedy like a kid at the nanny goat.
           I've seen him smoke. That stoop is in front of
           your husband's roadhouse James Small's, and
           James Small's for years.

Fingers: His father's name before him.

Mercy: No sign, though. No way to know who's
           running the show…

Fingers: Men like those Smalls, they don't waste money on
           signs, the paint, the wood, that will cost you.

Mercy: Hard times like these, makes sense.

Fingers: They never would, though, those Smalls, spend extra. And they don't care whether folks know them, who they are. Men like that, they don't think they need a name. It doesn't change anything... My husband would flick it away like so much cigarette ash... I never called him James. I never called him, just waited. It was at the midnight point that my husband would have his time—the relations—the act of love... What about this, now, can you hear this? You being a man.

Mercy: I'm sure I can... What is it?

Fingers: About the wanting a woman has for a man... The physical wanting.

Mercy: Lord God, that's love. That's a mercy.

Fingers: There is something in it. My husband is like a craftsman who has made that same chair every night, year after year. He knows how to put the hammer to the nail without much fuss, he never touched my face with his hands, never whispered any words, still, the smoothness of the regular relations could be counted on, and I relaxed, riding the animal inside me like it was a secret and private joy that I didn't have to share. Some ways I like that. It is just mine... My husband would always say, "Fingers, you will never love another man," as he went off, arching and twisting inside me... But as I held him there, pumping inside me, I knew that was wrong.

Mercy: I loved a woman once.

Fingers: How's that?

Mercy: Lord God, she was something to see, long and
            lean as a hard times summer, and a mercy to
            the eye… Loved me with her heart. I could see
            it just a bustin' outa her. And the way we would
            talk. 'Tween the two of us you couldn't tell where
            a man's voice started in and a woman's voice
            finished up: we were that close.

Fingers: Why are you tellin' me this?

Mercy: I thought I should say. You were tellin'–

Fingers: I don't need to hear it, though.

Mercy: I had a love there, see, but I could'na stay.
            Still, it was a true love.

Fingers: Then you're a fool, a foolish man… Do you think
            if I'd of ever had that I would ever have let go? I
            married up with my husband before I knew not
            just any man would do. I was a young girl and
            I thought that if a man, a man wanted you with
            what looked like desire, he's be loving you, and
            it wouldn't take no time for this young girl to be
            loving him back… The bar, James Small's Place,
            gave us a living.

Mercy: Even in hard times it was the only place on the
            blue side of town. We'd all make it down there.

Fingers: The farm hands and bosses.
            All the men on the blue side of town.

Mercy: I knew him then. We all called him sir, like he
            was some kind of gentry or politician.

James Small had what we wanted: long brown
glasses of beer and short hot shots of whiskey.
Lord God, that was a mercy.

Fingers: I never saw him there, though. My husband didn't
want me in that room. But I can see him there,
nodding at those farm hands. But not warm,
my husband was not warm. Ever.

Mercy: Still, he's recognizin' us, and givin' us that nod.
It seemed like enough for us farm boys, shufflin,'
and flushed in the cheeks, dirty overalls, boots
heavy with mud… Just him takin' us in and handin'
out beers. Lord God, that was a mercy, that drink.
James Small always looked sharp.

Fingers: Spit shine and shiny black suit, sharp creases.

Mercy: That's it. Sure.

Fingers: My husband always said,
"You keep me lookin' good, I'll stay good."
My husband always looked good.

Mercy: O mercy me, he did that. Like a king he looked…

Fingers: My husband didn't care, though, him bein' so sure
that the world owed him that. He is separate from
the rest of us, superior… I can't say I liked that
about him. I can't say I like him, even, only love.

Mercy: Good? He isn't like that, good, no.
Not like a good piece a pie, say.

Fingers: I am used to him, though. He is mine.
A woman can get used to things.

Mercy: That's sure.

Fingers: You hear that pause now in our talk...
            (They both listen to nothing.)

Mercy: I do, though I was about to launch in,
            I was holding back, mama having taught
            to be polite when a missus is talking…
            I can find some things to jaw on.

Fingers: Expect an echo of your own voice will have to
            serve ya, I believe James Small left the cart back
            at the house expecting someone to fill it with
            liquor to sell, you that someone?

Mercy: Wal', missus, just might be

SCENE SIX:

> *Further up the road where FARMBOY and*
> *TommyO have been sitting. MERCY appears*
> *pulling a cart made of wood, rough, two wheels*
> *weighed down, a barrel and some bottles.*

Mercy: Wal'lll now young brothers your a mercy on a
            lonely road to a gabby man.

TommyO: Wal' now sittin' after walkin only,
            not much to talk on.

Farmboy: Lo, brother.

Mercy: I do expect you might have something more to tell
then you think you got and you already sittin' tells
me that you got time to talk and you just ventured
out of the big world, too.

TommyO: 30 miles we been out there walkin' today we surely
did come from there, if thirty miles takes us back
to the big world.

Mercy: 30 miles, that's hard, hard walkin'.
Hard times like these… You all got anything to eat.
It'd be a mercy to share some.

Farmboy: Wal,' carrots.

Mercy: What's that.

Farmboy: Wal', carrots… and chicken.

Mercy: You'd be the shy one, I figure.

Farmboy: Not most times.

TommyO: Just sore of foot, with all that walkin'.

Mercy: Wal'lll, that would quiet a man down.

TommyO: It would.

Mercy: You hear that growling, that's this mans' stomach…
lord god, I am a hungry man… you sharing the
chicken and keeping the carrots?

Farmboy: We could.

TommyO: We weren't planning to, no.

Mercy: You change your minds, it'd be a mercy.

TommyO: Not done walking tho,
         it's all the food we're carrying.

Mercy: Hard to find a chicken, hard times like these.
          That fresh chicken?

TommyO: Plucked her outa some wild henhouse just this
        morning, didn't we, Farmboy ?

Farmboy: Sure did.

Mercy: I am not always a hungry man. It'd be a mercy
          and a kindness, you sharing it around, lord god,
          it would and you'd still have them carrots?

TommyO: Wal' now mercy is one thing and kindness another.

Farmboy: What's in the cart?

Mercy: No food, I am sad to say. Just a barrel of beer and
          some bottles of whiskey, taking 'em into the blue
          side of town, James Small's place.

Farmboy: Wait now, you telling me we made it to
         the blue side of things?

Mercy: A couple a dozen long strides that way,
          if you'd be the hurrying kind.

Farmboy: Whiskey for chicken, straight up?

Mercy: Some of them bottles could be broken, the roads being that rough, James Small won't notice that.

Farmboy: *(Swaps chicken for whiskey... Drinks)*
Brother that is something.

TommyO: *(Drinks)* Man, I like it, I do.

Mercy: A bite a that chicken fat will put a bit of fat on a hungry man and that's a mercy, hard times like these.

Farmboy: This town got a name, mister?

Mercy: Some folks call it coming some folks call it going... its not much of a town, got a grey side, a blue side and a touch of red... you see some farms, James Small's place, scrub of timber, you swallow hard, you might miss the whole thing.

Farmboy: Whiskey's good.

TommyO: And it's a pretty place seems like... lots a color in this here sky greens and red and violets and blue on the horizon.

Mercy: Ya see them colors? Most folks don't see all of that, just the gray, even with their eyes closed.

Farmboy: They keep drinkin' that whiskey they'd see all dem colors, and more, too.

TommyO: They surely would.

Mercy: You boys plan to keep roughin it, now?

Farmboy: We could stay put, I'm thinking, this bein' such a
           pretty place, with blue on the horizon.

Mercy: Still, it's a small place and a small place
           usually gets filled up hard times like these,
           you dona' wanna' trouble a place,
           get to fillin' it up too much.

TommyO: Wal'... we will take that into account.

Mercy: I knew you would.

TommyO: You wear that star for show or are you puttin'
           something behind it?

Mercy: This? Now brother, it's a part time star,
           keeps me in eggs and butter,
           but I like my eggs and butter.

TommyO: Funny town, tho... where the law hauls the
           whiskey, I think, I do.

Mercy: A man does what man can do, a little haulin,'
           a little lawin,' hard times like these.

Farmboy: Everything's beautiful here.

Mercy: Lord god, that's true, still you might wanna
           go easy on the bottle, son.

Farmboy: Everything's jumpin' up and down,
           TommyO, do you see it?

TommyO: Farmboy, I do, I do.

Mercy: A bit more of that chicken,
         make a man feel satisfied, brother.

TommyO: Wal,' I could use more of that whiskey, I could.

Mercy: I'll tell you what I'll do…
         we'll swap up whats left of that chicken
         and you boys take this here cart up the road
         and let James Small pay you for the hauling
         and the whiskey, and you might just drink
         some more along the way.

TommyO: Wal,' I donna know, it's pretty good chicken.

Farmboy: Whiskey! Whiskey!

Mercy: Couple miles up the road is all,
         and if you're courteous boy,
         James Small has got a wife
         and she'll let you sleep it off in the hay,
         and that's a mercy, too.

Farmboy: Let's go, Let's GO, TommyO.

TommyO: Wal,' I guess.
        (*Swaps chicken for whiskey*)

Mercy: Lord god. This is sweet, only thing is,
         TommyO, in the morning you boys keep
         on up the road, this place being filled up,
         what with the hard times.

TommyO: Wal,' it is a pretty place.

Mercy: It is still, be pretty still without you,
         best you keep going.

TommyO: Guess so.

SCENE SEVEN:
Back on FINGERS' porch.

Fingers: We had no children, my husband James Small and
           I don't think I would have missed that, nor griefed
           it, either, if it wasn't that the women of the grey
           side of town would whisper after me whenever I
           passed them on the road, how James Small's seed
           falls on hard ground, meaning me, that my womb
           must be hard and wrong, of course it couldn't
           be James Small's seed was lacking, him being
           so manly and cold and him so superior, like he'd
           fertile up the oceans and the mountains, too, if he
           put himself to it... it was this talk that made me
           flushed and red with anger and avoid the women
           of the grey side of town, and the blue side too, all
           of 'em, still there's not not much to do between
           visits with the husband and I got so restless,
           walking after sundown and before that midnight
           hour... after some weeks I got hungry for that
           twilight time, out under the oncoming purple black
           sky, walking hard, long hours of it, too...
           ...that's how I happened to be on the road when
           Mercy's cart, fulla my husband's liquor came
           storming down that hill.

           *(TOMMYO is hauling the cart while FARMBOY
           drives, they are both drinkin' whiskey and a lot has
           already been drunk.)*

Farmboy: WHOA, now TommyO, you're a good horse,
           you are TommyO.
           (Whinnying like a horse)
           Neigh, neigh hay hay hay ni ha ni ha ni ha hey hey.

Farmboy: O man, o man… go faster TommyO.

TommyO: I figure to go faster and faster, Farmboy,
           going down the hill, I do.

Farmboy: Stampede, TommyO, a wild stampede that tramps
           it all down, everything that's in a wild horse's way,
           faster and faster, TommyO… Brother, I am drunk,
           this fast and everywhere, this fast and I am flying.

           (The cart crashes hard and FARMBOY
            is thrown, screaming)

Farmboy: TommyO !!!

Fingers: Now that crash was something awful to see, that
           Farmboy's body flying across the sky leaping like
           a flame, whiskey and blood exploded everywhere.
           TommyO right after, eyes rolling in a red heat at
           the iris, screaming and spinning in wild circles
           popping out of the head, the momentum of the
           hill and the cart in a crash, that energy all gone in
           to his body, twisting and lurching, that screaming,
           I couldn't have that, I moved in hitting that
           TommyO, smacking him down hard, too…

           You can't have a crazy boy at you when a broken
           boy's blood is everywhere… and now everybody
           silent, my skirt's ripping felt loud, sharp sounds, I
           tied up those poor broken bone legs, It was the

blood that I needed to staunch, that blood
poring out would kill a boy, but it was his head
that worried me, the brain, that Farmboy
gibbering, strange sounds as if talking sounds
before words, huh, grrs, maa's, with these horrible
gulping sounds underneath 'em, I carried these
boys to the hay barn down the road, first that
Farmboy, jerking and wild in my arms, like an
animal after the trap has been sprung, TommyO
was harder, him being so drunk and filled with
terror, I had to drag him along, slapping him
repeatedly just to get him there...

I couldn't take them home, my husband's a hard
man and he would not have forgiven them Mercy's
cart and the wasted liquor, hard men are never
kind to broken boys, that's not a hard man's way.

Me, I felt anything but hard, soft and tender for
these wounded boys, the farm boy all scrunched
up and infant faced, TommyO slack and wretched
in his liquor and his shame, me I felt something
animal inside me, mewling and nursing towards
them like my intimate private self was a mamma
full up and awake on spotting her lost babes...
in the dark I left them there and walked away but
you don't walk away from that kinda feeling and
it stayed with me, even as my husband made his
midnight methodical love, me coming like there
were stars in heaven and that husband not being
the reason.

In the morning I went back there to change their
bandages, to touch their faces with my fingertips
but they were gone, just some clots of blood,
rough in the hay, gone.

SCENE EIGHT:

> *TOMMYO and FARMBOY sitting on the side of the road, morning.*

TommyO: You'd be lying there a long time, now Farmboy, you'd be waitin' on those bones to mend up on their own. I know that much.

Farmboy: More than I know, then, more'n me…

TommyO: What you got left after them bones broke, then?

Farmboy: Blue sky. Red eyes. Head spinnin.' Crack. Crack.

TommyO: Oh, brother. That was bad.
A boy needs more than that.

Farmboy: Well, that blue sky, me flying thru the air.
That was somethin.'

TommyO: Sure it was. We'll see it again.
Still, with them legs like that you'll never get anything like a constitutional.

> *(TOMMYO picks up FARMBOY wrapping his arms around him and shaking him up and down.)*

TommyO: I got ya now. Ya just lay into it. *(Shaking him)*
Ya gotta get that blood going now.

Farmboy: It hurts, TommyO, hurts.

TommyO: Sure, I know. I do. Hurts now but I seen a man get the atrophies and lose all them limbs. I donna wanna see that again. See, so we shake the blood… Get it goin Farmboy.

Farmboy: The bones go shakin' with the blood, TommyO. And that's that pain.

TommyO: Well, it'll get less, tho… And we'll be savin them limbs, you'll see I got ya, FarmBoy… We'll just walk in now.

Farmboy: Oh, no… Now I can't cant cant cant cant can not.

TommyO: You can, Farm Boy. You can. You gotta. We can't stop here. We wrecked that man's cart and there's a no telling what a man will do. Now I'm carryin ya. I'm pickin ya up now.

Farmboy: Nah–Yah ah ah

TommyO: O God, Holy God, He's a hurtin'
(Walking and carrying) Don't you let him hurt so… now, I'm tellin' ya god...
Don't a ya do it, and you tell that death to keep off, not this boy. There's other poor boys up the road. You can take one of them if you gotta and give' em to Farmboy's mama, if she be needin' the company…
the dead don't see, now do they?
It would make her no nevermind it…
I need this Farmboy.

TommyO: I could carry you, tho, a good long way, and I'da do it too, you're that special.
(They walk awhile)

This place, it'll do for us, Farm Boy, just some ol'
boxcars, maybe, but we'll lay up a while, outa the
wind and you'll heal up good outa the wind…
(listening)
What's this, now critters in here…
Hey. you critters I'll get a big stick an' clear
you out and finish you off, too…

(TOMMYO kills the wolf pups with a stick)

SCENE NINE:

*FINGERS' porch, daytime. FINGERS already there,
enter TOMMYO.*

TommyO: I'd be lookin' to work for somethin'—onions,
potatoes, a bit of bacon, if you had it, ma'am.
I'm a good worker, too. I am.

Fingers: Wal' now, it's only laundry tho women's work,
that's all I got to do.

TommyO: I'd do it tho, that women's work, and be happy
to get it, too if you had them things to spare—
the onions and things.

Fingers: You that hungry, boy?

TommyO: Wal', hungry, I am. There's no gettin' around that.
But it's not that, the reason for asking.

Fingers: What would it be then, if not the hunger?

TommyO: Sick friend I'd call it, Farmboy bein' all broke up
in the legs and all. It'd be to feed him see,
if you could see to it.

Fingers: Wal', I could stand the company.
I don't see folks much, as to talk to.

TommyO: Hard times, I guess. Folks'll be that way.

Fingers: I guess they do. Seems like I've seen you before.

TommyO: Wal', I'm on the gray side a-town, most days.
(TOMMYO is now washing the clothes.)

Fingers: Well, I have been there. Still, didn't I see
you on the road? In some kinda trouble?
That's how I remember it.

TommyO: Wal' no. I've never been in any of that trouble.

Fingers: Not at all?

TommyO: None to speak of. I'da knowed if I had, I would.

Fingers: I guess that's so . . . still.

TommyO: That your place up the hill?

Fingers: Wal', my husband's, James Small.

TommyO: Wal', now is it?

Fingers: James Small's. That's what they call it.
Chicken and beer.

TommyO: Whiskey, too, is it?

Fingers: Sure.

TommyO: Farmboy loves that whiskey.

Fingers: Not to your taste?

TommyO: Well, I will drink it.

Fingers: But?

TommyO: Like a good dog after he gets snakebit, you start
         nursing that whiskey, it don't know who you are
         it'll turn and bite you hard, too.

Fingers: Dog still wants it though . . .

TommyO: Wal'. You figure your husband he be wantin'
         to trade work for whiskey?

Fingers: I don't think he would, no.

TommyO: Maybe I'll try it, tho.
         Farmboy would love to get that whiskey.

Fingers: Ya ever kiss a woman, son? Like outta nowhere.
          Say spontaneous.

TommyO: Wal', no ma'am, I never even kissed one
         outta courtin' and on purpose.

Fingers: Wal', I think it would be good.

TommyO: Wal', I guess it might.

Fingers: What if you were to try, you think, you could.

TommyO: No. Wal', with a bottle of that whiskey in me, maybe.

Fingers: That's what it would take?

(They might kiss here)

SCENE TEN:
A few minutes later, the sound of a blow and TOMMYO runs onstage...

TommyO: You don't kill a man 'cause he's got somethin' that you want and he's in yer way about it... I don't.

No. Ya ask him first, modest and humble about it, too... Like he lives in the big house and is wearin' somethin' cool lookin, silk maybe. And you, you're hot and sweatin' it up, mud on your hands, and grit in your teeth. 'Cause him havin' somethin,' somethin' that you need just to keep breathin,' that puts you in the place of askin, askin like a field hand, if that's what it takes. And it's right that you should...

That man, he got his, and that is the big house. I asked that James Small for a bottle a' that whiskey, and I told him straight out that I didn't have any a' that money, but what I did have was two good hands and a strong back. But he dinna say a thing, just smokin and starin out, so I asked

him again. Could we swap? Makin it plain?
My work for that bottle? An he just smoked, like
I wasn't talkin,' even…So I'm mad, and shoutin',
I was. I won't say I wasn't. "HEY BROTHER, I'M
TALKIN TO YOU."'An he says, just smokin now, flat,
like his face is dead and he's not showing it. "Work.
I don't need your work, I got my own. Now that
bottle, I got that, too… And you need that, see,
you're the one in need. And you're shouting."

But, just smokin, this James Small.
Not laughin,' just the smokin. So I donna get
what he's tellin' me. So I say, "I'm needin' that
there bottle, now…"

And it's true, 'cause FarmBoy's legs is all broke up,
and he needs that pain killin whiskey. But I donna
tell him why. I don't. That's my business, and I got
my business.

But this James Small, he says, "No can do."
Like it's a fly, my need, and he's flickin' it away.
James Small, not even lookin at me, but at the sky,
like there's somethin up there better'n me, more
worth a look, say…

So I say, "Brother, I gotta take it. That bottle."
And I go and do it. Not lookin.' Not catchin' his
eye, not pushin' him, there… 'Cause I know. I do.
But ready, like I'm hunchin up on the balls of my
feet to run, see… 'Cause that bottle gettin to
Farm Boy, that's the thing…

Still, I don't feel him comin, he's that fast…
Just BUMP, and there's his pistol, a pistol I have
never seen he had, even… jammed into the
back of my head.

"You'll put it down," James Small, he says.
"Can't. Can't do that," I say, I do…
Knowin' it's true.

And he just pulls. The trigger clacks, I hear that,
and I got one second, maybe, 'fore I meet my
maker. But no, the bullet hits that bone, the one at
the bottom of the skull now, and stops there. It's a
punch, now. I won't say it's not. Like a bull takin' a
brick to the head and almost goin down, but not
dead. I'm not. James Small, not even tensing he
figures I'm so dead, and I lay into him with that
bottle, killing him with that bottle. Hittin' 'em hard.
I'm all jacked up, with my head goin' bang, and
pounding. And I lay him out with that bottle,
killing him with that bottle. You kill a man who puts
a pistol on you and fires it, too. At least, I do…

I took two more bottles of that whiskey, call me
criminal now, and headed back to Farmboy.

SCENE ELEVEN:
Back at FARMBOY's boxcars, enter TOMMYO.

TommyO: Hey Farmboy, you were sleepin' brother, you were
sleepin, you said you wouldn't be a sleepin.'

Farmboy: TommyO, TommyO.

TommyO: You got to stay wide awake, Farmboy.
Workin that stew pot.

Farmboy: Mercy was here, and he said that, too.

TommyO: Mercy empty out that stew pot because I was hopin' for somethin' being gut empty all night, I was.

Farmboy: Wal', sure that's rabbit stew over there.

TommyO: You done good, Farmboy.

Farmboy: Wal', I'm thirsty... for whiskey, I guess that's what.

TommyO: You are, huh? And why's that?

Farmboy: Wal', just thought, you usually find something...

TommyO: *(Pulling out whiskey)* I do, and I have. One for you.

Farmboy: TommyO! TommyO!

TommyO: And one for me.

Farmboy: *(Drinking)* Man, that's beautiful.

Farmboy: You make it to the Violet side of town, TommyO?

TommyO: You know I did do that.

Farmboy: And how was it?

TommyO: Wal' how? It was beautiful, that's how.

Farmboy: Tell it, tell it.

TommyO: I worked my way up to the edge of the violet side, with all them big houses, remember how I told you they got those lawns, but cut short like hayfield after hayin' time and how all them lawns is all shiny and violet cause it's all violet over there, everything is. And this is the softer of them lawns, too. Like you coulda lied down without bustin' out in tears.

I really cried out a rainstorm, I do. You ever seen silk, Farmboy? Cause those lawns is like that silk.

Farmboy: *(Half remembering)* Silk? Like cotton?

TommyO: No. No. Silk that makes cotton look like mud, silk floats up and easy like there's a sweet south wind in it all the time.

Farmboy: Oh, man. Oh, man.

TommyO: Yeah. That silk is somethin' and this lawn is like that. Wal,' first I laid in it and then I rolled, shakin' off my clothes, too, so it was the softest thing this side of heaven all over me. I coulda stayed there, too, but I knew he'd be a waitin, and wantin' somethin, so I rolled up still naked, all the way along that lawn, so I got to the front of that house, and the window wasn't it wide open.

Farmboy: What you rolled up all that way?

TommyO: All that way.

Farmboy: Musta took an hour. At least alone like that.

TommyO: Two hours. Two and a half-hours. It took a minute. I swear. It did.

Farmboy: Man, that is some lawn.

TommyO: And there were nothin' rough about it, those two and a half hours, neither. It was a pleasure to do it, and I'd do it again tomorrow. I love that lawn.

Farmboy: Man.

TommyO: But that farmhouse now, that was the real picture. A big farmhouse, like a farmhouse castle, big farmhouse kings and queens up in there, big farmhouse dragons and wizards and if they weren't so magic and invisible you could spot them all. And what all else you could think of, it would be in the farmhouse. The windows were open. Long wood tables laid out with violet glasses, all shiny in the moon. And platters heaped up and up with ham and sweet potatoes, biscuits, and apple pie at every place. Deep dish ones, too. Still steamin.' Like someone just loved them outta the oven, and there's no one there, just empty. Like the castle farmhouse was waiting on TommyO to come on in and help himself to it.

Man, Farmboy, for a minute I couldn't even move for such plenty. All of it glowing like God was just beneath it, but I recollected myself cause of the sudden I hear voices—down the hall, like the kings and queens is deciding now to come into dinner. Movin' slow and leisure like cause there's plenty of food. Time. There's plenty of everything. And I have ham, biscuits, and pie. Pie, Farmboy.

(Laying the food out)

Farmboy: Oh my. Oh my.

TommyO: We'll eat for days off all this.

Farmboy: That's all, TommyO, cause I was hopin?

TommyO: Hopin' what, Farmboy. Whiskey? and here it is!

(Both drink and laugh)

SCENE TWELVE:
Both boys asleep, by the fire. FINGERS watching.

Fingers: I'd gone back to watch them wolves getting there, as that TommyO had killed all the pups.

Pups'll die easy them not knowin anything and not runnin away, even... That drunken boy was too much for that "he" and "she" wolf. Seein those pups smashed and broken red against that grey sky. A boy with a big stick and blood on his hands. That's hard to beat. And wolves will know that... but they will hang around on a moonless night, waiting for a wolf murderin boy to slip up drink too much or sleep to deep, then them wolfs will have their vengeance. I did not figure to wait that long.

(Slipping behind the scarecrow)

Fingers: Crack. Crack. Farm Boy. Crack. Crack.

Mercy: (*Slippin in*) They're sleepin' now, Fingers,
          comfortable. Hard times like these it's hard to get
          comfortable. You comfortable, Fingers?

Fingers: You here for me, Mercy?

Mercy: You ain't done nothin yet, Fingers, an' Lord God,
          I'm hopin' you leave it at that…
          Have a sit and we'll talk it through.

Fingers: I prefer to stand.

Mercy: FarmBoy's got some nice rabbit. I'm a smellin.'
          You hungry, now?

Fingers: Not for meat.

Mercy: Me, I always am. It's a mercy. I can find that food
          or I'd be miserable, hard times like these.

Fingers: Move outa' this, Mercy. I want Tommy. He's mine.

Mercy: You scarin' that Farmboy, though.
          He's a young one, and that ain't right.

Fingers: And here's the truth, if I'm ever going to get to it.
          I like the relations, the smooth and regular of
          them, riding that animal inside that was… mine.

          All the God given pleasure that a man don't see,
          and he knows nothing of, either.

          My husband didn't come in at midnight. I lay in
          bed… And I figured him leanin' on his stoop,
          shadow goin' nowhere, the white gray of his
          smoke twisting up into that purple sky…

(Long pause)

But he didn't come, and I knew. Just layin' in the bed feelin' that pleasure go out of my body, the longer I waited, 'till I got to thinkin' maybe it will never come back. And that scared me.
So I got up. By now the morning birds were singin,' one of them open and insane, shrieking, a drunk man who had just found out the truth and can't stand what he knows.

There was light in the sky: red, squeezed tight, and seeping in around the edges. Blood in the water after the fish has been gutted…My husband wasn't on his stoop, but inside through the door, on the floor…

I saw him like that and hung back, knowing what was done. And then I buried him. That took days. But I didn't notice now; I stopped sleeping at night, staying away from the bed. Feeling the pleasure of that animal inside slide away, my fingers; twisting in that long hair…

Then I heard from one of the farm hands that TommyO had been seen running away from that blue side of town, two bottles of whiskey in his hands, and I knew…

That's the story as I know, and I know it true.

Mercy: It would have to be. I figured pretty much that way: hard times like these. The farm hands wanted to figure it something wilder, strangers with wild eyes and fiery vengeance in their hearts, but I knowed it would turn up somethin simpler. Just one of the folks goin after another, all over not havin enough and wantin more. Hard times like this, it would have to be... What you aim to do now, Fingers? Kill him, flat and final?

Fingers: Haven't thought it through.

Mercy: Lord God, I wish you would, now...
You kill him, I'd hafta come after you.

Fingers: I know it...

Mercy: He's a boy, roughin' it thru some hard times.
One that meant you no harm.

Fingers: Harm is what he gave me, though.

Mercy: I'm askin' you, as a mercy to me, then.

Fingers: You? Who are you to ask?

Mercy: We're friends, Fingers. Neighbors.

Fingers: Friends? Mercy, we're not friends. You gonna come to me, after midnight, and every night, fulla relations regular as rain, like a bright moon on a windy night? Most men don't know how a woman waits, but my husband, he knew.
He was cold as a knife blade on a winter night, but he knew. You gonna be that man, Mercy? That man my husband was?

Mercy: James Small, now he wouldna 'a wanted it this-a-way. Lord God, he wouldna.

Fingers: That man? My husband wouldn't even give it notice one way or the other. "Fingers you'll never love another man," like he knew somethin' I didn't want what he had. Needed it, too. It was me who lost, Mercy, me, and I had it to lose. That's not right.

Mercy: So why not just do it, then? So clear and all that. Why play with this Farm Boy, and cause him fear and fright? Thas' not right, Fingers. The Lord God knows it's not.

Fingers: Takes time, though, and a change of manner to work up to killin' a man, to teach that grief inside you to step aside and leave room for somethin' like vengeance. And maybe this Farmboy, being beloved of that TommyO, maybe he's earned his share of the blame, and hurtin,' too.

Mercy: He's a boy, though, hurtin', and not doin' much a' anything. It's not right, no how.

Fingers: Wal', it's not fair and proper, maybe, living… Still, there's a way, and maybe it's natural that way… Hurt for hurt.

Mercy: I canna abide it, though, Fingers. You're not crazy. Now I kin see that much.

Fingers: No. I'm not crazy.

Mercy: I'm tellin' you to put this aside.

Fingers: Or what? You gonna stop me, Mercy? You're not much of a lawman. You even have a gun?

Mercy: I could go and get one. Lord God, I could.

Fingers: You're not much of any kind of man, is what I think.
           See, I had one in my husband, James Small.
           And I know how that is.

Mercy: You griefin' enough to kill over a man.
           Where's the Mercy in that?

Fingers: How does a boy break both legs, Mercy?
           You ask your TommyO that. Crack. Crack.

SCENE THIRTEEN:
FARMBOY at the soup pot.

Farmboy: TommyO was right, tho. It got so them bones
           started mending and I got to like those shakes,
           the blood shaking thru. TommyO was strong
           and he could shake a fella…
           How he did it, gettin strong like that, I donna know.

           Before I broke them legs up I had a life, one I'd like
           to remember. I drank whiskey I know that much.
           And liked it too… Now I hunt rabbit and squirrel,
           crawling on my hands and elbows from one side
           of that clearing to the other, whistling 'em up.
           (Catches something, breaks its legs.)

           Donna like that killing. Makes my stomach flip and
           fly around in my body, 'cause I'm whistling 'em up
           sweet. Talking at 'em and the critters are always
           good like children, or clouds, or the way the wind
           blows when you get to crying all lonesome and

up in yourself. But Tommyo says I gotta do it.
'Cause we gotta eat and them critters
donna know nothing anyhow.
Me, I think they do… I seen their eyes…

Fingers: Crack. Crack. Farmboy.

Farmboy: What's that now? You ghosts, you get away.

Fingers: Did you tell him, Farmboy, that TommyO?
Did you tell him I am coming
and it's him I am after?

Farmboy: I did tell him, I did, but he says scarecrows don't
figure into any of this and they canna talk
nevermind it, I was to let it go.

Fingers: CRACK! CRACK! *(FINGERS goes)*

Farmboy: Now I was right scaret with all this crack crack
comin'and goin,' too scared to eat on anything but
TommyO he says I need that eatin' fore i can get
them legs to heal proper and i was to keep at that
soup pot and i figure i will like the way that meat
feels when it hits the belly…

Once I get that rabbit or squirrel or bird I cook'er
slow, getting that soup pot to go to boiling and
taking that time. It's hours before TommyO comes
back, and he likes it tender…

My cookin' brings out the neighbors, them wolves
I hear sniffin in the bushes. And this two footed
one comin' here, he's always hungry… And a
lawman, too, seems like. TommyO, says we treat
him careful.

Mercy: *(Sniffing the air)* Is that rabbit?
           Am I smellin' rabbit, Farmboy? You tell me.

Farmboy: Sure it is, Mercy.

Mercy: Well, mercy, mercy me…
           The smell alone could sustain a man,
           a Lord God lovin' man. Do I look proper and fit?
           Feeling lean and hungry, too hard times like these.

Farmboy: You look sharp, Mercy.

Mercy: That's a blessing, then. Good bones'll tell.
           But tidy? Tidied up? Farm Boy?

Farmboy: Tight and tidy, Mercy.

Mercy: Thank you, Farm Boy. You are a mercy you are.
           It's hard times. Hard times to look proper and fit.
           I could use some of that rabbit.

Farmboy: I'm sure-a-that.

Mercy: O, I would enjoy that rabbit.

Farmboy: You gotta wait on TommyO, though. Dinner time.

Mercy: Of course. I'm not rushing to dine. Still… I am
           hungry now and I do have to see that TommyO.
           A small piece, say, a shank or two?

Farmboy: TommyO says to wait, though.

Mercy: O, well. TommyO. Sure. I'd like to see him.

Farmboy: Sure...

Mercy: I'd wait to see him. Still, I could offer something
for the table... Green apples, say.

Farmboy: They're green? Really green?

Mercy: Well, they are not from here, Farm Boy.
I am a mobile man. I can move around.
See? Green!

Farmboy: Brother, that's a nice color.

Mercy: So, a clean swap then. Green apple for a shank
or two of that delicious hare?

Farmboy: Well, now. I got an apple just last week...

Mercy: You did? You did? You're saying no to a good
green apple, Farmboy?

Farmboy: Well, not exactly, but–

Mercy: I've got chocolate.

Farmboy: What?

Mercy: One bar, and it's still wrapped up.

Farmboy: You steal it, Mercy?

Mercy: Not likely, that. Me bein' a lawman, part time.
An' a good neighbor, too.

Farmboy: 'Cause TommyO says we don't steal nothing,
           that stealing brings trouble.
           And we donna want trouble. We don't.

Mercy: Brother. Amen to that. We don't. We are in
           agreement as to that. Still. It's chocolate, Farm
           Boy. Fine chocolate an' a mercy to the tongue.

Farmboy: Chocolate.

Mercy: CHOCOLATE, CHOCOLATE, CHOCOLATE.

Farmboy: All right, we swap it up.

Mercy: Yes, brother. Yes. We do!

           (Both eat happily.)

Mercy: That rabbit muscle will put muscle on your muscle.

Farmboy: This chocolate tastes better than anythin'
           I ever put my mouth to.

Mercy: It's a mercy a sweet like that.

Farmboy: A mercy and a miracle, like God's been
           a driftin' and a dreamin' with all that food.
           But now here she's a'comin, the real deal,
           and better than anything.

Mercy: Well, you are a young man, and heapin' it on,
           Farm Boy… Lord God. It's a mercy to
           hear a happy man.

Farmboy: That's how I figure it. I do.

Mercy: Yes, brother, a happy man, and with those busted
up legs... How does a boy get two busted legs?
Do you know?

Farmboy: Nothin to know. Just BOOM! one day, busted up.

Mercy: Well, sure. But did you fall? Get kicked by a horse?
A man doesn't just wake up busted up; he wakes
up and gets busted up. It's how he gets there.
That's what I'm askin.'

Farmboy: I donna know... I...
You best ask TommyO, I donna know.

Mercy: TommyO, he was there?

Farmboy: He found me there. And. 'Fore that I donna know.
Blue sky. Red eyes. Head spinnin. Crack. Crack.
Thas what I know. I do.
(Starts to cry)

Mercy: Well, now. Farmboy. What you seein?
'Cause I just wanna know.

Farmboy: Crack! Crack!

Mercy: Well, sure.

Farmboy: Do scarecrows talk, Mercy? Do you think?

Mercy: I haven't seen it, no...

Farmboy: 'Cause this one does. And crack. Crack.
She's comin' for TommyO.

Mercy: Lord God, that will be somethin to see.

Farmboy: I'm scared, though.
Scared through and through. I am.

Mercy: Hard times like these, brother, it'd be hard not
to be. What age you say you was, Farmboy?

Farmboy: 15. TommyO figures. 15 or thereabouts.

Mercy: Well, sure. Then you'd be a boy still, Farm Boy.
A boy'll get scared, and it's a blessing, too...
'Cause he'd be learnin with it,
that scared would be a teacher, say.

Farmboy: I aint thought about it, I aint.
Not like that. It's just... scared.

Mercy: You sleep much at night, Farm Boy?
'Cause it's night now... And boys now,
you boys get to sleep at night.

Farmboy: I'm waitin' on TommyO. He says to.

Mercy: Long nights, now... With these hard times folks
don't go out much, come sundown.

Farmboy: I guess not, no.

Mercy: Lord God, how they do stay put!
No money, is how I see it.

Farmboy: Sure. I do.

Mercy: The nights get long, if you're not one for sleeping. Lonely, I'd say.

Farmboy: Sure, they do.

Mercy: You sleep much, FarmBoy?

Farmboy: Not me, not with these legs I don't...
That pain'll keep you up.

Mercy: Sure, it will... TommyO keeps you company, though. You're not alone.

Farmboy: He goes a lot, you know. All over blue and gold and violet, too...
you ever see that violet side of town?

Mercy: Sure, I go... It's beautiful...
The sky is somethin' a' course, but the air...
Brother, that's a mercy, soft and easy on a man, breathin' in violet...

Farmboy: Wal,' I'd like that. Easy. I would.

Mercy: Air like that, a man can sleep, and dream, too.
No matter what the pain he's in.

Farmboy: Wal,' I'd like that sleepin.'

Mercy: Well, sure, I'm ready to go up that road and find that TommyO, leave you laying down 'cause that sleepin, it's a Mercy...

Farmboy: Mending up, I guess
(Mercy goes)

TommyO: (Entering quiet) Farmboy, Farmboy…
what did that Mercy want with us?

Farmboy: Wal' he's wantin to talk to you, TommyO?

TommyO: Is that particular, that it was me?

Farmboy: Seems to be, and that scarecrow
he's been lookin,' too. Talkin' at me.

TommyO: Them scarecrows they don't talk, I told you that.

Farmboy: She does, tho.

TommyO: How's them legs?

Farmboy: Mended up, I guess

TommyO: (Picking FARMBOY up) We gotta go, Farmboy,
we gotta go now,

(Enter FINGERS)

Fingers: Crack Crack.

Farmboy: O god, O god, that's scary!

TommyO: (Alert and ready to fight) Who is that? Who's there?

Fingers: You know me, TommyO.

TommyO: Wal,' we did that washin' together and you were kind to me, kind to a poor boy in a hard time. I remember. And grateful.

Fingers: *(Showing James Small's gun)* Still, that's not all of it, TommyO, you seen this before?

TommyO: I have, if it's that James Small's gun.

Fingers: It is. You killed my husband. He wasn't much in the way of kindness, but he was my husband. Mine.

TommyO: I didn't mean it tho, ma'am. I'd take it back if I could ma'am, I would.

Fingers: You ever lay up all night, night after night, with the moon in your bed, wrapping you and making you soft and full of light but knowin' that your man is gone for good and you'll never never have that love inside you again? Not ever in this life.

TommyO: I never have, ma'am, and I can't figure it, but I'm sorry. I'm sorry.

Fingers: You're sorry? It's not enough tho.

TommyO: No.

Fingers: You put that Farmboy down now.

Farmboy: Don't do it, TommyO. Don't you do it.

TommyO: I'll keep him here then, ma'am.

Fingers: *(Putting the gun to TOMMYO's head)*
           You know any prayers? Best just to say it now.

TommyO: Don't a figure God's much for
           beginners, tho. I don't.

           (Enter MERCY)

Mercy: Wal'lll now, lord god, I'm not too late, that's a
           Mercy. I went and got me a gun of my own, so
           I figured I'd be law man enough to stop you now.
           You best give up that gun.

Fingers: I don't think I will, tho—something not right
           and I won't have it. You won't shoot a woman.
           Would you, Mercy?

Mercy: Lord God, I don't wish to find out. I don't.

Fingers: Still, now's the time, I guess.

           (Both fire shots. BLACKOUT...)

SCENE FOURTEEN:
*FARMBOY alone, FINGERS alone, MERCY alone
facing the audience.*

Farmboy: About this time, we stopped livin on the gray side
           of town. We moved away from those box cars, too.

           Riding first in Mercy's cart. He'd rebuilt it just in
           case. Then when TommyO swelled down to right
           size, TommyO he worked up a kind of papoose,

so he could sling me on his back. James Small's
gun knew TommyO's head and must have liked it
because it misfired once again, TommyO feeling
popped and dizzy, the bullet just punchin' the back
of Tommy's skull and not plowing through. And
Fingers she weren't to die neither. Mercy being
more of a farmer than a lawman he'd loaded up
on rock salt that stung like a wasps nest, Fingers
said, with enough force to knock her over. When
the smoke cleared, she climbed back up, still
wanted to be fierce but the wind all took out of
her sails what with TommyO shakin his head and
still standin there, that's how Mercy figured it to
go, I guess.

Mercy: Lord God a mercy I'm a thankful man.
            What with everybody gettin' through
            that in one piece. No harm done.

Fingers: I could go over to the violet side of town
            and get me a gun that works.

Mercy: Still it's a mercy that gun didn't go. So's I won't
            be havin' to hang ya anytime real soon, a smart
            woman like you. It would be a mercy to us all
            if you would just see it.

Fingers: I'm still short a husband. My bed is cold.
            Nothing right there.

Mercy: Wal'lll, I have been thinkin' on that and
            given it some thought.

Fingers: Then you have been busy.

Mercy: I don't a do much around midnight, most times. And those relations could be a mercy and a blessing in hard times like these to a grateful man, if you could see your way to it.

Fingers: You ain't much of a man, tho, seems like.

Mercy: That could be, still, I might be the best one askin hard times like these, and I was man enough to knock you down with my shotgun and never blink over it.

Fingers: Wal', you were that.

Farmboy: And on and on they courted each other, until they decided to give each other a go with the relations and just get me and TommyO outta town and see just how quick everybody would forget about James Small's death. Seems like only Fingers thought about him at all, and now with Mercy with her, she'd have her hands full.

I broke down and I cried when they said we could not ride through the blue side of town and on into that violet side what with TommyO having lifted all that ham and biscuits and sweet whiskey.

Mercy figured them kings and queens of the violet side of town would still be on the lookout for me and TommyO. Oh, but brother I did want to roll naked on one a them silk lawns with the sky so violet and the moonlight rollin' so soft all around me. I can see it still. The violet place like that if I close my eyes and look careful.

— THE END —

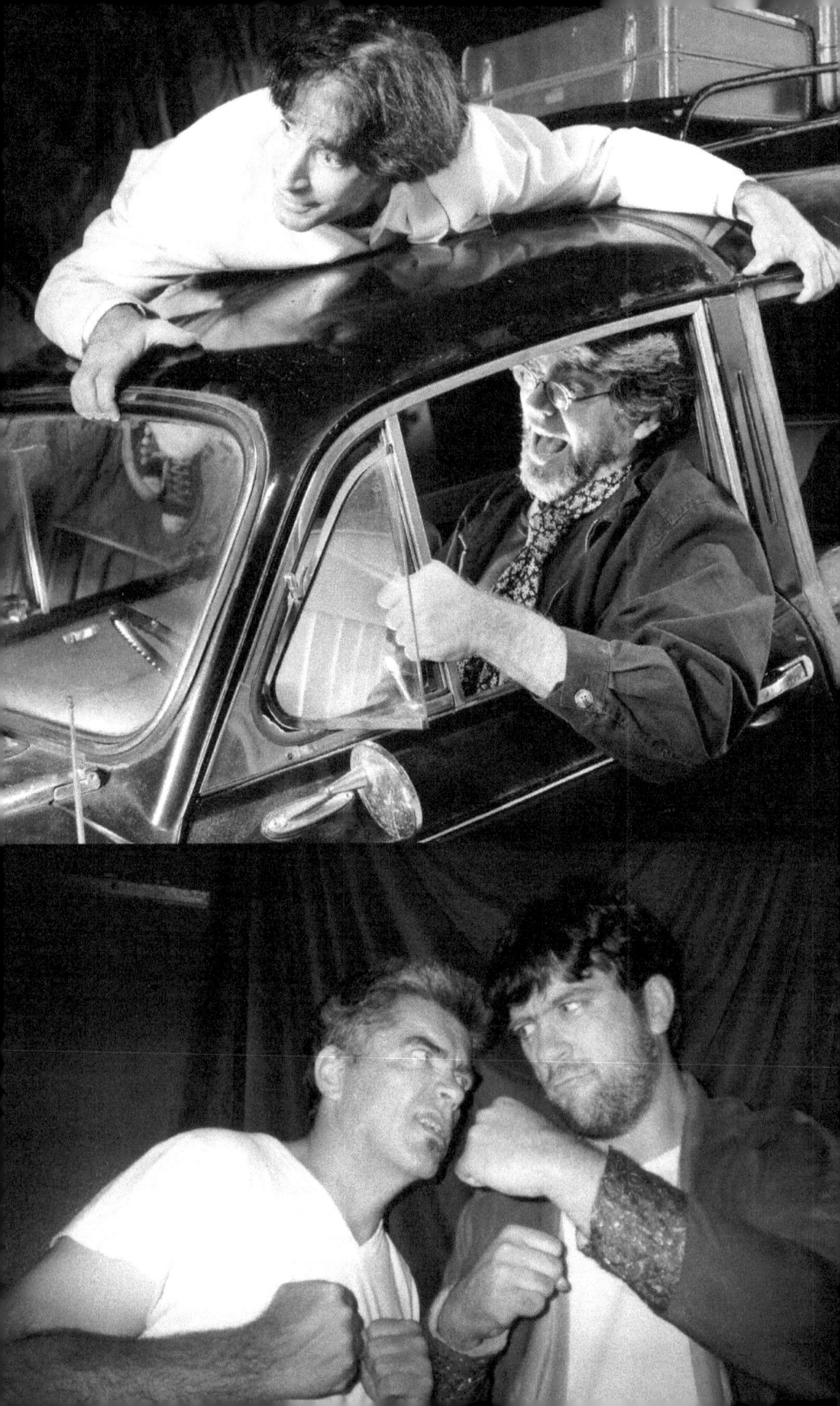

1991 to 2024

Memoribilia
& Ephemera

photo: Iwona Biedermann

434

LEFTY FIZZLE (*Beau's alter-ego/doppleganger*)
frontman of Maestro Subgum and the Whole, Chicago, 1989

Curious Theatre Branch started as a spin-off from my band: Maestro Subgum and The Whole

at the end of the eighties. Maestro was a good band then but more interested in swagger, drinking and making each other laugh than rehearsing or doing plays. I had met Jenny and invited her to work with us, she was billed as a special guest for those few years, we made two pieces as The Curious Theatre Branch: ITS ALL THE SAME FUCKING DAY which was just me, Jenny and the pianist Joe Huppert and FIVE VISIONS by Bertolt Brecht, which was me, Jenny, and Colm, who was still a kid.

By the time we wrote CAREENING IS A SKILL the band was in disarray, soon to be rebuilt even better! ….the Curious Theatre Branch moved quickly then, making plays fast; me, Jenny and Bryn Magnus providing scripts at— in retrospect—a breakneck pace. We had rent to pay and were chasing the pace of our peers, *Theater Oobleck*, who produced a lot of plays and had a lot of good writers in their group…

BEAU & COLM
Waiting for Godot

BEAU & MIKI
Musical Collaborators

TATTERED & WINCING by Beau O'Reilly, 2017

THE DOROTHY PROJECT
by Beau O'Reilly, 2003
Kat McJimsey

BEAU & JENNY: A PARTNERSHIP

Beau in consort with Jenny has explored, organically nurtured and defined a life of artistic collaboration in the realms of theatre, music, writing, teaching and in many dedicated forms of creative, family and community building.

The Curious Theatre Branch is often called a creative family...

Beau O'Reilly **STUDIO PORTRAIT**
/ by Joe Mazza, 2012

The Curious Theatre Branch is moving!
Farewell to Lunar Cabaret
Hello Rogers Park

New Moon
Vaudeville Benefit

Sat. Feb. 1st
TWO SHOWS!
7:00 P.M.
& 10:00 P.M.

featuring:

Ira Glass
Michael Zerang
Jamie O'Reilly
Greg Allen
Theater Oobleck
John Starrs · Cin Salach
Jeff Kowalkowski · Idris Goodwin
Kate O'Reilly, Michael & Max Greenberg
the Curious Theatre Branch
and special guests!

The Lunar Cabaret
2827 N. Lincoln Ave 60657

773.327.6666
call for reservations

$25 *or pay what you can*
(donations are tax deductible
and also accepted via mail)

www.curioustheaterbranch.com

THE SPEW POLICE...
SUFFERGUSH RETURNS & TWO-WHEELS GOOD
Mark Comiskey & Beau O'Reilly, 1994

THE WEIRDLY SISTERS
by Bryn Magnus
Theater Oobleck
Chicago, 1990

photos: Phil Cantor

CHICAGO'S RHINOFEST

At 35+ years and counting, the festival is Chicago's largest & longest running fringe festival that features works in theater and performance from Chicago companies and national artists alike.

logo:

The **RHINOCEROS THEATER FESTIVAL** began in 1988 as an offshoot of the Bucktown Arts Fest. In its first year it featured just two days of performances, including work by Beau O'Reilly and Jenny Magnus. When the founder moved away in 1990, he asked Beau O'Reilly and a ragtag group of local artists to keep the festival going, and Rhino Fest was born. The Curious Theatre Branch went on to produce the Rhino across many neighborhoods and venues over the years. The festival has platformed hundreds of local, international, emerging & established artists. Today the festival continues to foster Chicago's fringe theater arts community.

CROWTOWN by Beau O'Reilly, 1997
Colm O'Reilly, Jenny Magnus, Mark Komiskey, Beau O'Reilly, Vernon Tongues

BOY BASEMENT BATTLES THE DEMONS OF SLEEP
Colm O'Reilly & Guy Massey, 1994

THE SKRIKER by Caryl Churchill
Bethany Arrington (top) & Julie Williams
(bottom) Prop Thtr, Chicago, 2019

photos: Jeff Bivens

RUCK IN PIECES by Beau O'Reilly
Guy Massey (above) & Guy with Beau (below)
Lunar Cabaret, Chicago, 2001

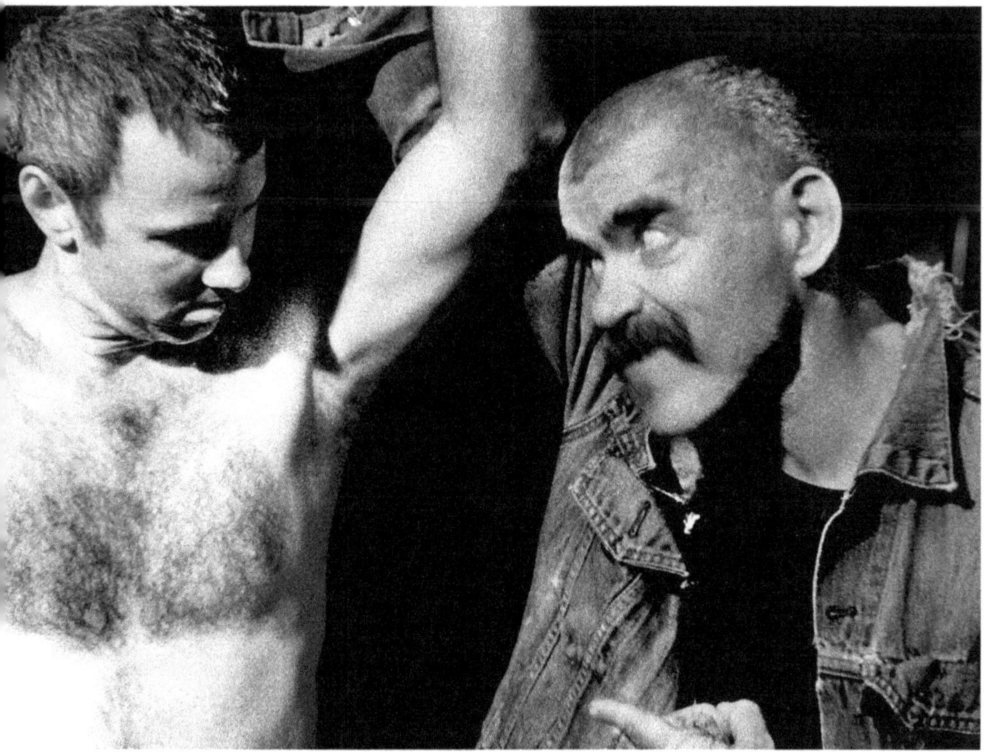

BEAU & JENNY, PUBLICITY STILL
for the PAC/Edge Festival, Chicago Athenaeum, 2004

SNAPSHOT Pre-Curious 1981 / **TRUCK IN PIECES** Sue Cargill 2002
NOT ONLY SLEEPING John Starrs & Beau O'Reilly, Lunar Cabaret 1993
PLAYING GOD Dir. by Matt Rieger, Prop Thtr 2015   447

photos: Kristin Basta

ENDGAME - **1991** by Samuel Beckett **/** Curious Theatre Branch–North Avenue
Dir. by Winifred O'Reilly w/ Chris O'Reilly, Beau O'Reilly, Trina O'Reilly, Ned O'Reilly

<< **ENDGAME** - **2006** by Samuel Beckett **/** Prop Thtr–Elston Avenue
Dir. by Jeff Bivens & Jayita Bhattacharya w/ Guy Massey, Beau O'Reilly,
Teresa Weed, Matt Wilson top: Guy & Beau / bottom: Jeff & Jayita rehearsal

PLAYING GOD
by Matt Rieger, Nov 2015, Prop Thtr
Photo by Jeffrey Bivens

STUDIO PORTRAIT
/ by Joe Mazza, 2012

LAST WEEK >>
Prop Thtr, 2016

RHINOCEROS by Eugene Ionesco
27th annual Rhinofest: Curious Ionesco Festival / Prop Thtr, 2016

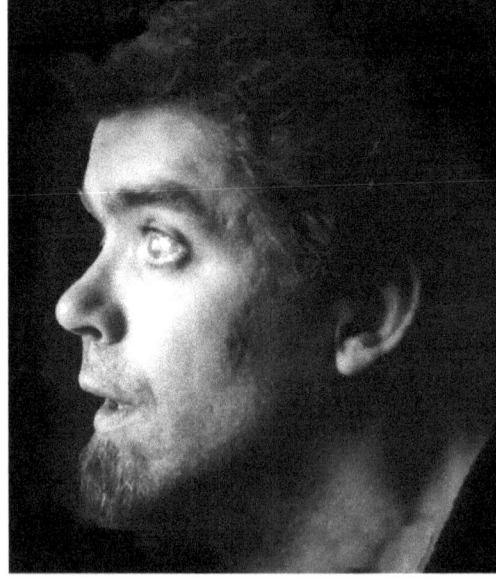

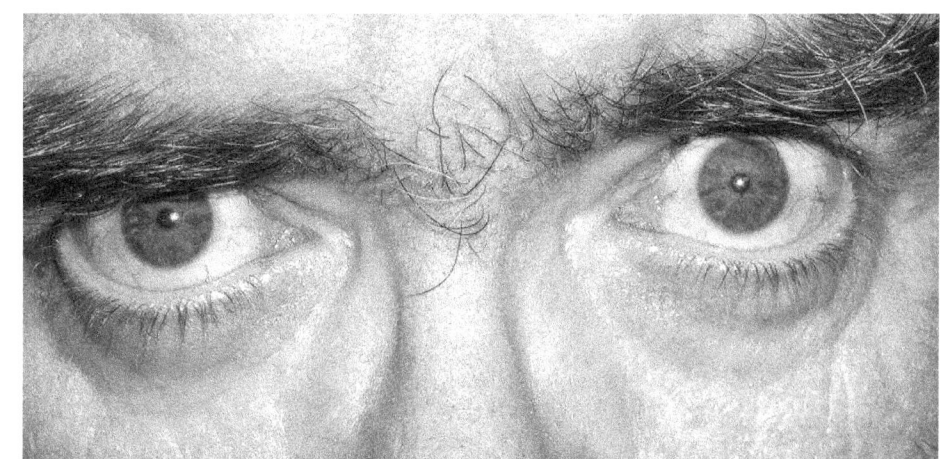

"THE FRINGE DWELLERS" profile by Justin Hayford in
CHICAGO SOCIAL magazine / Chicago, 2001

overleaf spread: **BEAU & JENNY** PORTRAIT by Joe Mazza, 2012

previous spread: **FOUR STORY ANIMAL**, 2020 / Kat McJimsey & Beau in
NOT ONLY SLEEPING, 1993 / Beau in **ENDGAME**, 1991 / BEAU'S STARE /
Beau & Julie in **PLAYING GOD**, 2015 *(written & directed by Matt Reiger)* /
Lefty Fizzle fronts **MAESTRO SUBGUM & THE WHOLE**, 1988 / Beau & Jenny in
THE TRIPS: A MADRAS PARABLE, 1996 *(written & directed by Jenny Magnus)*

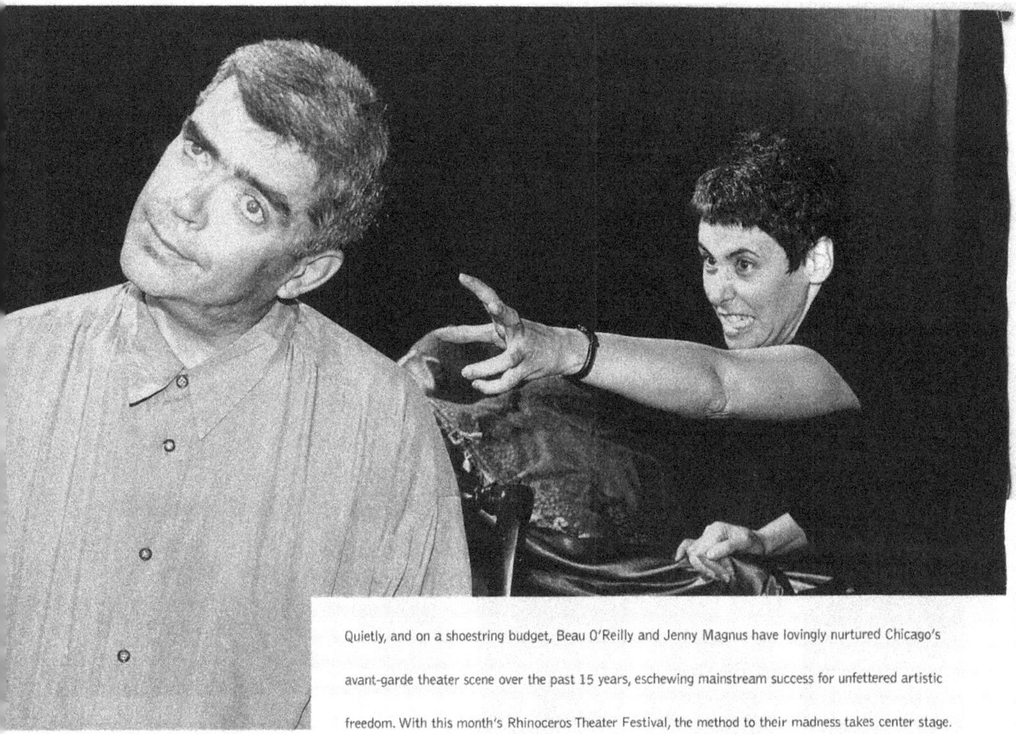

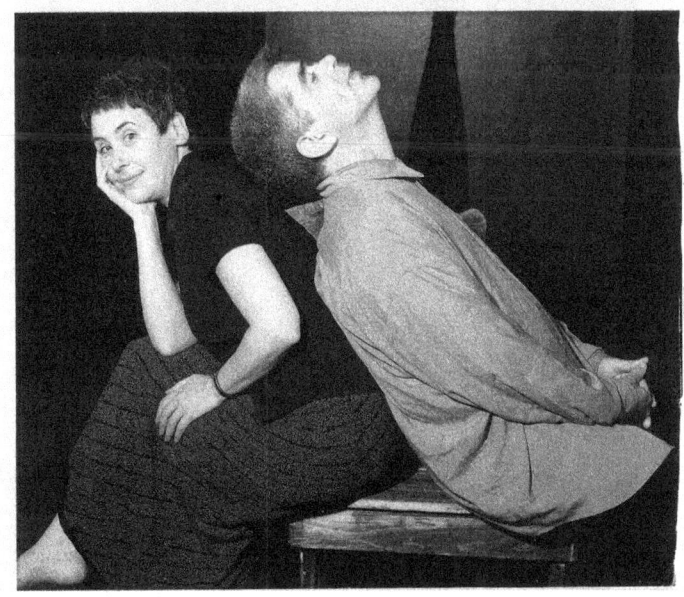

Quietly, and on a shoestring budget, Beau O'Reilly and Jenny Magnus have lovingly nurtured Chicago's

avant-garde theater scene over the past 15 years, eschewing mainstream success for unfettered artistic

freedom. With this month's Rhinoceros Theater Festival, the method to their madness takes center stage.

THE FRINGE DWELLERS   BY JUSTIN HAYFORD   PORTRAITS BY ROBERT WARNER

It would be difficult to find a group of people more exhausted in appearance than those crammed into the Lunar Cabaret tonight. Tucked away in a tiny Lakeview storefront on a strip of Lincoln Avenue once dominated by gay leathermen, this hub of Chicago's fringe theater scene feels jam-packed when 40 audience members show up at curtain time. But on this Monday evening in June it takes only six members of the venerable and iconoclastic Curious Theatre Branch huddled around a makeshift conference table to fill every inch of available space. The rest is taken up by the workaday mayhem of power tools, lighting instruments, loose-leaf scripts, take-out food, metal chairs, and a massive, unfinished set for a play scheduled to open in 10 days.

The Curious Theatre Branch has always fed on exhaustion. Under the unofficial tutelage of co-founders Jenny Magnus and Beau O'Reilly (the group has no hierarchical structure, so no one is truly "in charge") this small but dedicated band of avant-garde alchemists has boiled gritty street lyricism in dense literary torrents to produce some 57 imaginative, uncategorizable plays in 13 years. All were original works mounted on shoestrings. Like most members of the troupe, Magnus and O'Reilly have spent those years writing, performing, directing, designing,

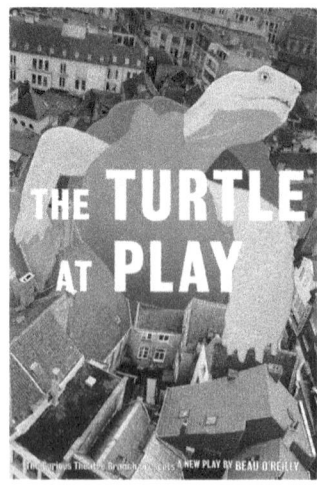

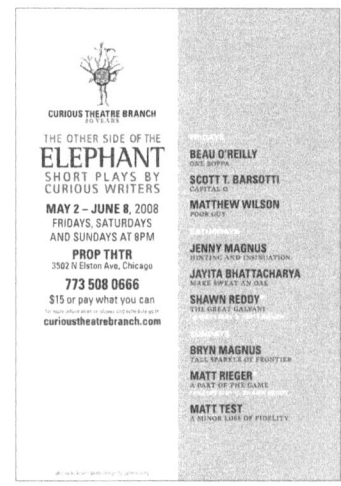

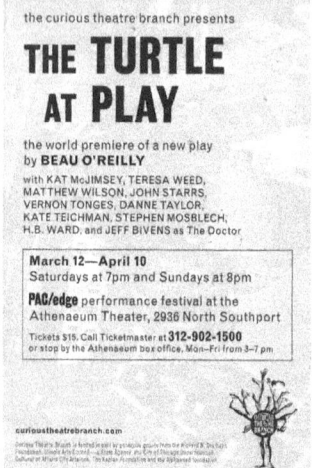

This spread & overleaf: Gallery of **BEAU'S CURIOUS PLAYS** 1991-2024

CURIOUS THEATRE BRANCH presents

OUR KATE TAKES A TRIP

a play by beau O'REILLY
directed by matt RIEGER
costumes by diane HAMM
stage manager: marlana may CARLSON

the players
stefan BRUN as DANDY
brian COLLINS as SAM
courtney KEARNEY as EMILY
judith HARDING as KATE
beau O'REILLY as SLUGGO
matt RIEGER as KK
john STARRS as WILL
john STARRS as 1st BARKEEP
john STARRS as 2nd BARKEEP

welcome to...

TATTERED and WINCING

a new play by Beau O'Reilly

Brought to you by the Curious Theatre Branch

A BEAU O'REILLY STORY AN

LAST WEEK

A NEW PLAY WRITTEN AND STAGE

BEAU O'REI

Technical Director Marlana Ca

ACTORS: Stefan Brün + Brook Celeste + Charlotte Hamilton +
Harding + Cat Jarboe + Barry Lohman + Lyle Mays + Shala M
Beau O'Reilly + Briavael O'Reilly + Winifred O'Reilly + Zelma O
+ Mike O'Brien + Matt Rieger + Julie Williams + Ryan V

BEAU O'REILLY IN THE ROLE OF A LIFETIME,
IN A NEW PLAY BY MATT RIEGER.

CURIOUS THEATRE BRANCH PRESENTS

PLAYING GOD

NOV 13–DEC 20 PROP THTR CURIOUSTHEATREBRANCH.COM

Curious Theatre Branch presents

TATTERED AND WINCING

a comedy about endings without an ending
by Beau O'Reilly

APRIL 29–MAY 14, 2017

PROP THTR

Tickets & info at curioustheatrebranch.com

judith HARDING / beau O'REILLY
performing in

SIXTY STORY ANIMAL

four works by
samuel BECKETT
at a price even you can afford

WHAT IS THE WORD   / ROCKABY
TEXT FOR NOTHING: ONE / THE OLD TUNE

followed by special guest
KELLYANN CORCORAN's solo extravaganza
GO
with works by barrie COLE / diana SLICKMAN / beau O'REILLY

Friday – Sunday   March 21 – 23   @ 7pm

LINKS HALL, 3111 N Western

$15 or pay what'cha can

This project is produced by CURIOUS THEATRE BRANCH
www.curioustheatrebranch.com

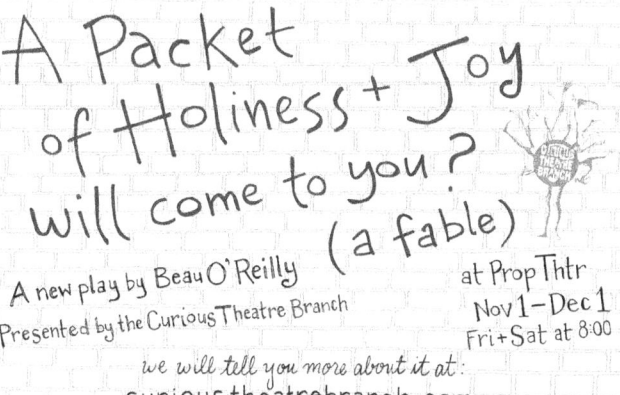

A Packet of Holiness + Joy will come to you? (a fable)

A new play by Beau O'Reilly
Presented by the Curious Theatre Branch

at Prop Thtr
Nov 1–Dec 1
Fri+Sat at 8:00

we will tell you more about it at:
curioustheatrebranch.com

IDLE THREATS

EVERYBODY HAS AN OPINION

Written by Idris Goodwin Directed by Stefan Brun
Starring Beau O'Reilly Ewa Boryczko Abby Cucci
Leo Asuncion and Idris Goodwin
Chicago Cultural Center - Studio Theater
Dec. 5 - Dec. 28
Thurdays and Fridays @ 7pm
Saturdays @ 4pm
78 East Randolph
$10 / $5 w/ student I.D.

Prop Theater
Jan. 10 - Feb
Fridays and Saturdays @ 8pm
Sundays @
4225 N. Lincoln Ave.
$10 General Admission

In association w/
Prop Theatre and

RATED

For Reservations and Information,
call 773-289-9506 or

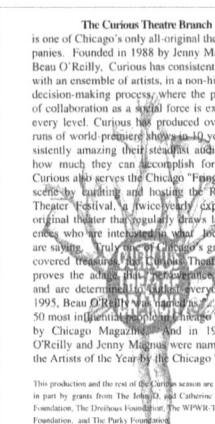

The Curious Theatre Branch
is one of Chicago's only all-original theater companies. Founded in 1988 by Jenny Magnus and Beau O'Reilly, Curious has consistently worked with an ensemble of artists, in a non-hierarchical decision-making process, where the philosophy of collaboration as a social force is explored on every level. Curious has produced over 40 full runs of world-premiere shows in 10 years, consistently amazing their steadfast audience with how much they can accomplish for so little. Curious also serves the Chicago "Fringe" theater scene by curating and hosting the Rhinoceros Theater Festival, a twice-yearly explosion of original theater that regularly draws large audiences who are interested in what local writers are saying. Truly one of Chicago's great undiscovered treasures, The Curious Theatre Branch proves the adage that "perseverance furthers", and are determined to tell everyone. In 1995, Beau O'Reilly was named as "one of the 50 most influential people in Chicago Theater..." by Chicago Magazine. And in 1996, Beau O'Reilly and Jenny Magnus were named among the Artists of the Year by the Chicago Tribune.

This production and the rest of the Curious season are made possible in part by grants from The John D. and Catherine T. MacArthur Foundation, The Dreihaus Foundation, The WPWR-TV Channel 50 Foundation, and The Parky Foundation.

For information and bookings, contact:
The Curious Theatre Branch
2827 N. Lincoln Avenue
Chicago IL 60657
773.327.0205
Jennlunar@extenct.com

The Third Degrees of J.O.Breeze
by Beau O'Reilly

August 20-30
New York Fringe
Theater Festival '98
Surf Realty
172 Allen Street
212.673.4182

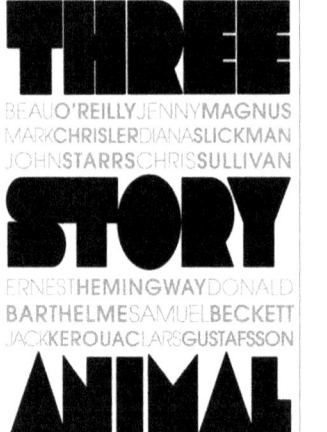

THREE
BEAU O'REILLY JENNY MAGNUS
MARK CHRISLER DIANA SLICKMAN
JOHN STARRS CHRIS SULLIVAN
STORY
ERNEST HEMINGWAY DONALD
BARTHELME SAMUEL BECKETT
JACK KEROUAC LARS GUSTAFSSON
ANIMAL
summer 2010 curioustheatrebranch.com

We lost a player, and that means we lost a play. What will we do now?

Mo and Motion sit on a bench, on a lawn, that is in Kansas. What have they seen?

Mark my words: If this play goes on longer than 42 minutes, I am walking off the stage. Pick it up, people.

APRIL 29 – MAY 14, 2017
curioustheatrebranch.com

TURN OFF YOUR PHONE, FRIEND

THERE IS NO INTERMISSION

THANK YOU FOR COMING

TATTTERED and WINCING
is...
Directed by Matt Rieger
Technical-Directioned by Marlana Carlson
Original-Musicked by Jenny Magnus
Beautifully Lit by Stefan Brün
with...
Props by Kate O'Reilly, Julie Williams, & Kelly Anchors
(that's a lot of clocks)
AND STARS...
Lyle Mays as Lyle/Armadillo/Coffeeshop Man
Barry Lohman as Barry/Armadillo/Coffee Man
Kelly Anchors as Kelly/Motion/Reva
Julie Williams as Julie/Narrator
Matt Rieger as Matt/Another Guy?/Nope Still Matt
AND!
Beau O'Reilly as Beau/Mo/The Old Man

the Curious Theatre Branch presents
whiskey in blue
...a play by Beau O'Reilly

FEATURING: KAT McCONNEY, PAUL LEISEN, KATHLEEN POWERS, and COLM O'REILLY
AT THE LUNAR CABARET
8:00PM FRIDAYS, SATURDAYS, and MONDAYS
2827 N LINCOLN AVE 773-327-6666
NOVEMBER 17 THROUGH DECEMBER 22

The Third Degrees of
J.O.Breeze
by Beau O'Reilly

Cast
Paul Tamney as J.O. Breeze
Bryn Magnus as Horace Treelander
Danny Thompson as The Captain
Marianne Fieber as Doris Doheny

Group Direction by
Beau O'Reilly and the cast (past and present)
Special Thanks to
Dana Wise, Ben Rayner, and Colm O'Reilly
Graphics by Colm O'Reilly

Come to Chicago and see The Curious Theatre Branch in
The Rhinoceros Theater Festival
September 11 to October 24
Performing *Small Together* by Bryn Magnus
and *7 Pounds of Mud* by Beau O'Reilly

462

THE CURIOUS THEATRE BRANCH PRESENTS
A NEW PLAY BY **BEAU O'REILLY**

TRUCK iN PIECES

A Tragic Comedy of Gentleness and Collapse

FEATURING BEAU O'REILLY, GUY MASSEY, AND SUE CARGILL ○ GROUP DIRECTED BY KAT McJIMSEY AND THE CAST
VIDEO BY ROBIN CLINE ○ SOUNDS BY COLM O'REILLY ○ SPECIAL APPEARANCE BY JOHN STARRS

PREVIEWS JULY 13 AND 14
JULY 20 – AUGUST 18
SATURDAYS 8:00PM ○ SUNDAYS 7:00PM
ADDITIONAL PERFORMANCES MONDAYS AUGUST 5 AND 12 7:00PM

THE LUNAR CABARET ○ 2827 NORTH LINCOLN AVE
INFO/RESERVATIONS: 773-327-6666 ○ $10 OR PAY WHAT YOU CAN

The Curious Theatre Branch presents

Truck in Pieces
a Tragic Comedy of Gentleness and Collapse

written by Beau O'Reilly

Truck	Beau O'Reilly
Rita	Sue Cargill
Father, Joey Buzz, Rodney, Hazel, Stiv, Eddie, Old Susan	Guy Massey
Judge, Waitress, Stage Manager	Katharine McJimsey

special appearances by John Starrs and Leo Asuncion

group directed by Kat McJimsey and the cast

lights: Kat McJimsey and Stefan Brün

video: Robin Cline

set stuff: Guy Massey and Kat McJimsey

poster/sounds: Colm O'Reilly
sounds include: Paul Butterfield's Better Days "It All Comes Back" Bobby Charles/Paul Butterfield
Muddy Waters "Why are People Like That" Bobby Charles
Glenn Gould "Sinfonia 9 in F minor" "Sinfonia 13 in A minor" J. S. Bach

typing, mailing and press: Michael Martin

outside eyes:
Teresa Weed, Colm O'Reilly, Michael Martin, Jenny Magnus, Stefan Brün

Sue thanks Fritz, Guy thanks KLB, Lisa thanks Crystal

writer's storytelling influences and help:
Barry Rosen, Joe Cardello, Michael Meyers, Jeff Oakes, Cassius Clay, Sonny Liston

story notes:
Kat McJimsey, Guy Massey, Sue Cargill, Teresa Weed, Winifred O'Reilly,
John Starrs, Shawn Reddy, Robin Cline, Jenny Magnus, Stefan Brün

This is The Curious Theatre Branch's 60th production.

See Bryn Magnus' new play in the Rhinoceros Theater Festival (Sept/Oct)

Take a Curious School acting class in the fall. Call Beau. 773.327.6666

The Curious Theatre Branch is:
Mark Comiskey, Marianne Fieber, Hallie Gordon, Paul Leisen, Bryn Magnus,
Jenny Magnus, Kat McJimsey, Beau O'Reilly, Colm O'Reilly, Shawn Reddy

Curious is funded in part by The Richard H. Driehaus Foundation,
The Gaylord and Dorothy Donnelly Foundation, and The Illinois Arts Council, a State Agency.

RHINO ART
by Sue Cargill 2016

HIT ME LIKE A FLOWER was remounted at Facility Theater in 2024

33 yrs later... after it premiered at Curious Theatre Branch-Morse Ave. in 1991

top: **HIT ME LIKE A FLOWER** 1991 & **EVANSTON OVER THERE** 2012
bottom: **ENDGAME** 1991 & **TALKING ABOUT GODARD** 1999

Beau O'Reilly in **HIT ME LIKE A FLOWER** / Facility Theater, Chicago 2024
facing page: as Lefty Fizzle, frontman for Maestro Subgum and the Whole 1999 >>

OUTRODUCTION

the Author's
AFTERWORD

I have written something like 80 plays, so

choosing this group of 14 for the books was both fun & impossible…

I wanted to represent my work from all periods and choose some of the two character plays, some ten actor ensemble pieces, some solo pieces. The oldest play dates back to 1991 and the most recent 2024… some of my favorite work didn't make this cut, the collaborations with **Jenny** and **Julie Williams**, **James Joyce** and **Shakespeare** seemed to warrant their own volume, the *Madelyn Plays* and the *Dorothy Project* are each over a hundred pages long and would have knocked out a lot of plays that did make it…so,…two more volumes to come!

Looking at all these plays and working on them again has been revitalizing and I am grateful to **Jackleg Press** and **Jen Harris** for their enthusiasm, to **Jason Greenberg** and **Art Works Design** for his book design and production skills. The School of the Art Institute of Chicago (SAIC) which gave me a modest grant. Oh, and special thanks to the **Amandes** brothers: **Paul and Tom**, to the playwright **Idris Goodwin**, **Drs. Henry Finn and Fred Ettner**, **Bill W**, who I forgot to add to the other lists…

…you all kept me going in times that might have been impossible.

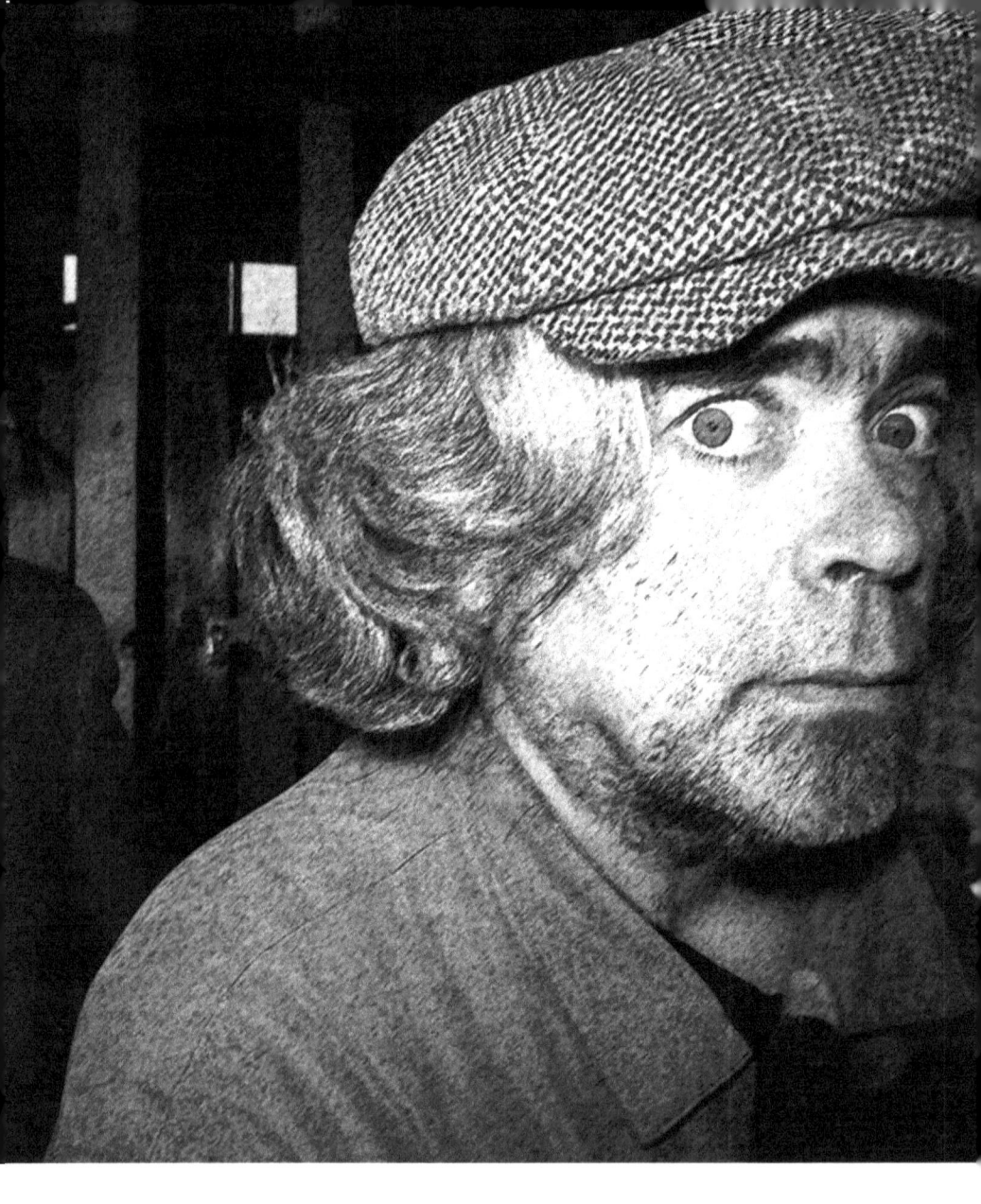

ARTIST
PROFILE

Beau O'Reilly is a founding member of **The Curious Theater Branch**. He has written over 80 pieces of new work for the theater, appeared frequently on *This American Life* and has co-curated the **Rhinoceros Theater Festival** for over thirty-five years...

Beau is a professor at the School of the Art Institute of Chicago... He has recorded and released over a dozen albums, both solo and with his bands, **Crooked Mouth** and **Maestro Subgum and the Whole**.

Beau has appeared as an actor in Harold Pinter's *The Caretaker*, *Waiting For Godot* [3 times], *Endgame* [3 times], *Under Milkwood*, the early plays of Bryn Magnus and Matt Reiger, and in Jenny Magnus' plays whenever invited... he has co-written plays with Julie Williams, Bryn and Jenny, Paul Amandes, Court Dorsey... he has directed plays by Ionesco, Carol Churchill, Sara Kane, Samuel Beckett and a dozen people you haven't heard of... Beau wrote 100 songs with Miki Greenberg and has written with ten other musicians since that collaboration ended...

Beau's **favorite actors** are Colm O'Reilly, Charles Laughton, Vicki Walden, Nichola Walker, Viola Davis, Denzel Washington, Julie Williams, Lena Brun, Jayita Bhattcharya, HB Ward, Guy Massey, Kate Teichman, Jenny Magnus, Matt Wilson, Stefan Brun, Christopher Walken, John Starrs, David Isaacson, Jeff Dorchen, Kelly Anchors, Kristi Lockhart, Matt Regier, Shaun Rosten, Kevin Sparrow, Jeff Bivens, Gena Rowlands, Mitch Salm.... his **favorite guitar player** is T-Roy Martin, with a long nod towards Jerry Garcia, Mike Bloomfield and Richard Thompson... **favored song writers:** Bob Dylan, Townes Van Zandt, Guy Clark, David Olney, Greg Brown, Michael Smith, Miki Greenberg, Jenny and T-Roy, Mose Allison, Elvis Costello, Lou Reed, Joni Mitchel, Vernon Tonges, Richard and Linda Thompson, Tom Waits, the McGarrigles, Jeff Kowalkowski, Leonard Cohen, Hunter and Garcia, John Lennon, and Bob Neuwirth.

Beau's favored writers: Caryl Churchill, Bryn Magnus, Dylan Thomas, Samel Beckett, Suzanne Lori-Parks, Imogen Binnie, A.T. Gruber, Murakami, Hemingway, Albee, Miranda July, Patti Smith, Jenny Magnus, Julie Williams, Elizabeth Bishop, Lars Gustafsson, Ruth Rendell, Rex Stout, Richard Stark, Barrie Cole, Mickle Maher, Chris Bower, Mark Chrysler, August Wilson, Don Delilo, Cecilie O'Reilly, Toni Morrison, John Cassavetes, Mike Leigh, Lydia Davis, James Tate... **favored vocal groups:** Crooked Mouth, 80 Foots, Maestro Subgum, the Five Blind Boys, Laura Nyro and Labelle, the Beatles, the Staple Singers, the Band, my brothers and sisters...

Special thanks, and they know why:
Chris Dyer, Janet DeSaulniers, Sarah Levine, Beth Nugent, Trudy and Felicia, Lunar Cabaret, Living In The Solution, the Madison Radioaktivists, Juicy John Pinks, UvuLittle, This American Life, ESS, Paul Leisen, Rory and Rhiannon, Court Dorsey, Matt Test, Sue Cargill, Ruben Whitaker, Crooked Mouth, Maestro Subgum, Jack the Dog, Ira Murfin, Teresa Weed, Ira Glass, Jim C, Bri and Nikki, Kate and Janet, Larry Odegaard, Barry Lohman, Danny Thompson, Brook Celeste, Jon and Stephanie, Shawn Reddy, the Billy Goats, Jason Greenberg, Jennifer Harris, Ned O'Reilly, Calvin Forbes, Kirk at Facility, Bob Jacobson, Sue Ann Jewers, Justin Hayford, Ralph Lozza, pie and coffee... & that is more than enough.   – *Beau*

<< Beau O'Reilly
gyrates in
The Weirdly Sisters

For more information visit my website: **beauoreilly.com**

"One of the most mesmerizing performances of the year came from Beau O'Reilly as Davies.... Colm O'Reilly and Jeff Bivens were uncompromisingly disturbed as Ashton and Mick, but Beau O'Reilly's disjointed transient Davies had an undercurrent of UNREALIZED THREAT that made you keep him in your eye, even if he was only fumbling around in the background. This was a great production, a study in how to convey absurdity to an audience in a way the audience can wrap its brain around."   *– Chicago Stage Review*

Beau O'Reilly in "The Caretaker"

We open Friday...

BEAU: Well, my idea is -- and, Sue, you're
    going to hate this -- oh you will -- believe
    me, you won't even want to <u>try</u> this --
    no, and that's okay, Sue -- really, it is, it is --
    but that you would leap into my arms and
    I'd catch you -- like a dancer thing.
(Silence.)
SUE: It's just I don't think Rita would --
BEAU: Yeah, fine.
GUY: Captain's log. Day 17. Tensions erupt
    among the crew.
SUE: I had this thought that Rita -- you know,
    she likes dogs so -- not a real dog but like
    I'd be on the phone carrying a cardboard dog.
(Silence.)
GUY: A cheese dog! Oh man! Picture a dog --
    and he's covered with popcorn -- <u>cheese</u>
    popcorn! Oh my God! I'm serious!
(BEAU and SUE stare unhappily at GUY. Silence.)
BEAU: I don't know about a cardboard dog, Sue.
    But we could ask the director. Kat?
KAT (looking under chair): Where's the director?
GUY (brightly): You know, I think it's going
    very well.

HAPPY FIVE-OH,
BEAU

ART CARDS / BIRTHDAY MILESTONES by Sue Cargill 2003 & 2008

Beau O'Reilly's Plays: Vol 1&2

and other Curious Theatre Branch titles in the
Contemporary Theater Collection are published by JackLeg Press.

For information on distribution of books in this series—
or to order copies—visit **www.jacklegpress.org**

Other **Jackleg Press** authors include:

V. Joshua Adams	Brigitte Lewis
Mark Baumgartner	Jenny Magnus
Scott Shibuya Brown	DK McCutchen
Michael Chin	Rita Mookerjee
Chloe Clark	Mamie Morgan
Rivka Clifton	Alexis Orgera
Brittney Corrigan	Zach Powers
Jessica Cuello	Karen Rigby
Barbara Cully	Jo Salas
Allison Cundiff	Maureen Seaton
Curious Theatre Branch	Kristine Snodgrass
Genevieve DeGuzman	Cornelia Spelman
Suzanne Frischkorn	Peter Stenson
Victoria Garza	Melissa Studdard
Reginald Gibbons	Jennifer Tseng
Joachim Glage	Gemini Wahhaj
Caroline Goodwin	Megan Weiler
Brett Hanley	David Welch
Summer Hart	Cassandra Whitaker
Kathryn Kruse	David Wesley Williams

www.ingramcontent.com/pod-product-compliance
Lightning Source LLC
Chambersburg PA
CBHW051129120626
46547CB00012B/727